ANNOTATED TE

SADLIER

VOCABULARY WORKSHOP®

ENRICHED EDITION

Level B

Jerome Shostak

Senior Series Consultant

Vicki A. Jacobs, Ed.D.
Associate Director, Teacher Education Program
Lecturer on Education
Harvard Graduate School of Education
Cambridge, Massachusetts

Series Consultants

Louis P. De Angelo, Ed.D.
Associate Superintendent
Diocese of Wilmington
Wilmington, Delaware

John Heath, Ph.D.
Professor of Classics
Santa Clara University
Santa Clara, California

Sarah Ressler Wright, NBCT
English Department Chair
Rutherford B. Hayes High School
Delaware City Schools, Ohio

Carolyn E. Waters, JD, Ed.S.
ELA/Literacy 6–12 Supervisor
Cobb County School District
Marietta, Georgia

Sadlier

Reviewers

The publisher wishes to thank for their comments and suggestions the following teachers and administrators, who read portions of the series prior to publication.

Teresa Appleby
English Teacher
Paxon Hollow Middle School
Marple Newtown District
Broomall, Pennsylvania

Laura Braun
Assistant Principal
Sawyer School
Chicago Public Schools
Chicago, Illinois

Eileen Brosnahan
Language Arts Teacher
St. Rita Catholic School
Dallas, Texas

Colleen DeGonia
Reading/Language Arts Teacher
Worth Junior High School
Worth, Illinois

Karen Berlin Ishii
Academic and Test Prep Tutor
New York, New York

Susan W. Keogh
Associate Director
Curriculum and Instruction
Lake Highland Preparatory
Orlando, Florida

Carol H. Rohrbach
Director of Curriculum and Staff Development
School District of Springfield Township
Oreland, Pennsylvania

Scott L. Smith
Teacher
Whitewater Valley Elementary
Harrison, Ohio

Patricia Stack
English Teacher
South Park School District
South Park, Pennsylvania

Sally F. Waller
English Teacher
Loyola Blakefield Middle School
Towson, Maryland

Cover: Concept/Art and Design: MK Advertising and William H. Sadlier, Inc.; Cover pencil: Shutterstock/VikaSuh. **Photo Credits:** Blend/Jose Luis Pelaez Inc: T7 *right*, T1. iStockphoto LP/Alex Slobodkin: T7 *left*; Grady Reece: T3; Sean Locke: T4. Ken Karp: T6 *top*. Photodisc/Amos Morgan: T8 *center*. Punchstock/Image Source: T8 *right*. Veer/Corbis: T2.

Printed in the United States of America.
ISBN: 978-0-8215-8027-1/6 7 8 9 10 RRDH 20 19 18 17 16

For additional online resources, go to vocabularyworkshop.com and enter the Teacher Access Code: VW13TB96TGLP3

CONTENTS

ENRICHED EDITION: NEW FEATURES

Vocabulary Workshop has for more than five decades been the leading program for systematic vocabulary development for grades 6–12. It has been proven a highly successful tool in helping students expand their vocabularies, improve their vocabulary skills, and prepare for the vocabulary strands of standardized tests.

This Common Core Enriched Edition of **Vocabulary Workshop** preserves and improves key elements of the program that have made it so effective, and it introduces important new features that make the series more comprehensive in scope and more current in its approach to vocabulary instruction, especially with respect to standardized testing and the **Common Core State Standards** for English Language Arts.

QR Codes

New QR (Quick Response) codes appear on the Reading Passage and Vocabulary in Context pages. The code can be read with a smartphone camera. To read the QR code, users may download any free QR code application to a smartphone. Snapping this code links students directly to the relevant **Vocabulary Workshop** Web site, where they can listen to iWords and audio passages, or take an interactive vocabulary quiz.

Use a smartphone camera and a QR code application to snap this code to link to the **Vocabulary Workshop** home page.

Reading Passages

New Reading Passages open each Unit of **Vocabulary Workshop**. At least 15 of the 20 Unit vocabulary words appear in each Passage. Students read the words in context in informational texts to activate prior knowledge and then apply what they learn throughout the Unit, providing practice in critical-reading skills. Idioms, adages, and proverbs used in Passages provide exposure to figurative language. Passage topics are high-interest and represent a variety of genres, including expository texts, informational essays, historical nonfiction, and biographies. Snap the code or go to the **Vocabulary Workshop** home page to listen to iWords, and hear modeled reading of each Unit Passage.

UNIT 4

*Read the following passage, taking note of the **boldface** words and their contexts. These words are among those you will be studying in Unit 4. As you complete the exercises in this Unit, it may help to refer to the way the words are used below.*

Coyotes in Legend and Myth

<Informational Essay>

In some of the most **spirited** Native American myths and legends, the main character is a trickster figure named Coyote. In these tales, Coyote is nearly always **controversial**, inspiring both admiration and disapproval. Sometimes he is wily and ingenious, while at other times he plays the **buffoon**. At first glance, such paradoxes may seem **bewildering**.

But Coyote's great achievement as a mythical figure is to break the **orthodox** mold. In the end, he cannot be easily classified. It is usually **fruitless** to predict how Coyote will behave in any given situation. He is a **virtual** bundle of contradictions. He is simultaneously a clown, a rebel, and a **wayward** troublemaker.

In myths and legends, the character Coyote displays some clear resemblances to the behavior of the animal known as *Canis latrans*. Like coyotes in real life, the story character is nearly always hungry. One of his primary concerns is to **procure** food to fill his belly. To this end, he **scurries** around, often in disguise and more than willing to cheat others.

One amusing tale about Coyote and cheating involves the challenge of a trader. This man dares Coyote to beat him in a deal. Far from being **disheartened**, Coyote accepts the challenge. He tells the man, though, that he needs to return home to collect his "cheating medicine." Coyote will need to borrow the trader's horse. Also, to make the horse comfortable, he will need to borrow the trader's clothes. Eagerly, the trader gives in to these requests. As Coyote rides off into the distance, the trader, who had hoped to **inflict** a defeat on Coyote, is left **mortified** and **wincing** with shame.

In another tale, an opponent turns the tables on Coyote, bearing out the truth of the old adage "set a thief to catch a thief." As often in trickster tales, Coyote has forged an **alliance** with his friend Iktome, or Spider. The two friends admire a beautiful rock named Iya. Coyote places his own blanket on the rock as a gift. When the weather turns colder, however, Coyote reclaims the blanket, despite Iktome's warnings. After Coyote refuses to return the blanket, Iya turns **hostile**. Rolling through the woods, he pursues the two friends. Finally, Iktome dashes down a hole to escape, abandoning Coyote. Iya then rolls over Coyote, flattening him out like a rug. The trickster has been beaten. At least, so it appears.

Coyote is never permanently defeated, however. In Native American legends and myths, he always has the power to return to life. In fact, many of these stories present Coyote as the creator of the world. In these tales, he fashions the universe from the **void** and makes people out of mud. Coyote is also featured as a culture hero who steals fire and gives it to human beings. This dimension of Coyote parallels the most famous deed of the Greek mythological hero Prometheus, who was punished by the gods for his theft of fire.

In fact, Coyote as a trickster resembles many of the best-known figures of world mythology, such as Loki in northern Europe, the fox Reynard in medieval France, the Japanese kitsune or seven-tailed fox, and the trickster/creator figure of Raven, who is also a hero in many Native American tales.

Audio

For iWords and audio passages, snap the code, or go to vocabularyworkshop.com.

50 • Unit 4

Unit 4 • 51

Writing Prompts

Students practice writing responses to two types of prompts. The first prompt refers to the Passage that introduced the Unit and encourages close reading of the text. The second prompt is modeled on those that appear on standardized tests, such as the SAT® and ACT®.*

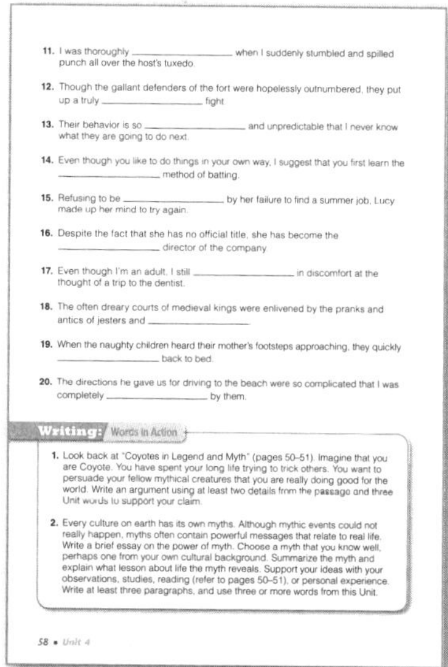

11. I was thoroughly ______________ when I suddenly stumbled and spilled punch all over the host's tuxedo.

12. Though the gallant defenders of the fort were hopelessly outnumbered, they put up a truly ______________ fight.

13. Their behavior is so ______________ and unpredictable that I never know what they are going to do next.

14. Even though you like to do things in your own way, I suggest that you first learn the ______________ method of batting.

15. Refusing to be ______________ by her failure to find a summer job, Lucy made up her mind to try again.

16. Despite the fact that she has no official title, she has become the ______________ director of the company.

17. Even though I'm an adult, I still ______________ in discomfort at the thought of a trip to the dentist.

18. The often dreary courts of medieval kings were enlivened by the pranks and antics of jesters and ______________.

19. When the naughty children heard their mother's footsteps approaching, they quickly ______________ back to bed.

20. The directions he gave us for driving to the beach were so complicated that I was completely ______________ by them.

Writing: Words in Action

1. Look back at "Coyotes in Legend and Myth" (pages 50–51). Imagine that you are Coyote. You have spent your long life trying to trick others. You want to persuade your fellow mythical creatures that you are really doing good for the world. Write an argument using at least two details from the passage and three Unit words to support your claim.

2. Every culture on earth has its own myths. Although mythic events could not really happen, myths often contain powerful messages that relate to real life. Write a brief essay on the power of myth. Choose a myth that you know well, perhaps one from your own cultural background. Summarize the myth and explain what lesson about life the myth reveals. Support your ideas with your observations, studies, reading (refer to pages 50–51), or personal experience. Write at least three paragraphs, and use three or more words from this Unit.

58 ■ Unit 4

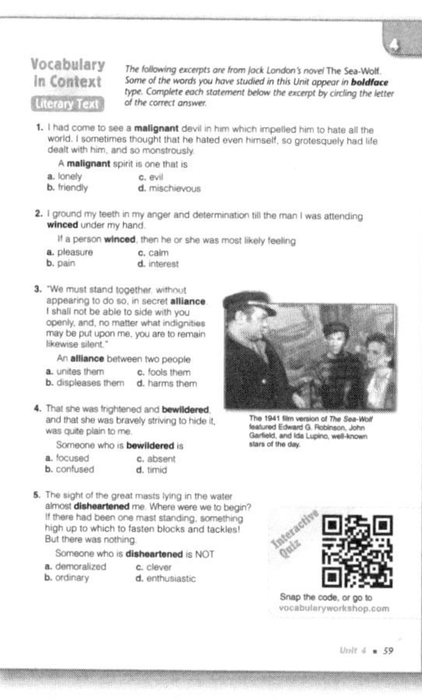

4

Vocabulary in Context

Literary Text

The following excerpts are from Jack London's novel The Sea-Wolf. *Some of the words you have studied in this Unit appear in* **boldface** *type. Complete each statement below the excerpt by circling the letter of the correct answer.*

1. I had come to see a **malignant** devil in him which impelled him to hate all the world. I sometimes thought that he hated even himself, so grotesquely had life dealt with him, and so monstrously.

   A **malignant** spirit is one that is
   a. lonely c. evil
   b. friendly d. mischievous

2. I ground my teeth in my anger and determination till the man I was attending **winced** under my hand.

   If a person **winced**, then he or she was most likely feeling
   a. pleasure c. calm
   b. pain d. interest

3. "We must stand together, without appearing to do so, in secret **alliance**. I shall not be able to side with you openly, and, no matter what indignities may be put upon me, you are to remain likewise silent."

   An **alliance** between two people
   a. unites them c. fools them
   b. displeases them d. harms them

The 1941 film version of *The Sea-Wolf* featured Edward G. Robinson, John Garfield, and Ida Lupino, well-known stars of the day.

4. That she was frightened and **bewildered**, and that she was bravely striving to hide it, was quite plain to me.

   Someone who is **bewildered** is
   a. focused c. absent
   b. confused d. timid

5. The sight of the great masts lying in the water almost **disheartened** me. Where were we to begin? If there had been one mast standing, something high up to which to fasten blocks and tackles! But there was nothing.

   Someone who is **disheartened** is NOT
   a. demoralized c. clever
   b. ordinary d. enthusiastic

Interactive Quiz

Snap the code, or go to vocabularyworkshop.com

Unit 4 ■ 59

Vocabulary in Context

The **Vocabulary in Context** pages contain excerpts from classic literature. Each excerpt uses one of the vocabulary words from the Unit and provides students with exposure to the vocabulary in the context of authentic literature. Multiple-choice questions give practice in standardized-test format. An interactive quiz using the Unit words is accessible by snapping the QR code on the page or by visiting **vocabularyworkshop.com**.

Word Study

In accordance with the Common Core State Standards, the **Word Study** pages address figurative language with instruction and practice using idioms, adages, and proverbs, as well as provide instruction on determining and applying denotation and connotation. This new section appears every three Units, after the Review.

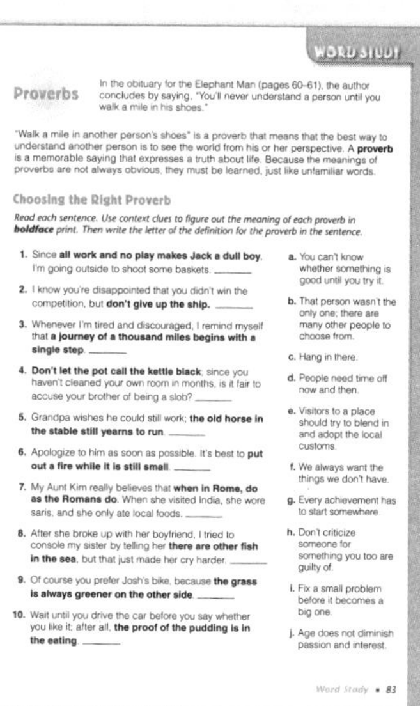

WORD STUDY

Proverbs

In the obituary for the Elephant Man (pages 60–61), the author concludes by saying, "You'll never understand a person until you walk a mile in his shoes."

"Walk a mile in another person's shoes" is a proverb that means that the best way to understand another person is to see the world from his or her perspective. A **proverb** is a memorable saying that expresses a truth about life. Because the meanings of proverbs are not always obvious, they must be learned, just like unfamiliar words.

Choosing the Right Proverb

Read each sentence. Use context clues to figure out the meaning of each proverb in **boldface** *print. Then write the letter of the definition for the proverb in the sentence.*

1. Since **all work and no play makes Jack a dull boy**, I'm going outside to shoot some baskets. ______
2. I know you're disappointed that you didn't win the competition, but **don't give up the ship.** ______
3. Whenever I'm tired and discouraged, I remind myself that **a journey of a thousand miles begins with a single step.** ______
4. **Don't let the pot call the kettle black**, since you haven't cleaned your own room in months; is it fair to accuse your brother of being a slob? ______
5. Grandpa wishes he could still work; **the old horse in the stable still yearns to run.** ______
6. Apologize to him as soon as possible. It's best to **put out a fire while it is still small.** ______
7. My Aunt Kim really believes that **when in Rome, do as the Romans do.** When she visited India, she wore saris; and she only ate local foods. ______
8. After she broke up with her boyfriend, I tried to console my sister by telling her **there are other fish in the sea**, but that just made her cry harder. ______
9. Of course you prefer Josh's bike, because **the grass is always greener on the other side.** ______
10. Wait until you drive the car before you say whether you like it; after all, **the proof of the pudding is in the eating.** ______

a. You can't know whether something is good until you try it.
b. That person wasn't the only one; there are many other people to choose from.
c. Hang in there.
d. People need time off now and then.
e. Visitors to a place should try to blend in and adopt the local customs.
f. We always want the things we don't have.
g. Every achievement has to start somewhere.
h. Don't criticize someone for something you too are guilty of.
i. Fix a small problem before it becomes a big one.
j. Age does not diminish passion and interest.

Word Study ■ 83

*SAT is a registered trademark of the College Board which was not involved in the production of, and does not endorse, this product. ACT is a registered trademark of ACT, Inc. which was not involved in the production of, and does not endorse, this product.

Vocabulary Workshop and the Common Core State Standards

The Common Core Enriched Edition of Vocabulary Workshop is aligned with and supports relevant and applic able standards contained in the Common Core State Standards for English Language Arts. The program is fully aligned with the Vocabulary Acquisition and Use standards and supports them with the kind of instruction, modeling, and practice that promote and cultivate corresponding vocabulary skills. Additionally, the Common Core Enriched Edition of Vocabulary Workshop addresses several Common Core Reading and Writing standards—in particular those associated with the role of vocabulary both in determining meaning and nuance within the broader context of reading, and in refining usage and expression in written and oral communication.

In this Teacher's Edition, the Common Core State Standards addressed in the form of instruction and/or practice in any given section of the Student Edition are indicated at the bottom of the corresponding page or pages. The standards are identified in an abbreviated notation. For example, "CCSS Vocabulary 4.c, 4.d" indicates that the vocabulary skill or skills represented on that page support Vocabulary Acquisition and Use standards 4.c and 4.d. Similarly, "CCSS Reading (Informational Text) 4, 6" is shorthand for Reading Standards for Informational Text 4, 6, and "CCSS Writing 1.c, 2.d" stands for Writing Standards 1.c and 2.d.

The full language of the corresponding Vocabulary, Reading (both Informational Text and Literature), and Writing standards for grade 7 is provided below. Note that in some instances, text is highlighted to show specific correlations between a particular skill and a more general standard. (A full correlation of the Vocabulary Workshop Common Core Enriched Edition program to the Common Core State Standards is available at **vocabularyworkshop.com**.)

Common Core State Standards for English Language Arts

Language Standards

(Grade 7)

Vocabulary Acquisition and Use

4. Determine or clarify the meaning of unknown and multiple-meaning words and phrases based on *grade 7 reading and content,* choosing flexibly from a range of strategies.

- **a.** Use context (e.g., the overall meaning of a sentence or paragraph; a word's position or function in a sentence) as a clue to the meaning of a word or phrase.
- **b.** Use common, grade-appropriate Greek or Latin affixes and roots as clues to the meaning of a word (e.g., *belligerent, bellicose, rebel*).
- **c.** Consult general and specialized reference materials (e.g., dictionaries, glossaries, thesauruses), both print and digital, to find the pronunciation of a word or determine or clarify its precise meaning or its part of speech.
- **d.** Verify the preliminary determination of the meaning of a word or phrase (e.g., by checking the inferred meaning in context or in a dictionary).

5. Demonstrate understanding of figurative language, word relationships, and nuances in word meanings.

a. Interpret figures of speech (e.g., literary, biblical, and mythological allusions) in context.

b. Use the relationship between particular words (e.g., synonym, antonym, analogy) to better understand each of the words.

c. Distinguish among the connotations (associations) of words with similar denotations (definitions) (e.g., *refined*, *respectful*, *polite*, *diplomatic*, *condescending*).

6. Acquire and use accurately grade-appropriate general academic and domain-specific words and phrases; gather vocabulary knowledge when considering a word or phrase important to comprehension or expression.

Reading Standards for Literature

(Grade 7)

Craft and Structure

4. Determine the meaning of words and phrases as they are used in a text, including figurative and connotative meanings; analyze the impact of rhymes and other repetitions of sounds (e.g., alliteration) on a specific verse or stanza of a poem or section of a story or drama.

Reading Standards for Informational Text

(Grade 7)

Key Ideas and Details

2. Determine two or more central ideas in a text and analyze their development over the course of the text; provide an objective summary of the text.

Craft and Structure

4. Determine the meaning of words and phrases as they are used in a text, including figurative, connotative, and technical meanings; analyze the impact of a specific word choice on meaning and tone.

6. Determine an author's point of view or purpose in a text and analyze how the author distinguishes his or her position from that of others.

Writing Standards

(Grade 7)

Text Type and Purposes

1. Write arguments to support claims with clear reasons and relevant evidence.

   c. Use words, phrases, and clauses to create cohesion and clarify the relationships among claim(s), reasons, and evidence.

2. Write informative/explanatory texts to examine a topic and convey ideas, concepts, and information through the selection, organization, and analysis of relevant content.

   d. Use precise language and domain-specific vocabulary to inform about or explain the topic.

3. Write narratives to develop real or imagined experiences or events using effective technique, relevant descriptive details, and well-structured event sequences.

   d. Use precise words and phrases, relevant descriptive details, and sensory language to convey experiences and events.

Production and Distribution of Writing

4. Produce clear and coherent writing in which the development, organization, and style are appropriate to task, purpose, and audience. (Grade-specific expectations for writing types are defined in standards 1–3 above.)

ENRICHED VOCABULARY APPROACH: Systematic Vocabulary Instruction

The VOCABULARY WORKSHOP program focuses on the words, their meanings, their ranges of application, and their uses in context. The approach is systematic because it begins with and builds upon a word list drawn from vocabulary that students will encounter in their reading. It provides students with the vocabulary skills they will need to achieve higher-level reading proficiency and to succeed at standardized tests.

With the introduction of reading passages and literary text, the Enriched Edition goes further than previous editions in integrating vocabulary instruction in the context of reading. (For a discussion of the importance of vocabulary in reading comprehension, see pages T31–T32. For more on how VOCABULARY WORKSHOP can be used to complement a literature program, see pages T33–T35.)

A cornerstone of the VOCABULARY WORKSHOP approach is intensive practice through varied and abundant "hands-on" exercises. This method provides both exposure to different meanings of the key words studied and coverage of the range of each key word through its appearance in many different contexts. The aim of the pattern of intensive practice is to embed the words in the students' active, daily-use vocabulary.

Grade-Level Placements

The chart below shows suggested grade placement for each Level of VOCABULARY WORKSHOP. In determining proper placement of a particular Level, consider the following:

- Grade placements are based on teacher experience and recommendations.
- Differences in grade are reflected in the difficulty of the words presented, the maturity of the sentences, and other contexts in which those words are used.
- Grade levels should not be taken too literally. Experimentation and the use of the program's online diagnostic materials will establish the correct placement of a particular Level in a given situation.

Grade Placements

Average Students		Above-Average Students	
Level	Grade	Level	Grade
A	6	A	5
B	7	B	6
C	8	C	7

Word Lists

Each Student Level presents 300 vocabulary words organized into 15 Units. Mastering these words will help students understand academic texts and increase their everyday language abilities.

For a discussion by Vicki A. Jacobs of the importance of academic vocabulary to reading comprehension, see pages T31–T32.

Criteria for Selection: The selection of **Vocabulary Workshop** words is based on four criteria: currency in and usefulness for present-day American oral or written communication; frequency on recognized high-utility and academic vocabulary lists; applicability to standardized tests; current grade-placement research.

General Sources: The lists of key words were developed from many sources: traditional, classic, and contemporary literature, including novels, short stories, essays, newspaper and magazine articles, plays, and films. Spelling and vocabulary lists recognized as valid bases for teaching language skills at the middle and secondary levels are used, as well as current subject-area textbooks, glossaries, and ancillary materials (especially for general, nontechnical terms).

Dictionary and Reference Sources: The following were the primary dictionary resources used for word (and definition) selection:

- *Webster's Third International Dictionary of the English Language* (unabridged)
- *Merriam-Webster's Collegiate Dictionary* (Ninth, Tenth, and online editions)
- *The American Heritage Dictionary of the English Language* (editions 1–4)
- *The Random House Dictionary of the English Language* (unabridged editions)
- *The Compact Edition of the Oxford English Dictionary*

Standard Word-Frequency Sources: Standard word-frequency studies were conducted to evaluate and revise the word list.

- *Primary* Dale-O'Rourke: *The Living Word Vocabulary*, Carroll-Davies-Richman: *The American Heritage Word Frequency Book*
- *Supplementary* Harris-Jacobsen: *Basic Reading Vocabularies*, Thorndike-Lorge: *The Teacher's Word Book of 30,000 Words*, Zeno-Ivens-Millard-Duvvuri: *The Educator's Word Frequency Guide*

"Sliding-Scale" Placement

Each word list works on a sliding scale based on the following principles: Any word that according to Dale-O'Rourke is known in a given grade is not presented in that grade. It is presented two or three grades earlier. Each grade level contains mostly words not known (according to Dale-O'Rourke) two or three grades later, with an admixture (in decreasing numbers) of words not known four or more grades later. The higher the grade, the larger the percentage of more difficult words contained in the word list.

Professional development papers discussing the research supporting the instructional approach of **Vocabulary Workshop** may be found in the Teacher Center of **vocabularyworkshop.com**.

PRINT COMPONENTS

This Enriched Edition of VOCABULARY WORKSHOP, Levels A–C, consists of an integrated array of print and digital components. Print materials for each Level include:

- Student Texts
- Teacher's Annotated Editions
- Test Booklets with Combined Answer Keys (Forms A and B)
- SAT-Type TEST PREP Blackline Masters (answers included)

Student Texts/Teacher's Annotated Editions

Each of the three Student Texts (Levels A–C) presents 300 key words and is organized in the same way: 15 Units of 20 words each and 5 Reviews following Units 3, 6, 9, 12, and 15. Preceding the first Unit is a section on types of questions students will find throughout the program. Concluding each Student Text is a Final Mastery Test.

In the Teacher's Annotated Editions, answers are shown for each student page. Correlations to Common Core State Standards are also noted on each page.

Reading Passages

New nonfiction Reading Passages open each Unit of VOCABULARY WORKSHOP. At least 15 of the Unit vocabulary words, as well as examples of figurative language such as idioms, adages, or proverbs, are used in each Passage. Students read the words in context to activate prior knowledge, and then they apply what they learn throughout the Unit and the Review.

Definitions

DEFINITIONS The definitions provided are clear, useful, and informal. The intent is to give students a reasonably good core idea of what each word means without extensive detail or secondary connotations. Generally, only a single meaning of maximum usefulness is given.

PART OF SPEECH Simple abbreviations give the part of speech with each definition. When a word functions as several parts of speech, the appropriate abbreviation appears before the corresponding definition.

PRONUNCIATION A simple set of diacritical marks presented at the beginning of every Student Text (inside front cover) indicates the pronunciation. Only one pronunciation is given for each word, except when a word changes its pronunciation in accordance with its use as different parts of speech (*ob′ ject* and *ob ject′*).

Students may utilize the **Online iWords Audio Program** for each Unit. Available at **vocabularyworkshop.com**, this program provides nearly four hours of spoken material per Student Text, including pronunciation and examples of usage.

ILLUSTRATIVE SENTENCE Concluding each key entry is an illustrative sentence. These sentences provide a context that clarifies the meaning of each word. By writing the word in such contextual settings, students begin to see how the word can be used effectively in their own writing.

SYNONYMS AND ANTONYMS Each word has a list of synonyms and/or antonyms if there is one or more of either for the word. By studying the given synonyms and antonyms, students will better understand the denotational family of words of which each key word is part; and by comparing specific usages of key words and their synonyms, students can better appreciate appropriate contexts for these words. Note that the lists of synonyms and antonyms are not exhaustive.

Choosing the Right Word

In this activity, students choose one of a pair of words that most satisfactorily completes the sentence. Completing this activity requires a thorough understanding of a range of a word's definitions.

Synonyms and Antonyms

In this section, students read phrases that include synonyms or antonyms for the Unit words. Students must choose the Unit word that matches the given synonym or antonym. Besides reinforcing meanings, this exercise provides students with further examples of usage and context.

Completing the Sentence

This activity provides a simple completion exercise in which students choose and write the word that logically and meaningfully fits into a blank in a given sentence.

When using this activity in the classroom, the teacher should bear in mind the following considerations:

- The sentences in this activity call for the literal or direct (as opposed to the metaphorical or extended) meaning of the words involved.
- The sentences are designed so that only one of the words fits in the given blank. Context clues have been placed in each sentence.
- The words are to be used as the part of speech given in Definitions. The only exceptions are: Nouns given in the singular in Definitions may be plural in the sentences; verbs given in the base form in Definitions may be used in any tense or form (including participial) required by the sentence.

Writing: Words in Action

New prompts provide practice with writing responses to two modes of writing. The first prompt is a text-dependent question that asks students to respond to the Reading Passage at the beginning of the Unit. The second prompt is modeled on those that appear on standardized tests. Students write their responses on a separate sheet of paper. Teachers should grade the responses using a rubric of their choice.

Vocabulary in Context/Literary Text

This activity provides Unit vocabulary words used in classic literature, which:

- gives examples of usage for the selected words,
- offers an opportunity to derive meaning from context, and
- provides practice in the sort of vocabulary exercises found on standardized tests.

Refer students to Student Text page 7 for an introduction to the strategies involved in studying vocabulary in context.

Review

A Review follows every three Units.

- Vocabulary for Comprehension: This section is designed to help students prepare for the critical-reading sections of standardized tests. Students read a Passage and then answer vocabulary-in-context and comprehension questions related to the texts.
- Two-Word Completions: Students practice with word-omission (cloze) exercises that appear on typical standardized tests, including the SAT.

Word Study

A Word Study section follows every Review. Exercises include instruction and practice with figurative language and relationships in meaning:

- Choosing the Right Idiom/Adage/Proverb
- Writing with Idioms/Adages/Proverbs
- Denotation and Connotation/Shades of Meaning
- Building with Classical Roots

The Final Mastery Test

The Final Mastery Test in the Student Text is a practice test of 70 items that gives students and teachers fair insight into how much progress has been made during the year and what kind of additional work is in order.

The purpose of the Final Mastery Test is threefold.

- It can serve as a dry run in preparation for the more formal (and secure) tests available as optional components of this program.
- It can serve as an informal evaluation of achievement to date.
- It can serve as a reinforcement activity.

Test Booklets (Optional)

Two Test Booklets (Form A and Form B) may be used to reduce the risk of answers being passed on. Though the formats of the Test Booklets are the same, the items tested in any given section are completely different. The contents are: a list of the 300 tested vocabulary words; a Warm-Up Test; 15 Unit Tests, each consisting of 25 items focusing on pronunciations, parts of speech, spelling, definitions, synonyms, antonyms, and sentence completions; and 5 Cumulative Tests of 52–110 items each.

TEST PREP Blackline Masters (Optional)

The TEST PREP component provides practice with SAT-type test questions and formats and also with review tests covering the corresponding Student Text. Prep Tests approximate the word-omission sections of the SAT and provide practice in the vocabulary-in-context strand with brief reading passages as well. Answer sheets in SAT-type test format develop student ease and familiarity with standardized testing materials. Mastery Tests are used when students have completed the corresponding group of three Units in the Student Text. Each test covers basic meanings, synonyms, antonyms, and sentence completions. Answer keys, including selected answer rationales, are provided for all tests.

DIGITAL COMPONENTS

Digital resources for each Level are available at **vocabularyworkshop.com** and include:

- iWords Audio Program
- Audio of Unit Passages
- Online Interactive Games
- Vocabulary in Context: Informational Text
- Diagnostic Tests and Cumulative Reviews
- Professional Development Videos
- Interactive Quizzes

The components have been designed for use in an integrated year-long vocabulary program, as suggested in the chart on pages T24–T26.

PDFs of the following materials may be found online for each level:

- Correlations to the Common Core State Standards
- Vocabulary in Context: Informational Text
- SAT and ACT Practice Worksheets
- Additional Practice and Quiz pages for each lesson
- Greek and Latin Roots Reference Guide
- Diagnostic Tests and Cumulative Reviews
- Pacing Guides
- Pronunciation Key

DIGITAL COMPONENTS *cont.*

iWords Audio Program

The VOCABULARY WORKSHOP iWords Audio Program provides students with pronunciations, definitions, and examples of usage for all program vocabulary words and word meanings. Students can visit **vocabularyworkshop.com** to listen to each word or download files of the words.

- The audio program is ideal for English Language Learners (ELL) and ELL classrooms.
- Students hear the recommended pronunciation of each word at least six times and are given two opportunities to pronounce each word themselves.
- Pronunciations are followed by brief definitions and examples of the word used in complete sentences.
- For recommendations on when to use iWords, see pages T24–T30.

Online Interactive Vocabulary Games

For each Level, students are provided interactive word games using the vocabulary presented in the Units. These activities include flashcards, crossword puzzles, word searches, "hangman," and Test Your Vocabulary questions. Additional Practice and Quiz pages including Interactive Quizzes provide more possibilities for academic assessment.

Vocabulary in Context: Informational Text

A Reading Passage that uses key Unit words provides another opportunity to read vocabulary in context. Each Passage is followed by multiple-choice questions for extra practice with nonfiction texts, the Unit vocabulary words, and question types found on standardized tests.

Diagnostic Test and Cumulative Reviews

- A **Beginning-of-Year Diagnostic Test** contains a sampling of words from the program to assess students' prior knowledge.
- After Units 3, 6, 9, 12, and 15, students can complete **Cumulative Review Tests**. Questions on Choosing the Right Meaning and Two-Word Completions provide practice on SAT-style questions. Activities on analogies and vocabulary enrichment are also included.

SAT and ACT Practice Worksheets

For teachers who wish to offer their students extra practice for the SAT or ACT, 45 standardized-test worksheets are available online for each Level. These practice worksheets are accessible only to teachers.

For each Level, there are 15 worksheets in standardized-test format for each of the following:

- comprehension and vocabulary skills assessed on the SAT and ACT,
- multiple-choice grammar and usage items included in the Writing section of the SAT and in the ACT, and
- step-by-step guidance in crafting a timed essay of the kind that is required on the SAT (and is optional on the ACT).

Teacher Resources

Available in PDF format:

- Correlations to the Common Core State Standards
- Pacing Guides
- Greek and Latin Roots Reference Guide
- Graphic Organizers
- Pronunciation Key

Online Student Assessment System (Optional)

The Web-based VOCABULARY WORKSHOP Online Student Assessment System allows teachers quickly and easily to create secure, interactive Unit practice and assessment pages that are automatically scored and provide students with immediate, prescriptive feedback. With a database of nearly 4,000 test items per Level, teachers have the option to individualize tests.

The Online Student Assessment System provides:

- the ability to create and edit question sets and tests,
- the ability to scramble answer choices and/or questions so that multiple versions of the same test can be administered securely,
- a wide assortment of question types: pronunciation, part of speech, spelling, definitions, synonyms, antonyms, sentence completions, sentence framing,
- formatted Unit tests, ready for immediate use,
- a secure portal to assign practice/test pages, with the option to print these pages,
- immediate feedback on each question,
- a detailed end-of-assignment report to help the teacher know exactly how students are progressing,
- the ability to track student progress through a comprehensive reporting system,
- a way to create detailed reports on class and individual student results, and
- the option to send practice/test pages and student results to learning management systems.

The VOCABULARY WORKSHOP Online Student Assessment System is a convenient and secure source of assessment and/or extra practice. The Online Student Assessment System is easy to use, either as needed or more systematically, as an integral part of the VOCABULARY WORKSHOP series. See pages T24–26 for recommendations on how it may be used in conjunction with the Student Text and other components.

IMPLEMENTING THE PROGRAM

VOCABULARY WORKSHOP not only provides vocabulary instruction but also teaches students a variety of other essential Language Arts skills. Teachers have many options for pacing VOCABULARY WORKSHOP'S activities to best meet the needs of their students and classes.

Planning and Pacing of Instruction

The charts on pages T24–T26 offer sample plans for weekly scheduling and for daily implementation of all components of the VOCABULARY WORKSHOP program. The charts are constructed to reflect the coverage of the Units in the Student Text and associated online resources on a 5-day and on a 10-day basis, and the Reviews on a 5-day basis. (Full-year schedules for both 5-day and 10-day plans are available at **vocabularyworkshop.com**.)

Weekly Schedules (5 days per unit and 10 days per unit)

5-Day Schedule	10-Day Schedule	Student Text and Online Resources	Implementation Plan
Week 1	**Weeks 1–2**	**Unit 1**	Complete VOCABULARY WORKSHOP activities in the book and online (see the "How to Use VOCABULARY WORKSHOP Exercises" charts on the following pages). Examine Best Practices on pages T28–T30 for further vocabulary activities. Additional Assessment: Assign Unit 1 Test from Test Booklets or from Online Assessment.
Week 2	**Weeks 3–4**	**Unit 2**	Follow procedure shown for Unit 1. Testing Options: Assign Unit 2 Test from the Test Booklets or from Online Assessment, and review Unit 1 Test to encourage deeper recall of all words.
Week 3	**Weeks 5–6**	**Unit 3**	Follow procedure shown for Unit 1. Testing Options: Assign Unit 3 Test from the Test Booklets or from Online Assessment, and review Units 1–2 Tests to encourage deeper recall of all words.
Week 4	**Week 7**	**Review Units 1–3**	Complete Review Units 1–3 activities, and ensure knowledge of all 60 vocabulary words as well as the mastery of other essential English skills. Mastery Tests Units 1–3 available as Test Prep Blackline Masters.

Note: For suggestions for the integration of the Diagnostic Test and Final Mastery Test into a full-year schedule, see the sample weekly schedules at **vocabularyworkshop.com**.

Daily Activities for Each Unit (5 Days)

How to Use the Student Text and Online Resources (at vocabularyworkshop.com) in 5 Sessions/Periods (See page T26 for a 10-Day Planner)

Assignment	Day 1	Day 2	Day 3	Day 4	Day 5
Class work	**1.** Review previous Unit's test results. **2.** Review word meaning and usage in context in the Unit's Reading Passage. **3.** Present any words not used in the Reading Passage.	**1.** Review Choosing the Right Word. **2.** Assign online SAT/ ACT Practice Worksheets.	**1.** Review Synonyms and Antonyms and also Completing the Sentence. **2.** Assign the first prompt for Writing: Words in Action.	**1.** Share excerpts (with vocabulary usage) from Writing: Words in Action. **2.** Assign Vocabulary in Context: Literary Text.	**1.** Assign Unit Test (Test Booklet or Online Assessment).
Homework	**1.** Download and listen to iWords. **2.** Assign Choosing the Right Word.	**1.** Assign Synonyms and Antonyms; Completing the Sentence. **2.** Assign online Unit games.	**1.** Assign the second prompt of Writing: Words in Action.	**1.** Assign online interactive quiz.	**1.** Have students read the next Unit's Reading Passage.

Daily Activities for the Review and Word Study Sections

How to Use the Student Text and Online Resources (at vocabularyworkshop.com) in 5 Sessions/Periods

Assignment	Day 1	Day 2	Day 3	Day 4	Day 5
Class work	**1.** Review previous Unit's test results. **2.** Assign Vocabulary for Comprehension.	**1.** Review SAT/ACT Worksheets and Two-Word Completions. **2.** Present Idioms/Adages/Proverbs.	**1.** Review Idioms/ Adages/ Proverbs. **2.** Present Denotation/ Connotation.	**1.** Review Denotation/ Connotation. **2.** Present Building with Classical Roots.	**1.** Assign Mastery Test (Test Prep Blackline Masters).
Homework	**1.** Assign online SAT/ ACT Practice Worksheets. **2.** Assign Two-Word Completions.	**1.** Assign Idioms/ Adages/ Proverbs. **2.** Assign online Unit games.	**1.** Assign Denotation/ Connotation. **2.** Assign online Unit games.	**1.** Review Building with Classical Roots.	**1.** Assign the next Unit's Reading Passage.

Daily Activities for Each Unit (10 Days)

How to Use the Student Text and Online Resources (at vocabularyworkshop.com) in 10 Sessions/Periods

Assignment	Day 1	Day 2	Day 3	Day 4	Day 5
Class work	**1.** Introduce vocabulary in context of the Unit's Reading Passage. **2.** Discuss two Unit words and their definitions.	**1.** Discuss two Unit words and their definitions.	**1.** Discuss two Unit words and their definitions.	**1.** Discuss two Unit words and their definitions. **2.** Have students play online Unit games and/or introduce an activity from Best Practices (T28-30).	**1.** Discuss two Unit words and their definitions. **2.** Assign the Interactive Unit Quiz.
Homework	**1.** Download and listen to iWords. Flashcards.' **2.** Complete the Definitions.	**1.** Assign Choosing the Right Word.	**1.** Assign Synonyms and Antonyms.	**1.** Assign Completing the Sentence.	**1.** Have students play online Unit games.

Assignment	Day 6	Day 7	Day8	Day 9	Day 10
Class work	**1.** Discuss two Unit words and their definitions **2.** Introduce one of the two Writing: Words in Action prompts	**1.** Discuss two Unit words and their definitions.	**1.** Discuss two Unit words and their definitions.	**1.** Discuss two Unit words and their definitions. **2.** Have students play online Unit games and/or introduce an activity from Best Practices.	**1.** Discuss two Unit words and their definitions. **2.** Assign Unit Test (Test Booklet or Online Assessment).
Homework	**1.** Complete Writing: Words in Action prompt assignment.	**1.** Assign Vocabulary in Context: Literary Text.	**1.** Assign online Practice Worksheets.	**1.** Assign online SAT/ACT Practice Worksheets	**1.** Assign audio passage and have students note context clues in margins.

Implementing the Weekly and Daily Schedules

The following may prove helpful when adapting the foregoing schedules to specific situations.

- As appropriate, review activities to monitor student progress (whole class or individual).
- Students need to recognize the value of learning vocabulary and completing the vocabulary exercises. Simply assigning words and the exercises for class work or homework does not provide intrinsic value for those who are learning new vocabulary. Teachers should model vocabulary usage and encourage students to learn the words to improve their speaking, writing, reading comprehension, and test scores (see "Best Practices" T28–T30 for suggestions).
- Activity order and timings are to some extent hypothetical. Teachers may switch items around and adjust timings as needed. Similarly, items may be modified or deleted.
- VOCABULARY WORKSHOP Units may also be adapted so that only 10 words are studied each week. The Online Assessment allows teachers to easily create quizzes for the first or second 10 words of a Unit, if desired. Students completing the exercises in VOCABULARY WORKSHOP can either wait until the second week to work on the activities, or they can identify the words they know and complete only those blanks that relate to the week's words being studied.

Student Study Guides

When students employ a review system for their vocabularies, they tend to learn the words and their meanings more thoroughly. Students may create flashcards or a vocabulary chart as two simple review methods. However, what students write down on their flashcards or charts may vary among learning styles.

For Basic Vocabulary Learners: Students should write the vocabulary word on one side of a flashcard (or in the first chart box), then a mnemonic device, synonym/brief definition of the word, and a short, student-created phrase incorporating the word on the back of the flashcard (or in chart boxes two, three, and four). Students then review by looking only at the word side of the flashcard or the first column of the chart (folding the paper so the other information is behind the first column) and seeing if they can remember the mnemonic device or phrase that enables them to recall the word's meaning.

For Kinesthetic Learners: Students may create a motion that goes with a vocabulary word definition, when possible. Students then write the word on one side of a flashcard (or in the first chart box), then the motion and a synonym/brief definition on the back of the flashcard (or in the second and third chart boxes). Students may review in the same way as is described above for basic learners.

For Visual/Artistic Learners: Students draw a picture that goes with each vocabulary word definition. Students may write the word on one side of a flashcard (or in the first chart box) and then draw the associated picture and write the synonym/brief definition on the back of the flashcard (or in the second and third chart boxes). Students then review in the same way as described above for basic and kinesthetic learners.

For Auditory Learners: In addition to the Basic Vocabulary Learner review sheet, teachers may strongly encourage these learners to review iWords on a daily basis to recall definitions.

BEST PRACTICES FOR USING VOCABULARY WORKSHOP IN THE CLASSROOM

Classroom experience and research have shown that repeated exposure to and varied application of vocabulary words embed meaning in students' minds. The more teachers and students utilize vocabulary in the Language Arts class period, the more likely students are to understand and use new vocabulary themselves.

Classroom Environment

Depending on the reading proficiencies of their students, teachers may differentiate and/or scaffold instruction to accommodate varying learning styles and modalities—for example, by reading aloud or having students read aloud the passages that introduce the Units.

To encourage students' use of vocabulary, teachers may post vocabulary words in the classroom—on bulletin boards, walls, or chalkboards/whiteboards. Students and teachers may bring in examples of vocabulary from print sources to be displayed in the classroom. Additionally, students may create visual representations or drawings of vocabulary words that can be posted in the classroom. Discuss which visual representations are the most appropriate and accurate representations of the vocabulary words.

Differentiation may be achieved through choice. Create a vocabulary choice menu of extension activities, such as using vocabulary words to write a poem or create an interactive presentation, that appeal to different learning modalities.

Recognition of Vocabulary Discovery and Usage

Students may share experiences in which they hear or use vocabulary outside of the classroom. Whether it is another teacher who said a vocabulary word, a television show or movie that incorporated vocabulary, or the student him- or herself who embedded a word in an assignment, it is important to recognize the use of academic vocabulary.

Daily Discussion and Review

Teachers may model vocabulary usage by including the words in their instructions or conversations with students. The more the teacher uses a word, the easier it is for students to understand the word's meaning and how to use it properly.

Teachers can have "Words of the Day" that students must incorporate into classroom activities. Whoever correctly uses the words the most might receive a reward.

During debates, discussions, or other times when students are conversing, teachers should require them to use the learned vocabulary words. A set minimum number of words can be established, and students who go above the minimum should be recognized for their efforts.

Any videos, songs, or art that students created to illustrate or act out the vocabulary words could be reviewed with the whole class.

When there is extra time, the class may review vocabulary words. See the "Vocabulary Projects and Games" section below for suggested activities.

Categorizing Vocabulary

When reviewing vocabulary words, students may categorize words as they relate to current events. By creating meaningful associations with each word, students more easily recall word meaning. Post the categories around the room and have students add to them during the year. Students can also create sentence strips for vocabulary words. Have students manipulate the strips to generate rankings and groupings. For an extra challenge, have students rank the words on a continuum.

Students can also learn vocabulary by creating more general categories. These categories can be as simple as "praise" or "insult" or as elaborate as students want (travel words, food words, etc.). When students learn new words, they can place them in the categories they have created.

Writing with Vocabulary

Students should incorporate at least one or two vocabulary words into their daily writing prompts, reading journals, or other forms of informal communication. Use pictures or photographs from magazines as an inspiration for writing.

Whenever students write formally for class (essays, stories, etc.), teachers may require a set minimum number of vocabulary words to be used, check to make sure that the usage is appropriate, and provide feedback. Students should highlight the vocabulary words in the writing. Read aloud essays and review the use of vocabulary for correct usage. Point out instances where the form of the words has been changed or a secondary meaning is used. Suggest ways for students to check their usage, such as replacing the vocabulary word in the sentence with its definition to see if it makes sense.

Teachers may also:

- Have students create puns that incorporate vocabulary. Example: "How dare you!" Tom said **indignantly**.
- Ask students to write poems for individual words. Example: "There once was a word called _____."
- Ask students to write a "Where I'm From" poem that explains both a word's origins and use, and that also traces its genealogy to related words.
- Have students write myths about the origins of individual words or groups of words.

Vocabulary Projects and Games

Students may create advertisements for a word to "sell" its uses. Example: "Race to your local dictionary and pick up the word _____. Whether frustrated with your social life or unhappy with a school assignment, this word can be used in a variety of ways...." Alternatively, teachers may have students sell a product, but have them use as many vocabulary words as possible to describe the item's attributes.

Students often learn words best when setting them to music. Students may write lyrics incorporating all (or most) of a Unit's vocabulary words/definitions and then perform, videotape, or record their finished products. Create a library of the videos and recordings for future classes to use.

Do a round-robin review of the words and their definitions. This activity can be teacher-directed or student-led. Begin with one student naming a vocabulary word, a second student defines it, then another gives the kinesthetic gesture the class gave the word, a fourth student puts the definition in his or her own words or provides a synonym or antonym. Another student uses the word in a sentence, and then another student finishes the activity by giving feedback on how the word was used in the sentence. Allow time after the activity for follow-up questions.

Create a "deck" of review cards, consisting of the word, the definition, a sentence with a blank where the vocabulary word would go, and the image for the word selected by the class. Have teams go head-to-head to see who can complete the sentence with the correct vocabulary word first.

Groups of students can act in skits or pantomimes that demonstrate a word's meaning; the rest of the class must guess the word being enacted.

Student groups may tell stories using vocabulary words. Groups should be created according to the ability and level of students.

Alternative Assessment

The following types of assessment may be used in addition to or in lieu of the objective-scoring materials provided in VOCABULARY WORKSHOP, Levels A–C.

- Teachers may have students write a story, song, poem, or essay incorporating vocabulary words (word list provided by the teacher). They can assign a topic or allow students to write about a topic they find interesting. Teachers should explain to students the rubric they will use to evaluate student writing before beginning the exercise.

- Teachers can write a series of true/false statements, each concerning a vocabulary word, and then have students decide whether the statements are true or false based on their understanding of the words.

- Students can use vocabulary words in conversations throughout the week. Students may either write down their statements or collect signatures from peers or adults who heard the student using each word. Students turn in their sheets at the end of the week. Teachers should review for correct usage for an assessment grade.

- Teachers should consider using a suggestion from "Writing with Vocabulary" or "Vocabulary Projects" as a final assessment.

ACADEMIC VOCABULARY AND READING COMPREHENSION

by Vicki A. Jacobs
Senior Series Consultant

As students advance to the higher grades, reading becomes more and more a matter of comprehending concepts that represent relationships among facts and information. At the same time, learning the academic vocabulary that represents those concepts becomes more critical to comprehension.

For example, to understand literature, students must read to understand more than a narrative's simple sequence of events. They need to know how to inquire about a text—about why an author chooses particular events or how an author uses characterization, imagery, and plot to develop a thematic statement. Students can memorize the definitions of the vocabulary of literature; but, more importantly, they need to be able to apply their understanding of the concepts that the vocabulary of literature represent.

Similarly, comprehension of content-area text requires more than locating and memorizing specific information; it also requires students to make meaning of the concepts, represented by disciplinary vocabulary, that relate facts to each other. To make conceptual connections among facts, readers first need to activate and organize the background knowledge and experience that they have gained from real-word experience (the "given") that will be relevant to understanding the "new" information and concepts that the text offers. Comprehension then becomes a complex matter of confirming or disconfirming the relationship between the students' "given" and the text's "new" and of resolving any differences. Successful readers skillfully identify relationships among facts and information, analyze and synthesize often-conflicting facts and points of view, and consolidate their learning by testing the validity of what they have comprehended and thus learned.

To comprehend increasingly sophisticated content-specific texts, students typically draw upon their knowledge of three kinds of vocabulary. The first is the language of everyday experience, the concrete words commonly used in conversation. The second is the academic language that content areas share (e.g., *argument*, *persuasion*, *analysis*, *synthesis*, *comparison*, and *contrast*)—although such words may represent different meanings depending on subject-matter (e.g., *conflict*, *resolution*, and *analysis* represent different concepts in the study of literature and history). The third kind of vocabulary represents the highly specialized concepts that are particular to particular content (e.g., *allegory*, *mitosis*, *sine*, *colonialism*).

Vocabulary also plays an integral role in both inquiry-based learning and reading comprehension. Both are cognitive processes that roughly involve the same three instructional stages: preparation, strategic guidance, and consolidation. An abbreviated description of these stages is given on the following page.

Stage I:

Preparation for Learning/Reading

Teachers:

- provide students with instructional means by which they can activate, extend, amend, and organize the "given"—the background knowledge (including vocabulary knowledge) and experiences that will be relevant to learning new concepts and the vocabulary that represents those concepts; and
- explain to students how their background knowledge and experience will be relevant to understanding a lesson or text's "new" central concepts and vocabulary.

Stage II:

Strategic Guidance of Learning/Reading

Teachers facilitate inquiry/comprehension by providing instructional means by which students can:

- investigate, enrich, deepen, and revise their understanding of a reading's key vocabulary and central concepts; and
- practice skills, including their understanding of new vocabulary.

Stage III:

Consolidation of Learning/Reading

Teachers provide students with the means to consolidate their learning/comprehension by:

- providing means by which they can probe the validity of their understanding (learning/comprehension) of new concepts and vocabulary; and
- preparing students to demonstrate their learning/comprehension (e.g., through the application of new concepts and vocabulary to novel contexts, comparison and contrast, and argument).

Above all, the comprehension and vocabulary strategies teachers use must support the kind of learning that their instructional goals require. For example, the strategies that teachers might use to help students memorize facts and information are very different from those they might use to support students' deep comprehension and understanding.

To become independent learners/readers, students depend on their teachers to be explicit with them about *what* instructional strategies they are learning, *how* they could use those strategies most effectively given varied purposes, and *why* such strategies work. Students need to know how to monitor the success of their learning/reading, recognize when learning or comprehension has broken down, have a ready store of learning/reading strategies, and be able to choose the most expedient strategy to correct their course. In other words, students need to learn how to learn as well as learn how to comprehend if they are to become independent, ongoing students of an academic discipline who are not only prepared to graduate from high school but also, in the language of the Common Core State Standards, to be "college and career ready."

CLASSIC LITERATURE TO USE WITH THE PROGRAM

Levels A–C

Lloyd Alexander *The Book of Three*

Laurie Halse Anderson *Speak*

William Armstrong *Sounder*

Natalie Babbit *Tuck Everlasting*

Ray Bradbury *Dandelion Wine*

Pearl S. Buck *The Good Earth*

Sheila Bumford *The Incredible Journey*

Frances Hodgson Burnett *The Secret Garden*

Sandra Cisneros *The House on Mango Street*

Sook Nyul Choi *Year of Impossible Good-byes*

Robert Cornier *The Chocolate War*

Karen Cushman *The Midwife's Apprentice*

Daniel Defoe *Robinson Crusoe*

Elizabeth B. De Trevino *I, Juan de Pareja*

Sir Arthur Conan Doyle *The Hound of the Baskervilles*

Esther Forbes *Johnny Tremain*

Paul Gallico *The Snow Goose*

Jean Craighead George *Julie of the Wolves*

William Goldman *The Princess Bride*

Rosa Guy *The Friends*

Virginia Hamilton *The House of Dies Drear*, and *M.C. Higgins, the Great*

Jean Wakatsuki Houston and James D. Houston *Farewell to Manzanar*

Norton Juster *The Phantom Tollbooth*

Rudyard Kipling *Just So Stories*

E.L. Konigsburg *The View from Saturday*

Harper Lee *To Kill a Mockingbird*

Madeline L'Engle *A Wrinkle in Time*

Julius Lester *Long Journey Home*

Lois Lowry *The Giver*, and *Gathering Blue*

Daniel P. Mannix *The Fox and the Hound*

Nicholasa Mohr *Going Home*

Walter Dean Myers *Hoops*

Mary Norton *The Borrowers*

George Orwell *Animal Farm*

Katherine Paterson *Jacob Have I Loved*

Ann Petry *Harriet Tubman: Conductor on the Underground Railroad*

Marjorie Kinnan Rawlings *The Yearling*

Jack Schaefer *Shane*

George Selden *The Cricket in Times Square*

Antoine de Saint-Exupéry *The Little Prince*

Elizabeth George Speare *The Sign of the Beaver*

Rex Stout *Fer-de-Lance*, and *The Golden Spiders*

Yoshiko Uchida *Journey Home*

H.G. Wells *War of the Worlds*

Laura Ingalls Wilder *Little House on the Prairie*

Laurence Yep *Dragon's Gate*

Additional Titles and Enrichment

Louisa May Alcott *Little Women*

Lewis Carroll *Alice's Adventures in Wonderland*

Willa Cather *My Antonia*

James Fenimore Cooper *The Deerslayer*

Charles Dickens *Oliver Twist*, *A Tale of Two Cities*, and *A Christmas Carol*

Carson McCullers *The Member of the Wedding*

To coordinate reading and vocabulary study, the following may prove helpful:

- Students may devote a notebook to vocabulary. As they encounter key words in their reading, they should head a page of the notebook with the word; copy the title of the work; and then indicate (a) the definition used in that sentence, (b) its part of speech, and (c) whether it is used in a literal or figurative sense.
- Students may then be instructed to check *Bartlett's Familiar Quotations* for other famous examples of the use of the key word in question. These quotations may be copied into the notebook and shared with others in the class.

Vocabulary in Context

VOCABULARY WORKSHOP uses excerpts from classic literature to show how a Unit's vocabulary words are used in context.

Level A Vocabulary in Context Literary Selections

Unit 1	Johann David Wyss	*Swiss Family Robinson*
Unit 2	Walt Whitman	*Leaves of Grass*
Unit 3	Jules Verne	*Twenty Thousand Leagues Under the Sea*
Unit 4	Edgar Rice Burroughs	*A Princess of Mars*
Unit 5	H.G. Wells	*The First Men in the Moon*
Unit 6	Mark Twain	*The Prince and The Pauper* and *"The Celebrated Jumping Frog of Calaveras County"*
Unit 7	Charles Dickens	*Oliver Twist*
Unit 8	Sir Arthur Conan Doyle	*The Adventures of Sherlock Holmes*
Unit 9	L.M. Montgomery	*Anne of the Island*
Unit 10	Edgar Allan Poe	"The Gold-Bug," "The Unparalleled Adventure of One Hans Pfaall," "Ms. Found in a Bottle," and "The Murders in the Rue Morgue"
Unit 11	Jack London	*White Fang*
Unit 12	Sir Arthur Conan Doyle	*Tales of Terror and Mystery*
Unit 13	L.M. Montgomery	*Anne of Green Gables*
Unit 14	Charles Dickens	*The Life and Adventures of Nicholas Nickelby*
Unit 15	Washington Irving	*The Legend of Sleepy Hollow*

Level B Vocabulary in Context Literary Selections

Unit 1	Edgar Allan Poe	"The Balloon Hoax," "The Mystery of Marie Roget," "Ms. Found in a Bottle," and "The Gold-Bug"
Unit 2	O. Henry	"The Cop and the Anthem," "The Coming-out of Maggie," "The Green Door," "Springtime á la Carte," and "Man About Town"
Unit 3	Sir Arthur Conan Doyle	*The Lost World*

Unit 4	Jack London	*The Sea-Wolf*
Unit 5	Charles Dickens	*Oliver Twist*
Unit 6	Sir Arthur Conan Doyle	*The Adventures of Sherlock Holmes*
Unit 7	Mark Twain	*A Connecticut Yankee in King Arthur's Court*
Unit 8	Jules Verne	*A Journey to the Center of the Earth*
Unit 9	Bram Stoker	*Dracula*
Unit 10	Victor Hugo	*The Hunchback of Notre Dame*
Unit 11	Mary Wollstonecraft Shelley	*Frankenstein*
Unit 12	Victor Hugo	*Les Misérables*
Unit 13	Jules Verne	*Around the World in 80 Days*
Unit 14	Hans Christian Andersen	*Andersen's Fairy Tales*
Unit 15	Sir Arthur Conan Doyle	*The Adventures of Sherlock Holmes* and *The Hound of the Baskervilles*

Level C Vocabulary in Context Literary Selections

Unit 1	Baroness Orczy	*The Scarlet Pimpernel*
Unit 2	O. Henry	"Brickdust Road," "Two Thanksgiving Day Gentlemen," "The Trimmed Lamp"
Unit 3	Henry David Thoreau	*Walden*
Unit 4	Edgar Allan Poe	"A Descent into the Maelström," "The Premature Burial," "The Pit and the Pendulum," "William Wilson"
Unit 5	Charles Dickens	*A Christmas Carol*
Unit 6	Jack London	*The Call of the Wild* and *White Fang*
Unit 7	Louisa May Alcott	*Little Women*
Unit 8	Stephen Crane	*The Monster and Other Stories* and *The Red Badge of Courage*
Unit 9	Mark Twain	*Life on the Mississippi*
Unit 10	Edgar Rice Burroughs	*Tarzan of the Apes*
Unit 11	E.M. Forster	*Where Angels Fear to Tread*
Unit 12	Sir Arthur Conan Doyle	*The Lost World*
Unit 13	George Eliot	*Silas Marner* and *The Mill on the Floss*
Unit 14	Robert Louis Stevenson	*Strange Case of Dr. Jekyll and Mr. Hyde*
Unit 15	Henry James	*The Turn of the Screw*

VOCABULARY STRATEGY: Roots and Affixes

One important way students build vocabulary is to learn the meaning of Greek and Latin word parts that make up many English words. These word parts consist of **prefixes**, **suffixes**, and **roots**, or bases. A useful strategy for determining the meaning of an unknown word is to "take apart" the word and think about those parts.

Following is a list of common prefixes. Knowing the meaning of a prefix can help students determine the meaning of a word in which the prefix appears.

Prefix	**Meaning**	**Sample Words**
bi-	two	bicycle
com-, con-	together, with	compatriot, contact
de-	down, away from, not	devalue
dis-/di-	apart, opposite	disloyal, diverse
fore-, pre-	before, ahead of time	forewarn, preplan
il-, im-, in-, ir, non-, un-	not	illegal, impossible, inactive, irregular, nonsense, unable
in-, im-	in, into	inhale, import
mid-	middle	midway
mis-	wrongly, badly	mistake, misbehave
re-	again, back	redo, repay
sub-, sup-	under, less than	submarine, subzero, support, supplant
super-	above, greater than	superimpose, superstar
tri-	three	triangle

Following is a list of common suffixes. Knowing the meaning and grammatical function of a suffix can help students determine the meaning of a word.

Noun Suffix	**Meaning**	**Sample Nouns**
-acy, -ance, -ence, -hood, -ity, -ment, -ness, -ship	state, quality, or condition of, act or process of	adequacy, attendance, persistence, neighborhood, activity, judgment, brightness, friendship
-ant, -eer, -ent, -er, -ian, -ier, -ist, -or	one who does or makes something	contestant, auctioneer, resident, banker, comedian, financier, dentist, doctor
-ation, -ition, -ion	act or result of	organization, imposition, election

Verb Suffix	**Meaning**	**Sample Verbs**
-ate	to become, produce, or treat	validate, salivate, chlorinate

-en	to make, cause to be	weaken
-efy, -ify, -ize	to cause, make	liquefy, glorify, legalize

Adjective Suffix	**Meaning**	**Sample Adjectives**
-able, -ible	able, capable of	believable, incredible
-al, -ic	relating to, characteristic of	natural, romantic
-ful, -ive, -ous	full of, given to, marked by	beautiful, protective, poisonous
-ish, -like	like, resembling	foolish, childlike
-less	lacking, without	careless

A root is the main part of a word to which prefixes and suffixes may be added. Many roots come to English from Latin. Knowing Greek, Latin, and even Anglo-Saxon roots can help students determine the meaning of a word.

In the Building with Classical Roots sections of this book students will learn more about some of these Latin and Greek roots and about the English words that derive from them.

Greek Root	**Meaning**	**Sample Words**
-aster-, -astro-	star	asteroid, astronaut, disaster
-auto-	self	autograph
-bio-	life	biography
-chron-, chrono-	time	chronic, chronological
-cosm-, -cosmo-	universe, order	microcosm, cosmopolitan
-cryph-, -crypt-	hidden, secret	apocryphal, cryptographer
-dem-, -demo-	people	epidemic, democracy
-dog-, -dox-	opinion, teaching	dogmatic, orthodox
-gen-	race, kind, origin, birth	generation, genetic
-gnos-	know	diagnostic
-graph-, -graphy-, -gram-	write	graphite, autobiography, telegram
-log-, -logue-	speech, word, reasoning	logic, dialogue
-lys-, -lyt-	break down	analysis, electrolyte, catalytic
-metr-, -meter-	measure	metric, kilometer
-micro-	small	microchip
-morph-	form, shape	amorphous
-naut-	ship	nautical

-phon-, -phone-, -phono-	sound, voice	phonics, telephone, phonograph
-pol-, -polis-, -polit-	city, state	police, metropolis, political
-scop-, -scope-	watch, look at	microscopic, telescope
-tele-	far off, distant, end	television, teleological
-the-	put or place	parentheses

Latin Root	**Meaning**	**Sample Words**
-cap-, -capt-, -cept-, -cip-	take	captive, concept, recipient
-cede-, -ceed-, -ceas-, -cess-	happen, yield, go	precede, proceed, decease, cessation
-cred-	believe	incredible
-dic-, -dict-	speak, say, tell	indicate, diction
-duc-, -duct-	lead, conduct, draw	educate, conduct
-fac-, -fact-, -fect-, -fic-	make	faculty, artifact, defect, beneficial
-ject-	throw	eject
-mis-, -miss-, -mit-, -mitt-	send	promise, missile, transmit, intermittent
-note-, -not-	know, recognize	denote, notion
-pel-, -puls-	drive	expel, compulsive
-pend-, -pens-	hang, weigh, set aside	pendulum, pension
-pon-, -pos-	put, place	component, position
-port-	carry	portable
-rupt-	break	bankrupt
-scrib-, -scribe-, -script-	write	scribble, describe, inscription
-spec-, -spic-	look, see	spectator, conspicuous
-tac-, -tag-, -tang-, -teg-	touch	contact, contagious, tangible, integral
-tain-, -ten-, -tin-	hold, keep	contain, tenure, retinue
-temp-	time	tempo
-ven-, -vent-	come	intervene, convention
-vers-, -vert-	turn	reverse, invert
-voc-, -vok-	call	vocal, invoke

DENOTATION, CONNOTATION, AND SHADES OF MEANING

The ***denotation*** of a word is its specific dictionary meaning. Here are a few examples:

Word	**Denotation**
hospitable	courteous
plague	pester
constituent	essential part

The ***connotation*** of a word is its **tone**—that is, the emotions or associations it normally arouses in people using, hearing, or reading it. Depending on what these feelings are, the connotation of a word may be *favorable* (*positive*) or *unfavorable* (*negative, pejorative*). A word that does not normally arouse strong feelings of any kind has a *neutral* connotation. Here are some examples of words with different connotations:

Word	**Connotation**
hospitable	favorable
plague	unfavorable
constituent	neutral

Every Word Study section of VOCABULARY WORKSHOP has two pages of instruction on and practice with the denotation and connotation of words. The exercises in this section will prepare students to meet the Craft and Structure requirements of the Common Core State Standards.

FIGURATIVE LANGUAGE

After every three Units of **Vocabulary Workshop**, there is a Review and a Word Study section, for a total of five Word Study sections per book. Each Word Study section contains a two-page lesson on idioms, proverbs, or adages. These three types of figurative language, especially problematical for ELL students, are important in light of the Common Core State Standards, which require students in grades 6–8 to demonstrate an understanding of figurative language by interpreting figures of speech in context and analyzing their role in the text. The Common Core directive that students read texts (both literary and informational) of increasing complexity means that students are more likely to encounter figurative expressions in their reading. Furthermore, these three types of figurative language frequently appear in standardized test items.

- An **idiom** is an informal expression whose literal meaning does not help the reader or listener figure out what the expression means. English is particularly rich in idioms and idiomatic expressions, such as "raining cats and dogs," "the apple of my eye," or "a dark horse."
- An **adage** expresses a common experience, often in the form of a phrase or sentence, such as "Time flies when you're having fun."
- A **proverb** is a statement that provides a lesson or a moral, such as "A stitch in time saves nine" and "A rolling stone gathers no moss."

Teachers may note with students that every language has its own idioms, proverbs, and adages. Students may find or think of examples from other cultures, especially if another language is spoken at home. Understanding the meaning of common English idioms, adages, and proverbs will improve reading ability and enrich students' writing.

How to Use the Word Study Lessons

The first page of each lesson refers to one of the introductory Reading Passages in the three preceding Units. An idiom, adage, or proverb is embedded in the Passage, where it is used in context. Students next encounter the idiom (or adage or proverb) on the first page of the Word Study section. Following instruction and examples of these figures of speech, students are given ten sentences containing different idioms (or adages or proverbs) in context and are asked to match each with its definition. The second page is a **writing exercise** in which students are required to write original sentences using twelve additional idioms (or adages or proverbs).

Enriching the Word Study Lessons

Teachers may suggest that students draw a cartoon that uses a proverb or an adage as a caption, or they might write brief narratives or fables with a proverb or adage as the moral. Standardized tests, such as the SAT, might use a proverb as a writing prompt; students are then asked to discuss the proverb, drawing from their personal experiences, observations, and reading. Students will practice writing such essays in the **Writing: Words in Action** activities during the course of the school year.

SADLIER

VOCABULARY WORKSHOP®

ENRICHED EDITION

Jerome Shostak

Senior Series Consultant

Vicki A. Jacobs, Ed.D.
Associate Director, Teacher Education Program
Lecturer on Education
Harvard Graduate School of Education
Cambridge, Massachusetts

Series Consultants

Louis P. De Angelo, Ed.D.
Associate Superintendent
Diocese of Wilmington
Wilmington, Delaware

John Heath, Ph.D.
Professor of Classics
Santa Clara University
Santa Clara, California

Sarah Ressler Wright, NBCT
English Department Chair
Rutherford B. Hayes High School
Delaware City Schools, Ohio

Carolyn E. Waters, JD, Ed.S.
ELA/Literacy 6–12 Supervisor
Cobb County School District
Marietta, Georgia

Reviewers

The publisher wishes to thank for their comments and suggestions the following teachers and administrators, who read portions of the series prior to publication.

Teresa Appleby
English Teacher
Paxon Hollow Middle School
Marple Newtown District
Broomall, Pennsylvania

Laura Braun
Assistant Principal
Sawyer School
Chicago Public Schools
Chicago, Illinois.

Eileen Brosnahan
Language Arts Teacher
St. Rita Catholic School
Dallas, Texas

Colleen DeGonia
Reading/Language Arts Teacher
Worth Junior High School
Worth, Illinois

Karen Berlin Ishii
Academic and Test Prep Tutor
New York, New York

Susan W. Keogh
Associate Director
Curriculum and Instruction
Lake Highland Preparatory
Orlando, Florida

Carol H. Rohrbach
Director of Curriculum and Staff Development
School District of Springfield Township
Oreland, Pennsylvania

Scott L. Smith
Teacher
Whitewater Valley Elementary
Harrison, Ohio

Patricia Stack
English Teacher
South Park School District
South Park, Pennsylvania

Sally F. Waller
English Teacher
Loyola Blakefield Middle School
Towson, Maryland

Cover: Concept/Art and Design: MK Advertising and William H. Sadlier, Inc.; Cover pencil: Shutterstock/VikaSuh. **Photo Credits:** akg-images: 103, 183. Alamy/AF archive: 135, 145; Archive Images: 141; Everett Collection Inc: 31; Friedrich Stark: 151; imageZebra: 70 *top*; JLImages: 65; Moviestore collection Ltd: 193; Photos 12: 59, 107; UK History: 60; United Archives GmbH: 117, 155; WoodyStock: 37. AP Images/Bettmann/Corbis: 33. Art Resource, NY/ SCALA/The Museum of Modern Art/ARS, NY/Chagall, Marc (1887–1985), *Birthday* (*L'Anniversaire*), 1915, oil on canvas, 31 3/4 X 39 1/4", acquired through the Lillie P. Bliss Bequest: 109; The Kobal Collection/CBS-TV: 131; First National: 41; United Artists: 173. Becker Medical Library, Washington University School of Medicine: 127 *bottom*. The Bridgeman Art Library/Metropolitan Museum of Art, New York, USA: 55; National Geographic Image Collection: 12; Romeo and Juliet from *Children's Stories from Shakespeare* by Edith Nesbit (1858-1924) pub. by Raphael Tuck & Sons Ltd., London (book illustration), Bacon, John Henry Frederick (1868-1914)/Private Collection: 93; Yale Center for British Art, Paul Mellon Collection, USA: 27. Corbis: 189; Bettmann: 97, 136 *bottom*, 137 *bottom*, 169, 179; Blend Images/Hill Street Studios: 110; moodboard/Mike Watson: 17; Reuters: 175 *top*. Digital Vision: 98. Getty Images/Archive Photos: 164 *right*; Gammo-Rapho/Raphael Gaillarde: 185; Hulton Archive/Central Press: 165; Photo Researchers/Richard Ellis: 99 *top*; Popperfoto: 136; Premium Archive/Bert Morgen: 146, 147 *bottom*; Sports Illustrated/Jerry Cooke: 147 *top*; Stone/Alejandro Balaguer: 70 *bottom*; Time & Life Pictures/Alfred Eisenstaedt: 75; Time & Life Pictures/Lee Lockwood: 108 *background* and *inset*. The Granger Collection, New York: 32 *bottom*, 184. The Image Works/Ann Ronan Picture Library/HIP: 79; Mary Evans Picture Library: 21; TopFoto: 175 *bottom*. Lebrecht Music & Arts Photo/Lebrecht Authors/*The Adventures of Oliver Twist* by Charles Dickens/Illustration by James Mahoney: 69. Minden Pictures/Nature Production/Shinji Kusano: 99 *bottom*. New York Public Library, Astor, Lenox and Tilden Foundations/Print Collection, Miriam and Ira D. Wallach Division of Art, Prints and Photographs: 32 *top*. Oxford University Press/Oxford Atlas of World History: 13. Photodisc: 32 frame, 60 *background*, 136 *top*, 137 *top*. Shutterstock/3d brained: 164 *left*; A-R-T: 13 scroll; Blue Lemon Photo: 22 *left*; Gregor Buir: 32 *background*; Iwona Grodzka: 22, 23 *top*; Jean Schweitzer: 146; Joao Virissimo: 22 *right*; Kesu: 23 *bottom*; Welena: 146 frame. St Bartholomew's Hospital Archives & Museum, North Wing, St Bartholomew's Hospital, West Smithfield London, EC1A 7BE/The Royal London Hospital Archives & Museum, The Royal London Hospital, Whitechapel, London, E1 1BB: 61. Stockbyte: 13 *background*, 185 *background*. SuperStock/Clover: 185; Image Asset Management Ltd: 126 *left*; Minden Pictures: 98; Rubberball: 127 *top*; Yoshio Tomi: 71. Wikipedia: 12, 126 *right*. World Health Organization: 174.

Illustration Credits: Tim Haggerty: 46, 84, 122, 160, 193. Lazlo Kubinyi/Gerald & Cullen Rapp: 88–89. Ron Tanovitz: 50–51.

Address inquiries to Permissions Department,
William H. Sadlier, Inc.,
9 Pine Street, New York, New York 10005-4700.

Printed in the United States of America.
ISBN: 978-0-8215-8007-3
3 4 5 6 RRDH 19 18 17 16 15

For additional online resources, go to vocabularyworkshop.com and enter the Student Access Code: VW13SB6RFF2MJ

ENRICHED EDITION: New Features

For more than five decades, **VOCABULARY WORKSHOP** has proven to be a highly successful tool for guiding systematic vocabulary growth and developing vocabulary skills. It has also been shown to help students prepare for standardized tests.

New in this edition are the **Reading Passages, Writing, Vocabulary in Context,** and **Word Study** activities. Nonfiction, high-interest passages use 15 or more of the Unit vocabulary words in context. Two writing prompts require a response to the reading and provide practice in writing for standardized tests. New Vocabulary in Context activities present words from the Unit as they are used in classic works of literature. After every three units, Word Study activities, developed in conjunction with Common Core State Standards requirements, provide practice with idioms, adages, and proverbs, as well as denotation and connotation and classical roots.

Look for the new **QR** (Quick Response) codes on the **Reading Passage** and **Vocabulary in Context** pages. QR codes can be read with a smartphone camera by downloading any free QR code application to a smartphone. Snap the code to listen to iWords and an audio of the Reading Passage for the Unit or to take an interactive quiz. With iWords you can listen to one word at a time or download all of the words in a Unit to listen to them at your convenience.

The new structure of VOCABULARY WORKSHOP is made up of 15 Units. Each Unit consists of the following sections: a **Reading Passage, Definitions, Choosing the Right Word, Synonyms and Antonyms, Completing the Sentence, Writing,** and **Vocabulary in Context**. Together, these exercises provide multiple and varied exposures to the taught words—an approach consistent with and supportive of research-based findings in vocabulary instruction.

Five **Reviews** cover Vocabulary for Comprehension and Two-Word Completions. Vocabulary for Comprehension is modeled on the reading sections of standardized tests, and as in those tests, it presents reading comprehension questions, including specific vocabulary-related ones, that are based on a reading passage.

A **Final Mastery Test** assesses a selection of words from the year with activities on Synonyms, Antonyms, Analogies, Two-Word Completions, Supplying Words in Context, Word Associations, and Choosing the Right Meaning.

In each level of **VOCABULARY WORKSHOP**, 300 key words are taught. The words have been selected according to the following criteria: currency and general usefulness; frequency of appearance on recognized vocabulary lists; applicability to, and appearance on, standardized tests; and current grade-level research.

ONLINE COMPONENTS

vocabularyworkshop.com

At **vocabularyworkshop.com** you will find iWords, an audio program that provides pronunciations, definitions, and examples of usage for all of the key words presented in this level of **VOCABULARY WORKSHOP**. You can listen to one word at a time or download all of the words of any given Unit. You will then be able to listen to the audio program for that Unit at your convenience.

At **vocabularyworkshop.com** you will also find **Audio Passages, interactive vocabulary quizzes, flashcards, games and puzzles** that will help reinforce and enrich your understanding of the key words in this level of **VOCABULARY WORKSHOP**.

CONTENTS

iWords Audio Program available at **vocabularyworkshop.com**.

VOCABULARY STRATEGY: Using Context

The **context** of a word is the printed text of which that word is part. By studying the word's context, we may find **clues** to its meaning. We might find a clue in the immediate or adjoining sentence or phrase in which the word appears; in the topic or subject matter of the passage; or in the physical features—such as photographs, illustrations, charts, graphs, captions and headings—of a page itself.

The **Vocabulary in Context**, **Vocabulary for Comprehension**, and **Choosing the Right Meaning** exercises that appear in the Units, the Reviews, and Final Mastery Test provide practice in using context to decode unfamiliar words.

Three types of context clues appear in the exercises in this book.

A ***restatement clue*** consists of a *synonym* for or a *definition* of the missing word. For example:

The ______________, lively puppy ran around in circles when let out into the yard.

a. spirited **b.** humdrum **c.** fallible **d.** casual

In this sentence, *lively* is a synonym of the missing word, *spirited*, and acts as a restatement clue for it.

A ***contrast clue*** consists of an *antonym* for or a phrase that means the opposite of the missing word. For example:

"It seemed to me that the race was easy," I said,

"But many of the runners found it (**grueling, transparent**)."

In this sentence, *easy* is an antonym of the missing word, *grueling*. This is confirmed by the presence of the word *but*, which indicates that the answer must be the opposite of *easy*.

An ***inference clue*** implies but does not directly state the meaning of the missing word or words. For example:

Like most ______________ the young reporter was looking to make big changes in the paper, but his attempts were always put down by the ______________ editor, who liked things to stay the same.

a. buffoons . . . hostile **c.** beneficiaries . . . notorious
b. dynasties . . . piecemeal **d.** firebrands. . . stodgy

In this sentence, there are several inference clues: (a) the phrase *make big changes* suggests *firebrand*; (b) the words *liked things to stay the same* suggest the word *stodgy*. These words are inference clues because they suggest or imply, but do not directly state, the missing word or words.

VOCABULARY STRATEGY: Word Structure

Prefixes, **suffixes**, and **roots**, or **bases**, are word parts. One strategy for determining an unknown word's meaning is to "take apart" the word and think about the parts. Study the prefixes and suffixes below to help you find out the meanings of words in which they appear.

Prefix	Meaning	Sample Words
com-, con-	together, with	compatriot, contact
de-,	down, away from, not	devalue
dis-, di-	apart, opposite	disloyal, dichromatic
il-, im-, in-, ir, non-, un-	not	illegal, impossible, inactive, irregular, nonsense, unable
sub-, sup-,	under, less than	submarine, support
super-	above, greater than	superimpose, superstar

Noun Suffix	Suffix Meaning	Sample Nouns
-acy, -ance, -ence, -hood, -ity, -ment, -ness, -ship	state, quality, or condition of, act or process of	adequacy, attendance, persistence, neighborhood, activity, judgment, brightness, friendship
-ant, -eer, -ent, -er, -ian, -ier, -ist, -or	one who does or makes something	auctioneer, contestant, resident, banker, comedian, financier, dentist, doctor
-ation, -ition, -ion	act or result of	organization, imposition, election

Verb Suffix	Meaning	Sample Verbs
-ate	to become, produce, or treat	validate, salivate, chlorinate
-efy, -ify, -ize	to cause, make	liquefy, glorify, legalize

Adjective Suffix	Meaning	Sample Adjectives
-able, -ible	able, capable of	believable, incredible
-al, -ic	relating to, characteristic of	natural, romantic
-ful, -ive, -ous	full of, given to, marked by	beautiful, protective, poisonous
-ish, -like	like, resembling	foolish, childlike
-less	lacking, without	careless

A **base** or **root** is the main part of a word to which prefixes and suffixes may be added. On the Classical Roots page of the Word Study section, you will learn more about Latin and Greek roots and the English words that derive from them. The following lists may help you figure out the meaning of new or unfamiliar words.

Greek Root	Meaning	Sample Words
-cryph-, -crypt-	hidden, secret	apocryphal, cryptographer
-dem-, -demo-	people	epidemic, democracy
-gen-	race, kind, origin, birth	generation
-gnos-	know	diagnostic
-lys-, -lyt-	break down	analysis, electrolyte, catalytic

Latin Root	Meaning	Sample Words
-cap-, -capt-, -cept-, -cip-	take	captive, concept, recipient
-cede-, -ceed-, -ceas- -cess-	happen, yield, go	precede, proceed, decease, cessation
-fac-, -fact-, -fect-, -fic-	make	faculty, artifact, defect, beneficial,
-tac-, -tag-, -tang-, -teg-	touch	contact, contagious, tangible, integral
-tain-, -ten-, -tin-	hold, keep	contain, tenure, retinue

For more prefixes, suffixes, and roots, visit **vocabularyworkshop.com**.

VOCABULARY AND READING

Word knowledge is essential to reading comprehension. Your knowledge of word meanings and ability to think carefully about what you read will help you succeed in school and on standardized tests, including the SAT, the ACT, and the PSAT.

New **Reading Passages** provide extra practice with vocabulary words. Vocabulary words are boldfaced to draw students' attention to their uses and contexts. Context clues embedded in the passages encourage students to figure out the meanings of words before they read the definitions provided on the pages directly following the passages.

Students read excerpts from classic literature in the **Vocabulary in Context** exercises. Each excerpt includes one of the Unit vocabulary words as it is used in the original work. Students can use what they learn about the word from its use in context to answer questions on the definition.

The **Vocabulary for Comprehension** exercises in each review consist of a nonfiction reading passage followed by comprehension questions. The passages and questions are similar to those that you are likely to find on standardized tests.

Kinds of Questions

Main Idea Questions generally ask what the passage as a whole is about. Often, but not always, the main idea is stated in the first paragraph of the passage. You may also be asked the main idea of a specific paragraph. Questions about the main idea may begin like this:

- The primary or main purpose of the passage is. . .
- The passage is best described as. . .
- The title that best describes the content of the passage is. . .

Detail Questions focus on important information that is explicitly stated in the passage. Often, however, the correct answer choices do not use the exact language of the passage. They are instead restatements, or paraphrases, of the text.

Vocabulary-in-Context Questions check your ability to use context to identify a word's meaning. Use line references to see how and in what context the word is used. For example:

- **Testimonial** (line 8) is best defined as. . .
- The meaning of **detest** (line 30) is. . .

Use context to check your answer choices, particularly when the vocabulary word has more than one meaning. Among the choices may be two (or more) correct meanings of the word in question. Choose the meaning that best fits the context.

Inference Questions ask you to make inferences or draw conclusions from the passage. These questions often begin like this:

- It can be inferred from the passage that. . .
- The author implies that. . .
- Evidently the author feels that. . .

The inferences you make and the conclusions you draw must be based on the information in the passage. Your own knowledge and reasoning come into play in understanding what is implied and in reaching conclusions that are logical.

Questions About Tone show your understanding of the author's attitude toward the subject of the passage. Words that describe tone, or attitude, are "feeling" words, such as *indifferent*, *ambivalent*, *scornful*, *astonished*, *respectful*. These are typical questions:

- The author's attitude toward . . . is best described as. . .
- Which word best describes the author's tone?

To determine the tone, pay attention to the author's word choice. The author's attitude may be positive (respectful), negative (scornful), or neutral (distant).

Questions About Author's Technique focus on the way a text is organized and the language the author uses. These questions ask you to think about structure and function. For example:

- The final paragraph serves to. . .
- The author cites . . . in order to . . . .

To answer the questions, you must demonstrate an understanding of the way the author presents information and develops ideas.

Strategies

Here are some general strategies to help you as you read each passage and answer the questions.

- Read the introduction first. The introduction will provide a focus for the selection.

- Be an active reader. As you read, ask yourself questions about the passage—for example: What is this paragraph about? What does the writer mean here? Why does the writer include this information?

- Refer to the passage when you answer the questions. In general, the order of the questions mirrors the organization of the passage, and many of the questions include paragraph or line references. It is often helpful to go back and reread before choosing an answer.

- Read carefully, and be sure to base your answer choices on the passage. There are answer choices that make sense but are not based on the information in the passage. These are true statements, but they are incorrect answers. The correct answers are either restatements of ideas in the text or inferences that can be drawn from the text.

- Consider each exercise a learning experience. Keep in mind that your ability to answer the questions correctly shows as much about your understanding of the questions as about your understanding of the passage.

WORKING WITH ANALOGIES

A verbal analogy expresses a relationship or comparison between sets of words. Normally, an analogy contains two pairs of words linked by a word or symbol that stands for an equal (=) sign. A complete analogy compares the two pairs of words and makes a statement about them. It asserts that the relationship between the first—or key—pair of words is the same as the relationship between the second pair.

In the **Analogies** exercises in the Final Mastery Test, you will be asked to complete analogies—that is, to choose the pair of words that best matches or parallels the relationship of the key, or given, pair of words. Here are two examples:

1. **maple** is to **tree** as
   - **a.** acorn is to oak
   - **b.** hen is to rooster
   - **c.** rose is to flower
   - **d.** shrub is to lilac

2. **joyful** is to **gloomy** as
   - **a.** cheerful is to happy
   - **b.** strong is to weak
   - **c.** quick is to famous
   - **d.** hungry is to starving

In order to find the correct answer to exercise 1, you must first determine the relationship between the two key words, **maple** and **tree**. In this case, that relationship might be expressed as "a maple is a kind (or type) of tree." The next step is to select from choices a, b, c, and d the pair of words that best reflects the same relationship. The correct answer is (c); it is the only pair whose relationship parallels the one in the key words: A rose is a kind (or type) of flower, just as a maple is a kind (or type) of tree. The other choices do not express the same relationship.

In exercise 2, the relationship between the key words can be expressed as "joyful means the opposite of gloomy." Which of the choices best represents the same relationship? The answer is (b): "strong means the opposite of weak."

Here are examples of some other common analogy relationships:

Analogy	Key Relationship
big is to **large** as **little** is to **small**	**Big** means the same thing as **large**, just as **little** means the same thing as **small**.
brave is to **favorable** as **cowardly** is to **unfavorable**	The tone of **brave** is **favorable**, just as the tone of **cowardly** is **unfavorable**.
busybody is to **nosy** as **klutz** is to **clumsy**	A **busybody** is by definition someone who is **nosy**, just as a **klutz** is by definition someone who is **clumsy**.
cowardly is to **courage** as **awkward** is to **grace**	Someone who is **cowardly** lacks **courage**, just as someone who is **awkward** lacks **grace**.
visible is to **see** as **audible** is to **hear**	If something is **visible**, you can by definition **see** it, just as if something is **audible**, you can by definition **hear** it.
liar is to **truthful** as **bigot** is to **fair-minded**	A **liar** is by definition not likely to be **truthful**, just as a **bigot** is by definition not likely to be **fair-minded**.
eyes are to **see** as **ears** are to **hear**	You use your **eyes** to **see** with, just as you use your **ears** to **hear** with.

There are many different kinds of relationships represented in the analogy questions you will find in the Final Mastery Test, but the key to solving any analogy is to find and express the relationship between the two key words.

UNIT 1

Note that not all of the 20 Unit words are used in this passage. *Humdrum*, *hurtle*, *recompense*, *trivial*, and *truce* are not included.

Read the following passage, taking note of the ***boldface*** *words and their contexts. These words are among those you will be studying in Unit 1. It may help you to complete the exercises in this Unit if you refer to the way the words are used below.*

CCSS Vocabulary: 4; Reading (Informational Text): 4, 6. (See pp. T14–15.)

The Times of Zheng He

<Narrative Nonfiction>

Zheng He was born in the year 1371, in the Chinese province of Yunnan. He was descended from a Persian who had been governor of Yunnan over a century before, in the early days of the Mongol-led Yuan **Dynasty**. The family retained its connections to the Mongol rulers of China through those years. But nothing is **interminable** in this world. A change was in the wind. About the time Zheng was born, the Ming clan asserted itself as the new ruling dynasty in China. Ming armies pushed the Mongols out of China and back to their homeland in Mongolia, an **adjacent** country in the north, dry and rather **barren**.

While Zheng was still a boy, pockets of Mongol loyalists remained in certain areas of China, not least in the southern province of Yunnan. Unrest erupted wherever loyalists lived. Zheng was about ten years old when political turmoil **disrupted** his life, forever altering its course. His father was killed in 1381 during the Ming army's conquest of Yunnan. Zheng was captured and sent to the court of Prince Zhu Di, son of the Ming emperor. If the boy was **sullen** and withdrawn at first, he did not remain so for long. He became one of the prince's trusted advisors, gradually **insinuating** himself into a position of respect. In time, Prince Zhu Di sought to depose his own nephew, who had become the second Ming emperor. When the hour came, he relied on Zheng's assistance. And when the insurrection proved successful, Zhu Di had become the third Ming emperor of China, and Zheng He was now the right hand to the emperor.

Emperor Zhu Di of the Ming Dynasty

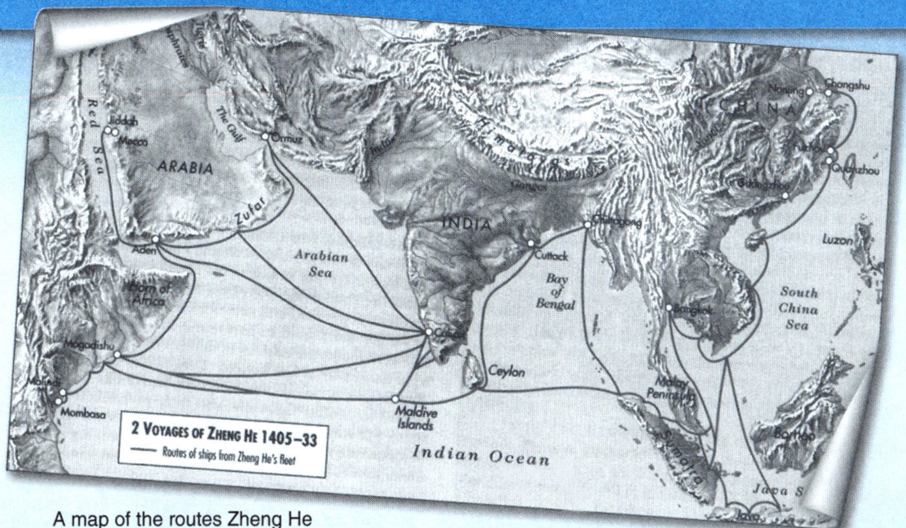

A map of the routes Zheng He took during his expeditions

This adventure was only a **foretaste** of what lay ahead for Zheng He. The new emperor had ambitious plans to **renovate** China after years of **vicious** war had reduced the population and stalled production to a **trickle**. The emperor planned to restore the economy, promote construction, maintain order and protect the borders, stimulate culture and learning, and extend China's influence throughout the world. As part of his vision, he sponsored a series of massive naval expeditions, appointing Zheng to be chief envoy and leader of the fleet.

Zheng led six expeditions for the emperor, his own prestige increasing with each notch in his **résumé**. The first expedition set off in 1405, with about 300 huge ships and nearly 30,000 men. At the time, it was the largest fleet ever to have sailed from China.

The main purpose of the expeditions was not exploration, or conquest, or commerce, but diplomacy. Zheng's giant fleet and the soldiers who manned it made a strong impression wherever they went. They projected an image of Chinese wealth and power. The troops were rarely called on for a display of force; the size of the fleet was intimidating enough. Wherever Zheng **alighted**, he had an opportunity to **interrogate** the locals for news, meet with local elites to exchange gifts and information, and represent the interests of the Chinese emperor.

The emperor died in 1424. His successors did not continue his maritime policy. Zheng He led one more fleet in 1433. He died during this last great expedition and was buried at sea. Seeds of foreign relations planted during his lifetime **germinated** even after he was gone.

The Hall of Supreme Harmony, one of China's greatest buildings, was built in 1406 for the Ming emperor Zhu Di.

Audio

For iWords and audio passages, snap the code, or go to **vocabularyworkshop.com**.

Definitions

Note the spelling, pronunciation, part(s) of speech, and definition(s) of each of the following words. Then write the appropriate form of the word in the blank spaces in the illustrative sentence(s) following. Finally, study the lists of synonyms and antonyms.

1. adjacent
(ə jās′ ənt)

(*adj.*) near, next to, adjoining

Boston and its **adjacent** suburbs were severely flooded after three days of heavy rain.

SYNONYMS: alongside, nearby, neighboring
ANTONYMS: faraway, distant

2. alight
(ə līt′)

(*v.*) to get down from, step down from; to come down from the air, land; (*adj.*) lighted up

The passengers hurried to **alight** from the small airplane.

The sky was **alight** with a red glow as the fire raged in the distance.

SYNONYMS: (*v.*) dismount, land, touch down
ANTONYMS: (*v.*) mount, board, take off

3. barren
(bar′ ən)

(*adj.*) not productive, bare

In contrast to the rich land we left behind, the plains appeared to be a **barren** landscape.

SYNONYMS: unproductive, sterile, desolate, arid
ANTONYMS: fertile, fruitful

4. disrupt
(dis rəpt′)

(*v.*) to break up, disturb

Even the loud demonstration on the street below was not enough to **disrupt** the meeting.

SYNONYMS: upset, displace, disorder
ANTONYMS: organize, arrange

5. dynasty
(dī′ nə stē)

(*n.*) a powerful family or group of rulers that maintains its position or power for some time

The Han **Dynasty** of China was in power for about 400 years.

SYNONYMS: ruling house, regime

6. foretaste
(fôr′ tāst)

(*n.*) an advance indication, sample, or warning

The eye-opening first scene of the new play gave the audience a **foretaste** of things to come.

SYNONYMS: preview, anticipation

CCSS Vocabulary: 4.c., 4.d. (See pp. T14–15.)

7. germinate (jər′ mə nāt)

(*v.*) to begin to grow, come into being

After he interrogated the suspect, suspicion began to **germinate** in the inspector's mind.

SYNONYMS: sprout, shoot up, burgeon
ANTONYMS: wither, die, stagnate, shrivel up

8. humdrum (həm′ drəm)

(*adj.*) ordinary, dull, routine, without variation

All household tasks are **humdrum**, according to my brother, who never helps with them.

SYNONYMS: monotonous, prosaic, boring
ANTONYMS: exciting, thrilling, exhilarating

9. hurtle (hər′ təl)

(*v.*) to rush violently, dash headlong; to fling or hurl forcefully

After separating from its booster rocket, the capsule began to **hurtle** through space.

SYNONYMS: speed, fly, catapult, fling
ANTONYMS: crawl, creep

10. insinuate (in sin′ yü āt)

(*v.*) to suggest or hint slyly; to edge into something indirectly

The attorney attempted to **insinuate** that the witness's testimony was false.

SYNONYM: imply
ANTONYMS: barge in, broadcast

11. interminable (in tər′ mə nə bəl)

(*adj.*) endless, so long as to seem endless

We had an **interminable** wait in the hot, crowded train station.

SYNONYM: never-ending
ANTONYMS: brief, short, fleeting

12. interrogate (in ter′ ə gāt)

(*v.*) to ask questions, examine by questioning

Two detectives helped the young, inexperienced officer to **interrogate** the suspect.

SYNONYMS: question, query

13. recompense (rek′ əm pens)

(*v.*) to pay back; to give a reward; (*n.*) a payment for loss, service, or injury

My grandparents were happy to **recompense** the little girl who found their lost puppy.

As **recompense**, the landlord offered all tenants a month free of rent.

SYNONYMS: (*v.*) repay; (*n.*) compensation

14. renovate (ren′ ə vāt)

(*v.*) to repair, restore to good condition, make new again

The young couple brought in an architect and a contractor to help them ___renovate___ the old house.

SYNONYMS: repair, recondition

15. résumé (rez′ ə mā)

(*n.*) a brief summary; a short written account of one's education, working experience, or qualifications for a job

The job applicant gave a copy of her ___résumé___ to the person in charge of the employment agency.

SYNONYM: synopsis

16. sullen (səl′ ən)

(*adj.*) silent or brooding because of ill humor, anger, or resentment; slow moving, sluggish

The ___sullen___ student sat down in the back of the classroom.

SYNONYMS: grumpy, surly, peevish, morose
ANTONYMS: cheerful, blithe, vivacious

17. trickle (trik′ əl)

(*v.*) to flow or fall by drops or in a small stream; (*n.*) a small, irregular quantity of anything

The water began to ___trickle___ from the rusty old pipe.

The runoff, which is quite heavy in the spring, dwindles to a ___trickle___ by late summer.

SYNONYMS: (*v.*) dribble, drizzle, drip; (*n.*) small amount
ANTONYMS: (*v.*) gush, pour, flood; (*n.*) deluge

18. trivial (triv′ ē əl)

(*adj.*) not important, minor; ordinary, commonplace

The general left all ___trivial___ details to subordinate officers.

SYNONYMS: insignificant, trifling
ANTONYMS: important, weighty

19. truce (trüs)

(*n.*) a pause in fighting, temporary peace

After tense negotiations, the warring nations reluctantly agreed to a five-day ___truce___.

SYNONYM: cease-fire; ANTONYMS: war, warfare

20. vicious (vish′ əs)

(*adj.*) evil, bad; spiteful; having bad habits or an ugly disposition; painfully severe or extreme

The ___vicious___ rumor was damaging to their budding friendship.

SYNONYMS: wicked, malicious
ANTONYMS: good, kind, kindly, mild

CCSS Vocabulary: 4.c., 4.d. (See pp. T14–15.)

Choosing the Right Word

*Select the **boldface** word that better completes each sentence. You might refer to the passage on pages 12–13 to see how most of these words are used in context.*

Pep rallies raise team spirit and are rarely humdrum.

1. Our team spirit is so high that there is never a (**sullen, trivial**) reaction from players who aren't chosen to start a game.

2. Sometime in mid-August, you can view the spectacular Perseid meteor shower, as comet debris (**hurtle, alight**) through space and enter Earth's atmosphere.

3. The principal asked the students not to hang around in front of the houses and other buildings (**adjacent to, alighting**) the school.

4. The administration had no major scandals, but it was also (**barren, sullen**) of outstanding accomplishments.

5. I am angry not because she criticized me but because she made remarks that were untrue and (**trivial, vicious**).

6. I'd been looking forward to the new TV series on Monday nights, but the first episode turned out to be just another (**humdrum, adjacent**) detective story.

7. Are we going to allow minor disagreements to (**disrupt, recompense**) the club that we have worked so hard to organize?

8. He said that he was going to ask only "a few casual questions," but I soon saw that he wanted to (**recompense, interrogate**) me thoroughly.

9. Even the most (**humdrum, vicious**) work can be interesting if you regard it as a challenge to do the very best you can.

10. Representatives from both nations met to negotiate a (**dynasty, truce**) to give each side a chance to care for its wounded.

11. If the sights we've seen today are a true (**recompense, foretaste**) of what lies ahead, we're in for some real treats.

12. For three generations, their family has formed one of the leading automotive (**truces, dynasties**) of this country.

13. As he grew old, the torrent of beautiful music that he had produced for so many years was reduced to a mere (**foretaste, trickle**).

14. "The program the usher handed you contains a brief (**résumé, hurtle**) of the action of the opera you are about to see," I replied.

15. When we are having fun, time rushes by, but even five minutes in the dentist's waiting room may seem (**adjacent, interminable**).

CCSS Vocabulary: 4.d. (See pp. T14–15.)

16. What would you consider an adequate (**résumé, recompense**) for having worked so many extra hours on the job?

17. The flight attendant asked the passengers to make sure that they had all their personal belongings before (**disrupting, alighting**) from the aircraft.

18. Regardless of who started this silly quarrel, isn't it time for us to declare a (**dynasty, truce**) and work together for the best interests of the school?

19. What we want to do is (**recompense, renovate**) the old house without harming its charm and beauty.

20. With flattery and clever half-truths, the newcomers (**insinuated, renovated**) themselves into the inner circle of the organization.

21. Planted in the fertile soil of her imagination, the seed of a great idea soon (**germinated, disrupted**) into a workable proposal.

22. The way to be successful at a job is to carry out all instructions carefully, even though you think some of them are (**trivial, sullen**) or silly.

23. Only twenty yards from the finish line, the horse stumbled and (**hurtled, insinuated**) its rider to the ground.

24. When I saw a big "A" on my term paper in English, I felt that I had been fully (**germinated, recompensed**) for all my hours of hard work.

25. The senator's speech seemed (**interminable, vicious**) as he droned on for an hour.

Synonyms

*Choose the word from this Unit that is the same or most nearly the same in meaning as the **boldface** word or expression in the phrase. Write that word on the line. Use a dictionary if necessary.*

1. **intimate** that it was her fault — insinuate
2. chased by the **savage** bear — vicious
3. decided to **fix up** the old theater — renovate
4. sit through an **uneventful** play — humdrum
5. his attempt to **descend** from the plane — alight
6. sent a **job history** to the company — résumé
7. sign a binding **armistice** to end the fighting — truce
8. **race** through space — hurtle
9. a **petty** matter not worth pursuing — trivial
10. to **reimburse** her expenses — recompense

CCSS Vocabulary: 5. (See pp. T14–15.)

Antonyms

*Choose the word from this Unit that is most nearly opposite in meaning to the **boldface** word or expression in the phrase. Write that word on the line. Use a dictionary if necessary.*

1. to **move slowly** down the narrow path ___hurtle___
2. definitely a **momentous** decision ___trivial___
3. leads a **lively** existence ___humdrum___
4. hope to continue their **battle** ___truce___
5. would **rip off** his idea ___recompense___

Completing the Sentence

From the words in this Unit, choose the one that best completes each of the following sentences. Write the correct word form in the space provided.

1. As we sat at the side of the lake, we enjoyed watching the wild geese swoop down and ___alight___ on the surface of the water.
2. She was so happy and grateful that I felt more than ___recompensed___ for all that I had tried to do to help her.
3. After the big party, cleaning up, which was supposed to take "just a few minutes," proved to be an almost ___interminable___ job.
4. Although they lived in a house ___adjacent___ to ours, we never really got to know them well.
5. In only a few days, the seeds that I had planted in the fertile soil of the garden began to ___germinate___ and take root.
6. When I applied for the job, I left a(n) ___résumé___ of my previous work experience with the personnel office.
7. Our carefully laid plans were completely ___disrupted___ by a sudden and totally unexpected turn of events.
8. The "coming attractions" shown before the main feature gave us a distinct ___foretaste___ of what the next film would be like.
9. Though they didn't say it in so many words, they did ___insinuate___ that I was responsible for the accident.
10. I never would have thought that so bitter and long-lasting a quarrel could result from such a(n) ___trivial___ and unimportant cause.

CCSS Vocabulary: 4.a., 5. (See pp. T14–15.)

11. In the 11th century, a foreign warlord invaded the country and set up a(n) ___dynasty___ that ruled for more than 250 years.

12. After the warring nations had agreed to a(n) ___truce___, they faced the far more difficult task of working out a real peace.

13. Although the building is old and needs repair, we are convinced that we can ___renovate___ it without spending a lot of money.

14. During the exciting chase, the police cars ___hurtled___ through the town.

15. Though my dog Rover is huge and fierce-looking, children are fond of him because he doesn't have a(n) ___vicious___ disposition.

16. We need large sums of money to keep our school system going, but we are getting only a(n) ___trickle___ of funds from the state.

17. Many people who lead rather ___humdrum___ lives get a great thrill from watching the exciting adventures of TV and movie superheroes.

18. The judge said to the lawyer, "You have a right to ___interrogate___ the witness, but there is no need to bully her."

19. The suspect's only reaction to the detective's question was a wry smile and ___sullen___ silence.

20. As the drought continued without a letup, the once fertile farmlands of the region slowly became ___barren___ "dust bowls."

Writing: Words in Action

Answers to both prompts will vary.

1. Look back at "The Times of Zheng He" (pages 12–13). Imagine that you are Zheng He near the end of his life. What do you think are your greatest accomplishments? How would you like to be remembered? Write a journal entry, using at least two details from the passage and three Unit words.

2. What do you think are the qualities, or personality traits, that make a person successful? Write a brief essay in which you define success and describe at least three qualities a person needs in order to achieve it. Support your views with specific examples from your own observations, studies, reading (refer to pages 12–13), or personal experience. Write at least three paragraphs, and use three or more Unit words.

Writing prompt #2 is modeled on that of standardized tests.

 CCSS Vocabulary: 6; Writing: 1.c., 2.d., 3.d., 4. (See pp. T14–15.)

Vocabulary in Context: Informational Text for Unit 1 is available online at **vocabularyworkshop.com**.

Vocabulary in Context

Literary Text

*The following excerpts are from four short stories by Edgar Allan Poe. Some of the words you have studied in this Unit appear in **boldface** type. Complete each statement below the excerpt by circling the letter of the correct answer.*

1. As the original design was to cross the British Channel, and **alight** as near Paris as possible, the voyagers had taken the precaution to prepare themselves with passports directed to all parts of the Continent. ("The Balloon-Hoax")

When voyagers **alight** from their means of transportation, they

a. take off
b. step down
c. reach up
d. move to

2. These phenomena were occasioned by the expansion of the gas, through increase of heat in the atmosphere, and the consequent **disruption** of the minute particles of ice with which the network had become encrusted during the night. ("The Balloon-Hoax")

A **disruption** of ice particles involves

a. breaking them up
b. arranging them
c. melting them
d. ruining them

Poe published "The Mystery of Marie Roget" in 1850.

3. "In respect to the **insinuations** leveled at Beauvais, you will be willing to dismiss them in a breath. You have already fathomed the true character of this good gentleman." ("The Mystery of Marie Roget")

Insinuations are statements that are

a. stated clearly
b. proven to be false
c. thought to be true
d. hinted at or implied

4. . . . Our attention was again arrested by the appearance of the sun. It gave out no light, properly so called, but a dull and **sullen** glow without reflection, as if all its rays were polarized. ("Ms. Found in a Bottle")

A **sullen** glow would be

a. gloomy
b. romantic
c. healthy
d. bright

5. "This mistake made a difference of about two inches and a half in the 'shot'—that is to say, in the position of the peg nearest the tree; . . . of course the error, however **trivial** in the beginning, increased as we proceeded with the line. . . ." ("The Gold-Bug")

Something that is **trivial** is definitely NOT

a. accurate
b. small
c. important
d. petty

Snap the code, or go to **vocabularyworkshop.com**

UNIT 2

Note that not all of the 20 unit words are used in this passage. *Entrepreneur*, *homicide*, *lubricate*, *regime*, and *unscathed* are not included.

*Read the following passage, taking note of the **boldface** words and their contexts. These words are among those you will be studying in Unit 2. It may help you to complete the exercises in this Unit if you refer to the way the words are used below.*

CCSS Vocabulary: 4; Reading (Informational Text): 4, 6. (See pp. T14–15.)

In Poor Taste

<Letter to the Editor>

To the Editor:
RE: "Fast-Food Ads Target Kids"
(*Business section, October 29*):

Our children are sitting ducks in an advertising war. The "combatants" are the food and beverage companies, advertising agencies, and media corporations **pelting** kids with a dangerous diet of junk food and soft drink ads.

I am no troublesome **firebrand**. I am a nurse at a middle school. I am also the mother of three school-age children. I am writing to express my **indignation** and frustration at the **indifference** of those trying to get one over on the public and, specifically, our kids.

Turn on any children's TV show or visit a website that **caters** to kids. You'll be bombarded with cute characters proclaiming how cool it is to eat Brand "X" cereal or Brand "Y" convenience food. Web sites are full of banner ads and interactive games with commercial content. The problem is, most young children don't have the sophistication to understand the power of persuasive commercials. They think if their favorite animated dragon says eating sugar-laden gooey treats is good for you, it must be so.

According to the Centers for Disease Control and Prevention, childhood obesity in the United States has nearly tripled in the past 30 years. Being significantly overweight is a dangerous health **hazard**. Plus, rates for both diabetes and asthma are soaring. Experts say the rise in both is linked to the rise in childhood obesity. Good health is **indispensable** for a long and happy life. Our youngest generation is **poised** to become the unhealthiest in history.

Despite these alarming facts, the food industry and their advertisers use every **available** media outlet to promote and sell their products. Although their marketing techniques don't break any laws, pushing food and drinks low in nutritional value and high in sugar, salt, and fat is unethical. Instead of encouraging kids to make good food choices, most of these companies use misleading tactics that **hinder** healthy eating goals. In fact, a recent university study found that, on any given day, one-third of American children and teens eat fast food.

In an ideal world, I'd like all food advertisements aimed at kids banned from children's programming. But I know that's not realistic. After all, we're talking about a multibillion-dollar industry. So I demand that companies involved in the making, marketing, and selling of food be required to be far more **transparent** in their advertising to children. I also demand that regulating agencies such as the Federal Trade Commission set far tougher policies. It's painfully clear that self-regulating guidelines for the food industry are not working.

As a nurse and mom, it is **customary** for me to be concerned about the health of kids. I will keep doing all I can to **dissuade** them from choosing junk food over healthy food. I will also continue to **plague** junk-food peddlers and the government officials who **mutually** benefit from leaving things as they are.

Human beings are, after all, just human. We'll always have our bad habits. But cigarette advertising has been banned from the airwaves. Alcohol advertising is strictly regulated. So why do we allow advertising for junk food?

K.D. Nettles, R.N.
Yarmouth, Maine

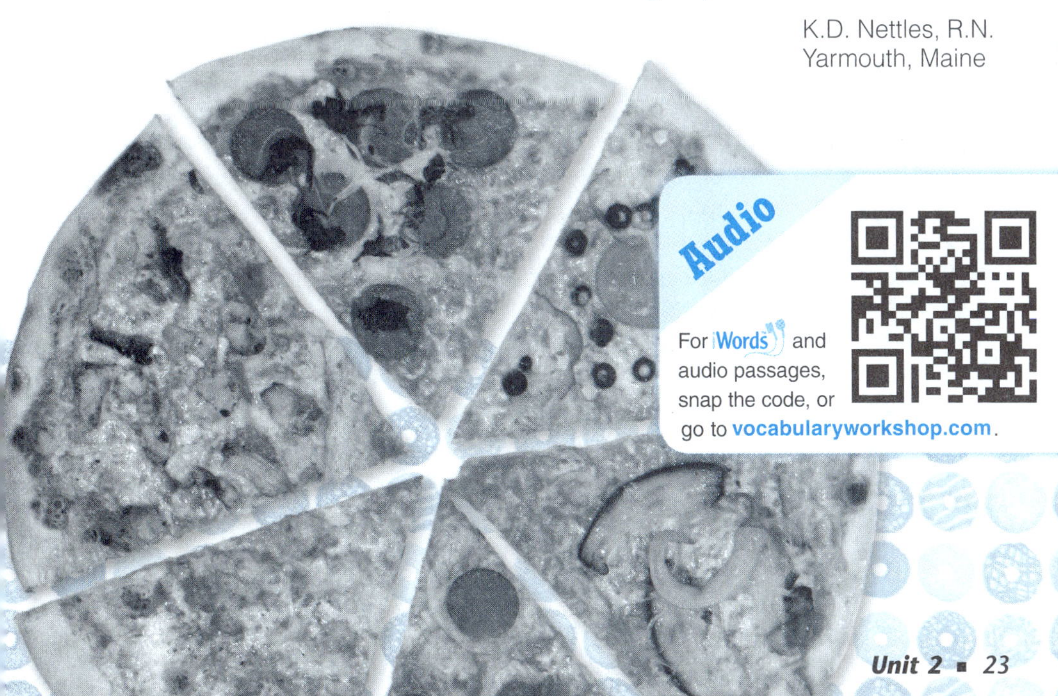

Note the spelling, pronunciation, part(s) of speech, and definition(s) of each of the following words. Then write the appropriate form of the word in the blank spaces in the illustrative sentence(s) following. Finally, study the lists of synonyms and antonyms.

1. available (ə vā′ lə bəl)

(*adj.*) ready for use, at hand

Bean sprouts and bean curd are **available** in the Chinese market on Main Street.

SYNONYMS: obtainable, on hand
ANTONYMS: unobtainable, not to be had

2. cater (kā′ tər)

(*v.*) to satisfy the needs of, try to make things easy and pleasant; to supply food and service

Our grandmother cared for the twins all summer, but she refused to **cater** to their every whim.

SYNONYMS: pamper, indulge, gratify
ANTONYMS: frustrate, deny, refuse

3. customary (kəs′ tə mer ē)

(*adj.*) usual, expected, routine

The **customary** tip given to a waiter for service is 15–20 percent of the bill.

SYNONYMS: regular, normal, traditional
ANTONYMS: strange, odd, untraditional

4. dissuade (dis wād′)

(*v.*) to persuade not to do something

Despite offering big raises and bonuses, the boss was unable to **dissuade** workers from quitting.

SYNONYM: talk out of
ANTONYMS: persuade, talk into

5. entrepreneur (än trə prə nər′)

(*n.*) a person who starts up and takes on the risk of a business

In the first year of business, an **entrepreneur** often assumes losses for the sake of future profits.

SYNONYM: businessperson

6. firebrand (fī′ ər brand)

(*n.*) a piece of burning wood; a troublemaker; an extremely energetic or emotional person

A rash young **firebrand**, the new editor of the newspaper strove to expose corruption in the mayor's office.

SYNONYMS: hothead, agitator
ANTONYMS: peacemaker, pacifier, conciliator

CCSS Vocabulary: 4.c., 4.d. (See pp. T14–15.)

7. hazard (haz′ ərd)

(*n.*) risk, peril; (*v.*) to expose to danger or harm; to gamble

Snow tires can help eliminate the **hazard/hazards** of driving on icy roads.

When asked to predict when the long drought would end, the meteorologist would not **hazard** a guess.

SYNONYMS: (*n.*) danger; (*v.*) venture

8. hinder (hin′ dər)

(*v.*) to delay; to stop or prevent from happening

The all-day rain predicted for tomorrow will definitely **hinder** our plans for a picnic at the lake.

SYNONYMS: interrupt, impede, block, thwart
ANTONYMS: encourage, further

9. homicide (hom′ ə sīd)

(*n.*) the killing of one person by another

It did not take the jury members too long to find the drifter guilty of **homicide**.

SYNONYM: manslaughter

10. indifference (in dif′ rəns)

(*n.*) a lack of interest or concern

The outcome of the rugby match between the two teams is a matter of complete **indifference** to me.

SYNONYMS: apathy, unconcern
ANTONYMS: interest, concern, enthusiasm

11. indignant (in dig′ nənt)

(*adj.*) filled with resentment or anger over something unjust, unworthy, or mean

Angered by the editorial in the newspaper, my mother wrote an **indignant** letter to the editor.

SYNONYMS: offended, resentful, outraged, exasperated
ANTONYMS: pleased, delighted, elated

12. indispensable (in di spen′ sə bəl)

(*adj.*) absolutely necessary, not to be neglected

Oxygen is a gas that is **indispensable** to life processes on this planet.

SYNONYMS: essential, crucial
ANTONYMS: unnecessary, nonessential

13. lubricate (lü′ brə kāt)

(*v.*) to apply oil or grease; to make smooth, slippery, or easier to use

The workers had to **lubricate** the equipment regularly so that production would not suffer.

SYNONYM: oil

CCSS Vocabulary: 4.c., 4.d. (See pp. T14–15.)

14. mutual (myü′ chü əl)

(*adj.*) shared, felt, or shown equally by two or more

During the course of the summer, the adoring couple formed a ______**mutual**______ admiration society.

SYNONYMS: two-sided, joint, shared, reciprocal
ANTONYMS: one-sided, unilateral

15. pelt (pelt)

(*v.*) to throw a stream of things; to strike successively; to hurry

The children resisted the urge to ______**pelt**______ the cars with snowballs.

SYNONYMS: bombard, shower

16. plague (plāg)

(*n.*) an easily spread disease causing a large number of deaths; a widespread evil; (*v.*) to annoy or bother

In the 14th century, a ______**plague**______ spread by infected rats wiped out about one-fourth of the population of Europe.

Mosquitoes will ______**plague**______ the campers if they forget to wear insect repellent on the hike.

SYNONYMS: (*n.*) epidemic, pestilence; (*v.*) pester, vex
ANTONYMS: (*n.*) boon, blessing

17. poised (poizd)

(*adj., part.*) balanced, suspended; calm, controlled; ready for action

The captain and other members of the crew were ______**poised**______ for takeoff.

SYNONYMS: (*adj.*) collected, self-confident, ready
ANTONYMS: (*adj.*) nervous, tense

18. regime (rā zhēm′)

(*n.*) a government in power; a form or system of rule or management; a period of rule

The present ______**regime**______ in that country came to power through democratic elections.

SYNONYM: rule

19. transparent (trans par′ ənt)

(*adj.*) allowing light to pass through; easily recognized or understood; easily seen through or detected

The students could see the other class through the ______**transparent**______ glass door.

SYNONYMS: clear, translucent, obvious
ANTONYMS: frosted, sooty, smoky, unclear, indistinct

20. unscathed (ən skathd′)

(*adj.*) wholly unharmed, not injured

Remarkably, the captain and the entire crew emerged from the wreck ______**unscathed**______.

SYNONYMS: unhurt, sound, intact
ANTONYMS: injured, damaged, hurt

CCSS Vocabulary: 4.c., 4.d. (See pp. T14–15.)

Choosing the Right Word

*Select the **boldface** word that better completes each sentence. You might refer to the passage on pages 22–23 to see how most of these words are used in context.*

1. In Shakespeare's *Macbeth*, after the (**homicide, entrepreneur**) of the Scottish King Duncan, the sleepwalking Lady Macbeth cries that she cannot clean her bloodstained hands.

2. Antibiotics can be a very effective means of (**catering, hindering**) the spread of some diseases.

3. Queen Victoria began her (**entrepreneur, regime**) in 1837 at the age of 18 and ruled until her death in 1901, a period known as the "Victorian Age."

4. All during that nightmarish period, I found myself (**plagued, dissuaded**) by fears about the future.

5. The public's (**indifference, hazard**) to government may be measured by the number of people who don't vote.

6. When the salesclerk replied rudely to my polite inquiry about the price of the garment, I became a bit (**transparent, indignant**).

"Here's the smell of the blood still: all the perfumes of Arabia will not sweeten this little hand."

7. Because I am a creature of habit, I can't do anything in the morning without first having my (**customary, mutual**) cup of coffee.

8. The judge explained to the jury that killing someone in self-defense may be considered justifiable, or noncriminal, (**homicide, plague**).

9. Unfortunately, nothing any of us said could (**dissuade, cater**) Ned from his plan to quit his job.

10. Though I have no means of knowing for sure where Joe and Miguel happen to be, may I (**hazard, lubricate**) the guess that they're in the gym?

11. Innocent or guilty, no one involved in a major political scandal ever comes away from it entirely (**dissuaded, unscathed**).

12. Young (**entrepreneurs, regimes**) have made millions from start-up companies that develop and sell apps for smartphones and tablets.

13. The aid that we have (**indignantly, mutually**) given each other during the years has enabled both of us to overcome many problems.

14. You cannot ignore me for months on end and then take it for granted that I will be (**available, customary**) whenever you want me.

15. Your excuse for missing practice was so (**transparent, indispensable**) that even a child would have seen right through it.

CCSS Vocabulary: 4.d. (See pp. T14–15.)

16. The fire that started from smoldering embers in the chimney totally destroyed the house, but fortunately everyone in the family escaped (**unscathed, indignant**).

17. When the new (**hazard, regime**) took power, it canceled or reversed most of the policies of its predecessor.

18. A little courtesy can do much to (**dissuade, lubricate**) the machinery of our everyday social life.

19. In Shakespeare's day, an actor who displeased the audience might find himself (**poised, pelted**) with a barrage of rotten vegetables.

20. Do you agree with the criticism that many television programs shamelessly (**cater, dissuade**) to the lowest tastes?

21. When my 8-year-old sister started up a successful chain of lemonade stands, I knew we had a budding (**entrepreneur, firebrand**) in the family.

22. Southern (**firebrands, hazards**) agitating for a complete break with the Union helped speed the coming of the Civil War.

23. On our long camping trip, we learned that we could get along without many things that we had considered (**indispensable, indifferent**).

24. It seems that only last year she was an awkward child, but now she is a charming and (**poised, unscathed**) young woman.

25. The locksmith says we should (**hinder, lubricate**) the lock to keep it functioning.

Choose the word from this Unit that is the same or most nearly the same in meaning as the ***boldface*** *word or expression in the given phrase. Write the word on the line. Use a dictionary if necessary.*

1. is **vital** to the good of the community — indispensable
2. found guilty of **murder** — homicide
3. met the new **impresario** of sports entertainment — entrepreneur
4. began to **pepper** the windshield with hailstones — pelt
5. lucky to survive the battle **unimpaired** — unscathed
6. is considered a **rabble-rouser** by colleagues — firebrand
7. was needed to **grease** the bicycle chain — lubricate
8. hired to **provide** food for the wedding guests — cater
9. thrived under the new **administration** — regime
10. wants to **discourage** her from taking the job — dissuade

 CCSS Vocabulary: 5. (See pp. T14–15.)

The synonyms and antonyms here do not appear on the Definitions page.

Antonyms

Choose the word from this Unit that is most nearly opposite in meaning to the ***boldface*** *word or expression in the phrase. Write that word on the line. Use a dictionary if necessary.*

1. an **unambitious assistant** in a struggling company ____entrepreneur____
2. was **wounded** in the explosion ____unscathed____
3. **overjoyed** when the candidate lost ____indignant____
4. an arid climate that **dried out** our sinuses ____lubricated____
5. **unusual** healing methods ____customary____

Completing the Sentence

From the words in this Unit, choose the one that best completes each of the following sentences. Write the correct word form in the space provided.

1. It takes a special kind of bravery to face the ____hazards____ of life in the jungle.
2. Although the legislators have done nothing to further the passage of the bill, they haven't tried to ____hinder____ the process either.
3. Only a really hard-hearted person could show such ____indifference____ to the plight of the homeless who wander our streets.
4. When the wounded shopkeeper died, the charges against the person who had been arrested were raised from robbery to ____homicide____.
5. It took the authorities quite some time to put down the riot that a few rash ____firebrands____ had managed to start.
6. Angry at the call, the crowd began to ____pelt____ the referee with all kinds of refuse.
7. A sense of humor is ____indispensable____ if you are to cope with all the strains and difficulties of everyday life.
8. Mother prepares wholesome and tasty meals, but she says she is not going to ____cater____ to the special tastes of six different children.
9. Because the seat covers in the car were ____transparent____, we could see the attractive pattern of the upholstery underneath.
10. At the front desk, a(n) ____indignant____ guest was angrily complaining about the shabby treatment he had received from the staff of the hotel.

CCSS Vocabulary: 4.a., 5. (See pp. T14–15.)

11. Though the habit of taking a siesta in the afternoon may seem strange to a foreigner, it is quite **customary** in this part of the world.

12. Until it was almost too late, the hunters did not see the leopard crouching in a tree, **poised** to leap on them.

13. The guidance counselor tried to **dissuade** me from taking the job because she thought the work would be too high-pressure for me.

14. Eventually, the army toppled the country's democratic **regime** and set up a military dictatorship in its place.

15. Most of the homeowners in this area have tried in vain to overcome the **plague** of crabgrass that threatens to overrun their lawns.

16. When we **lubricate** the engine of a car, we try to cut down the friction at every point.

17. Having spent many years as political opponents, the two senators have since developed a(n) **mutual** respect for each other.

18. With the emergence of market economies in Eastern Europe have come hordes of **entrepreneurs** seeking business opportunities there.

19. Although we arrived at the stadium only a few minutes before the game, we found that many good seats were still **available**.

20. No one has ever been able to explain to my satisfaction how any person can walk **unscathed** across beds of hot coals.

Writing: Words in Action

Answers to both prompts will vary.

1. Look back at "In Poor Taste" (pages 22–23). Write a letter to the editor responding to K.D. Nettles's argument. What, if anything, do you think should be done to regulate food ads on TV programs for children? Respond to at least two of K.D. Nettles's key points, and use three Unit words in your letter to the editor.

2. You are on a student committee to improve lunches served in the school cafeteria. Write a brief persuasive essay suggesting three specific changes you think should be made. Be sure to explain why such changes are necessary. Support each of your suggestions with examples, facts, personal observations, and the reading (refer to pages 22–23). Write at least three paragraphs, and use three or more words from this Unit.

Writing prompt #2 is modeled on that of standardized tests.

CCSS Vocabulary: 6; Writing: 1.c., 2.d., 3.d., 4. (See pp. T14–15.)

Vocabulary in Context: Informational Text for Unit 2 is available online at **vocabularyworkshop.com**.

Vocabulary in Context

Literary Text

The following excerpts are from short stories by O. Henry in his collection The Four Million. *Some of the words you have studied in this Unit appear in* ***boldface*** *type. Complete each statement below the excerpt by circling the letter of the correct answer.*

1. On the opposite side of the street was a restaurant of no great pretensions. It **catered** to large appetites and modest purses. Its crockery and atmosphere were thick; its soup and napery thin. ("The Cop and the Anthem")

   Whenever someone is **catered** to, he or she is

   a. refused
   b. shaped
   c. gratified
   d. opened

2. But what was this? Instead of the **customary** humble and grateful thanks from the non-escorted one there was to be perceived a high-poised head, a prideful dimpling at the corners of a broad mouth, and almost a sparkle in a dull brown eye. ("The Coming-out of Maggie")

   Things that are **customary** are

   a. untraditional
   b. expected
   c. unexpected
   d. shocking

O. Henry wrote stories about people he saw on the streets of New York and other cities where he lived.

3. When he had travelled a few yards further he glanced at the card **indifferently**. Surprised, he turned it over and looked again with interest. ("The Green Door")

   Whenever you glance **indifferently**, you show that you are NOT

   a. clumsy
   b. cautious
   c. casual
   d. intrigued

4. **Mutual** satisfaction resulted from the agreement. Schulenberg's patrons now knew what the food they ate was called even if its nature sometimes puzzled them. ("Springtime á la Carte")

   Mutual satisfaction is

   a. unusual
   b. one-sided
   c. shared
   d. immense

5. People passed, but they held me not. [Women's] eyes rayed upon me, and left me **unscathed**. Diners, . . . shop-girls, confidence men, panhandlers, actors, highwaymen, millionaires and outlanders hurried, skipped, strolled, sneaked, swaggered and scurried by me; but I took no note of them. ("Man About Town")

   Someone who is left **unscathed** is

   a. wounded
   b. untouched
   c. lonesome
   d. comfortable

Snap the code, or go to
vocabularyworkshop.com

UNIT 3

Note that not all of the 20 Unit words are used in this passage. *Drone*, *literate*, *loom*, and *oration* are not included.

Read the following passage, taking note of the ***boldface*** *words and their contexts. These words are among those you will be studying in Unit 3. It may help you to complete the exercises in this Unit if you refer to the way the words are used below.*

 CCSS Vocabulary: 4; Reading (Informational Text): 4, 6. (See pp. T14–15.)

Lunch at Delmonico's

<Diary Entry>

October 18, 1876

I've had little rest since arriving in New York on business. Harriet and I feel at home at the Fifth Avenue Hotel, which has proved a fine and **downright** respectable establishment. Today she set off early, in a quick and **animated** spirit, to meet with a certain ladies' group downtown. No doubt the whole **brood** spent the afternoon discussing women's suffrage. That topic has entirely absorbed my wife's attention of late, whenever she has not been **seething** with excitement about going to the theater. I've promised Harriet I will **indulge** myself by joining her along with her sister and Mr. Treadwell at the theater this evening.

Lorenzo Delmonico, the restaurant's namesake

The food here in New York City is quite good. It seems the art of cooking, and with it the sport of eating, **culminates** on this very avenue at Delmonico's. Of course, I'd heard it said that Delmonico's is the finest restaurant in the city, or even in the country. But there's no substitute for having a look at the facts yourself. I've been to the Delmonico's at Madison Square three times already for business luncheons. I daresay I've managed to **verify** the rumors.

Everything at Delmonico's has the **luster** of elegance and good taste. The walls are lined with great mirrors. The furnishings are fine mahogany. Silver chandeliers hang from a painted ceiling. In the center of the main

View of Delmonico's restaurant on the corner of Fifth Avenue and 26th Street, New York City, c. 1888

Society people dining at Delmonico's in New York City, c. 1890

dining room there is a large fountain surrounded by flowers. This room enjoys a view of Fifth Avenue, and the well-placed diner can see a well-kept lawn and the trees and gardens of Madison Square. If he forgets to look up from his table, he'll be delighted almost as much by the craft of every **miscellaneous** detail, from the tablecloth to the silverware. I kept my eye open for an Astor or Vanderbilt to walk in, but I have yet to see one of the many wealthy and powerful men who frequent Delmonico's.

The menus are entirely in French. I confess at first I was somewhat **peevish** and put-off at being forced to choose between guessing what I should order and begging the help of some translator. The **upright** waiters of the establishment have been of some help in this regard, although my New York associates seem almost as well acquainted with the menu. A few **constituents** of the menu alarmed me—there was one dish consisting primarily of snails. But my companion on that occasion, Mr. Jameson, managed to **goad** me into trying it. After my initial shock, I found it a delicate and perfectly delicious dish. I was also persuaded to try the delicious Lobster à la Wenberg. I'm told this is a new concoction of the chef's. I must say, however, that having sampled a great variety of dishes that were new and **unique** to me, I began last night to **hanker** for a good piece of beef. The Steak Delmonico I enjoyed for lunch this afternoon was as fine a cut as I've tasted anywhere out West. The chef cooks them to the customer's preference. I ordered mine rare and slightly **singed**.

In fact, I've just returned from that meal, which I took alone. It's left me in fine spirits (whoever said "the more the merrier" got it wrong). For the moment, I've forgotten about the work ahead of me tomorrow. I suppose an evening at the theater with Harriet and the Treadwells will do me some good after all.

For iWords and audio passages, snap the code, or go to vocabularyworkshop.com.

Definitions

Note the spelling, pronunciation, part(s) of speech, and definition(s) of each of the following words. Then write the appropriate form of the word in the blank spaces in the illustrative sentence(s) following. Finally, study the lists of synonyms and antonyms.

1. animated (an′ ə māt id)

(*adj.*) full of life, lively, alive; (*part.*) moved to action

After the game the sportscaster found the winning team to be in an **animated** mood.

SYNONYMS: (*adj.*) energetic, vigorous
ANTONYMS: (*adj.*) lifeless, dead, flat

2. brood (brüd)

(*n.*) a family of young animals, especially birds; any group having the same nature and origin; (*v.*) to think over in a worried, unhappy way

The mother bird fed her **brood**.

The pioneers did not **brood** over the hardships they suffered on the long journey.

SYNONYMS: (*v.*) ponder, meditate, worry, agonize

3. constituent (kən stich′ ə wənt)

(*n.*) an essential part; a voter who elects a representative

In our district, almost every **constituent** is dedicated to participating in the voting process.

SYNONYMS: element, component

4. culminate (kəl′ mə nāt)

(*v.*) to reach a high point of development; to end, climax

The president's military advisors hoped the overseas action would not **culminate** in disaster.

SYNONYMS: conclude, terminate; ANTONYMS: begin, initiate, kick off

5. downright (daůn′ rīt)

(*adv.*) thoroughly; (*adj.*) absolute, complete; frank, blunt

Our neighbor, who chopped down our tree and destroyed our fence, is just **downright** mean.

The actor felt like a **downright** fool when he forgot his lines.

SYNONYMS: (*adj.*) total, out-and-out

6. drone (drōn)

(*n.*) a loafer, idler; a buzzing or humming sound; a remote-control device; a male bee; (*v.*) to make a buzzing sound; to speak in a dull tone of voice

The steady **drone** of the engine put us all to sleep.

The speaker **droned** on and on, ignoring the fact that much of the audience had left.

SYNONYMS: (*n.*) bum, do-nothing; (*v.*) hum, buzz, purr
ANTONYM: (*n.*) hard worker

CCSS Vocabulary: 4.c., 4.d. (See pp. T14–15.)

7. goad (gōd)

(*v.*) to drive or urge on; (*n.*) something used to drive or urge on

The sergeant had to ___**goad**___ the reluctant soldiers into action.

The cowhand used a ___**goad**___ to prod the sluggish cattle.

SYNONYMS: (*v.*) prod, spur on
ANTONYMS: (*v.*) curb, check, restrain

8. hanker (haŋ′ kər)

(*v.*) to long (for), to desire

Now after three weeks on the road, I really ___**hanker**___ for home-cooked meals and my own bed.

SYNONYM: yearn

9. indulge (in dəlj′)

(*v.*) to give in to a wish or desire, give oneself up to

Sometimes the members of a losing team will ___**indulge**___ in self-pity.

SYNONYMS: oblige, humor, coddle, pamper
ANTONYMS: deny, refuse

10. literate (lit′ ə rət)

(*adj.*) able to read and write; showing an excellent educational background; having knowledge or training

Compared with others in the colonial settlement, she was a highly ___**literate**___ young woman.

SYNONYM: educated; ANTONYMS: unlettered, ignorant

11. loom (lüm)

(*v.*) to come into view; to appear in exaggerated form; (*n.*) a machine for weaving

The climbers were awestruck to see the peak ___**loom**___ up before them.

The antique ___**loom**___, once used to make cloth, was on display in the crafts museum.

SYNONYMS: (*v.*) emerge, surface, hover, tower

12. luster (ləs′ tər)

(*n.*) the quality of giving off light, brightness, glitter

The polished gold dome atop the state capitol shone with a starry ___**luster**___.

SYNONYMS: gloss, sheen, shine
ANTONYMS: tarnish, dullness

13. miscellaneous (mis ə lā′ nē əs)

(*adj.*) mixed, of different kinds

A collection of ___**miscellaneous**___ items was gathering dust in the attic.

SYNONYMS: varied, assorted, motley
ANTONYMS: identical, uniform, homogeneous

14. oration (ô rā′ shən)

(*n.*) a public speech for a formal occasion

Cicero's ___**orations**___ in the Roman Senate are still studied by speakers today.

SYNONYM: address

15. peevish (pē′ vish)

(*adj.*) cross, complaining, irritable; contrary

Although the members of the tour group were usually in good humor, hunger made them ___**peevish**___.

SYNONYMS: crabby, testy, stubborn
ANTONYMS: agreeable, amiable, even-tempered, pleasant

16. seethe (sēth)

(*v.*) to boil or foam; to be excited or disturbed

Mother would ___**seethe**___ with rage each time she learned that a dog had been mistreated.

SYNONYMS: churn, simmer, stew

17. singe (sinj)

(*v.*) to burn slightly; (*n.*) a burn at the ends or edges

Getting too close to the flame of the campfire caused the camper to ___**singe**___ his eyelashes.

A ___**singe**___ from a cigar ash had destroyed the last word in the document.

SYNONYMS: (*v.*) scorch, char
ANTONYM: (*v.*) incinerate

18. unique (yü nēk′)

(*adj.*) one of a kind; unequaled; unusual; found only in a given class, place, or situation

Most people would agree that finding an elephant in one's bathtub would constitute a ___**unique**___ situation, even in one's dreams.

SYNONYMS: unparalleled, distinctive
ANTONYMS: ordinary, commonplace, run-of-the-mill

19. upright (əp′ rīt)

(*adj.*) vertical, straight; good, honest; (*adv.*) in a vertical position

The senator showed her ___**upright**___ character by voting for bills she believed to be morally right.

The patient was finally standing ___**upright**___.

SYNONYMS: (*adj.*) perpendicular, virtuous
ANTONYMS: (*adj.*) horizontal, prone, dishonest, corrupt

20. verify (ver′ ə fī)

(*v.*) to establish the truth or accuracy of, confirm

The reporter hurried to ___**verify**___ the source of the controversial statement.

SYNONYMS: prove, validate, substantiate
ANTONYMS: disprove, discredit

CCSS Vocabulary: 4.c., 4.d. (See pp. T14–15.)

Choosing the Right Word

*Select the **boldface** word that better completes each sentence. You might refer to the passage on pages 32–33 to see how most of these words are used in context.*

When it was completed in 1930, New York's Chrysler Building was the world's tallest structure.

1. Even those who do not like New York must admit that it is a truly (**unique, literate**) city, quite unlike any other in the world.

2. The American people must take action right now to deal with the problem of pollution that (**looms, seethes**) so large on our horizon.

3. You may make friends very easily, but if you continue to be so (**peevish, upright**), you aren't going to keep them for long.

4. The (**luster, loom**) of her reputation as a friend of humanity has grown brighter with the years.

5. All of the students in Sandra's advanced weaving class are making small rugs on their portable (**looms, goads**).

6. Glenn has such a store of (**miscellaneous, downright**) information in his head that we have nicknamed him "The Encyclopedia"!

7. It's all right for us to disagree, but let's argue about the facts only, without (**indulging, hankering**) in name-calling.

8. "If you choose to play with fire," I warned them, "you run the risk of (**animating, singeing**) your fingers."

9. Probably no (**oration, luster**) in American history is so well known and beloved as Lincoln's address on the battlefield of Gettysburg.

10. Neither threats nor force will (**indulge, goad**) me into doing something that in my heart I know is wrong.

11. Instead of (**droning, brooding**) about the misfortunes that have befallen you, why don't you go out and do something to correct the situation?

12. The man was not just "a little careless" in handling the club's funds; he was (**downright, upright**) dishonest!

13. It was really difficult to hear the speaker because of the steady (**oration, drone**) of airplanes landing, taxiing, and taking off.

14. Each year the professional football season (**culminates, broods**) in the Super Bowl.

15. Modern scientists often try to (**loom, verify**) their ideas and theories by conducting extensive experiments in their laboratories.

CCSS Vocabulary: 4.d. (See pp. T14–15.)

16. This magazine is published not for a mass circulation but for a very small audience of highly (**peevish, literate**) people.

17. By Friday afternoon, all of us were (**indulging, hankering**) for a relaxing, enjoyable weekend.

18. I have my doubts about people who spend too much time telling the world how noble and (**upright, downright**) they are.

19. The school board candidate delivered a stirring, twenty-minute (**constituent, oration**) on her plans for lowering the district's dropout rate.

20. An important (**constituent, oration**) of what is commonly called luck is the willingness to take chances when an opportunity appears.

21. The last thing I heard before falling asleep was the (**goad, drone**) of their voices as they continued their endless discussion of politics.

22. In his many years in Congress, he has been (**animated, culminated**) mainly by a strong desire to help the underdogs in our society.

23. Anyone who strives to be (**unique, literate**) in American literature should be familiar with the strange, mysterious tales of Edgar Allan Poe.

24. Though the colonies had long (**seethed, singed**) with resentment at the British, the cauldron of their discontent did not boil over into rebellion until 1776.

25. On a cold night, what I (**brood, hanker**) for most is a hot bowl of chicken soup.

Synonyms

*Choose the word from this Unit that is the same or most nearly the same in meaning as the **boldface** word or expression in the phrase. Write that word on the line. Use a dictionary if necessary.*

1. the key **ingredient** in the process — constituent
2. despite the danger that **appears** ahead — looms
3. **trained** in a new computer language — literate
4. an **utter** disaster — downright
5. offered a **singular** opportunity — unique
6. gave a long **sermon** — oration
7. the **murmur** of the bored crowd — drone
8. **crave** Paris in the springtime — hanker (for)
9. lost some of its **brilliance** with each performance — luster
10. attempted to **incite** others into action — goad

 CCSS Vocabulary: 5. (See pp. T14–15.)

Antonyms

*Choose the word from this Unit that is most nearly opposite in meaning to the **boldface** word or expression in the phrase. Write that word on the line. Use a dictionary if necessary.*

1. was completely **unschooled** in physics and calculus ______ literate ______
2. had a deserved reputation as a **workaholic** ______ drone ______
3. summarized their demands in **a few words** ______ oration ______
4. the **receding** danger ______ looming ______
5. a campaign that will **commence** in a week ______ culminate ______

Completing the Sentence

From the words in this Unit, choose the one that best completes each of the following sentences. Write the correct word form in the space provided.

1. I'm normally fairly even-tempered, but I can become ______ peevish ______ and irritable when I'm tired or frustrated.

2. The dull conversation became much more ______ animated ______ when it turned to a subject in which we were all interested.

3. Indian elephant keepers usually use a short wooden ______ goad ______ to control and direct the movements of their huge charges.

4. Those books that do not fit logically under any of the subjects indicated will be placed in a group labeled "______ miscellaneous ______."

5. I don't know which is worse—parents who are too strict with their children or parents who ______ indulge ______ them too much.

6. The mayor will deliver her annual Fourth of July ______ oration ______ in City Square right after the parade.

7. When storm clouds ______ loomed ______ on the horizon, we hurried to find shelter.

8. The man was the prime suspect in the crime until two eyewitnesses came forward to ______ verify ______ his alibi.

9. Larry has the ______ unique ______ distinction of being the only student in our school ever to win varsity letters in four sports.

10. When I saw how handsome my father looked in his brand-new jacket, I ______ hankered ______ for one exactly like it.

11. Like some storm-tossed sea, her inventive brain **seethes *or* seethed** with all kinds of new and imaginative answers to old problems and questions.

12. How pleasant it is for us city dwellers to smell the new-mown hay and listen to the **drone** of bees in the clover patch!

13. The resentment of the American colonists against the harsh policies of the British government **culminated** in armed rebellion.

14. In every election, the candidates try to persuade their **constituents** that they know how to solve the problems and issues that most concern them.

15. Like the traffic guard at a school crossing, the mother hen directed her large **brood** across the yard toward a torn sack of feed.

16. We put supports around the tree that had been partially uprooted by the storm, and it was soon standing **upright** again.

17. I believe in being careful, but Dan is **downright** miserly when it comes to spending money.

18. Because of limited resources, only one half of the population of that underdeveloped nation is **literate**.

19. The sunlight shining on her hair gave it an almost metallic **luster**.

20. "You're just supposed to **singe** the meat," I shouted at him in dismay, "not burn it to a crisp!"

Writing: Words in Action

Answers to both prompts will vary.

1. Look back at "Lunch at Delmonico's" (pages 32–33), a diary entry written in October 1876 by a wealthy businessman. Write the diary entry that Harriet, his wife, might have written about her thoughts and activities on the very same day. Use at least two details from the passage and three Unit words.

2. Published diaries, such as those of Anne Frank or Samuel Pepys, offer firsthand accounts of certain historical events or eras. However, some people believe that diaries can only offer one-sided views of complex issues. In your opinion, is it helpful to learn about the past from a specific person's personal experiences? Explain your reasoning in a short essay. Use examples from your reading (pages 32–33), studies, and personal observations. Write at least three paragraphs, and use three or more words from the Unit.

Writing prompt #2 is modeled on that of standardized tests.

CCSS Vocabulary: 6; Writing: 1.c., 2.d., 3.d., 4. (See pp. T14–15.)

Vocabulary in Context: Informational Text for Unit 3 is available online at **vocabularyworkshop.com**.

Vocabulary in Context

Literary Text

The following excerpts are from the novel The Lost World *by Sir Arthur Conan Doyle. Some of the words you have studied in this Unit appear in* ***boldface*** *type. Complete each statement below the excerpt by circling the letter of the correct answer.*

1. We had not gone thirty yards before a great black opening **loomed** in the wall. We turned into it to find that we were in a much larger passage than before. Along it we hurried in breathless impatience for many hundreds of yards.

If something **loomed**, it

a. disappeared
b. emerged
c. opened
d. collapsed

2. The atmosphere was poisonous and horrible. After tripping and stumbling over these lumps of decay, I came suddenly against something hard, and I found that an **upright** post was firmly fixed in the center of the hollow.

Something that is **upright** is

a. intense
b. vertical
c. corrupt
d. airless

3. . . . I saw white-bearded men rising and shaking their fists at the obdurate Professor. The whole great audience **seethed** and simmered like a boiling pot. The Professor took a step forward and raised both his hands.

If something **seethed**, then it was NOT

a. annoyed
b. upset
c. calm
d. unusual

In 1925, Harry O. Hoyt directed a film based on *The Lost World*.

4. The air was calm, full of the eternal hum of insects, a tropical chorus of many octaves, from the deep **drone** of the bee to the high, keen pipe of the mosquito.

A **drone** is a(n)

a. part of a flower
b. outcome
c. shade of yellow
d. buzzing sound

5. "The object of my journey was to **verify** some conclusions of Wallace and of Bates, which could only be done by observing their reported facts under the same conditions in which they had themselves noted them."

When you **verify** a conclusion, you

a. confirm it
b. question it
c. publish it
d. disprove it

Snap the code, or go to **vocabularyworkshop.com**

Vocabulary for Comprehension

*Read the following passage in which some of the words you have studied in Units 1–3 appear in **boldface** type. Then answer the questions on page 43.*

This passage discusses the llama, an amazing and extremely useful animal.

(Line)

For thousands of years, the llama has been a working animal. In fact, in the **barren**, rugged highlands of Peru, this **unique** animal has for centuries proved to be a reliable beast of burden, carrying heavy packs to lowland markets. Then, about one hundred years ago, the llama was brought to the United States. In this country, however, the llama has added to its **résumé** by gaining some unusual work experience, so strange in fact that here its "odd job" has all but replaced its **customary** use as a pack animal.

Because of its tendency to work hard, eat cheaply, go many miles without water, and get along well with people and other animals, the llama has proved to be a match for many other working animals. Yet it is not just in **trivial** matters, such as carrying golf bags (although llamas do serve as caddies) or in maintaining hiking trails (they do work for the National Park Service), that llamas have distinguished themselves in this country. In fact, in the United States the llama's true calling seems to be in "predator protection," acting as a kind of fantastic "sheepdog."

Interestingly, llamas make good "guard dogs" for the following reasons: They are quick studies, learning in a few days what it might take a dog a year to master. Also, llamas and sheep get along famously. Most important, llamas have a natural distaste for coyotes, the sheep's main predator, and they don't get frazzled in the face of danger. When brazen predators approach the herd, llamas aggressively chase away the intruders.

So serious is this problem that in the United States **vicious** predators have killed millions of dollars worth of sheep in the past few years. Although efforts have been under way to destroy the coyotes, the thinking now is to focus on protecting the sheep. It would seem that the best way to do that is to "hire" a llama. In fact, when interviewed in an Iowa study, half the llama-owning sheep farmers reported sheep losses down to zero since getting a llama, which just goes to show that there's nothing like having a good guard dog, especially when it's a llama.

CCSS Vocabulary: 4.a.; Reading (Informational Text): 2, 4, 6. (See pp. T14–15.)

1. The main purpose of the passage is to
   a. explain the difference between llamas and sheepdogs
   (b.) inform the reader about a nontraditional use of llamas
   c. persuade the reader of the benefits of raising llamas
   d. describe the physical characteristics of a llama
   e. describe a typical day in the life of a llama

2. The meaning of **barren** (line 3) is
   a. lush
   b. productive
   c. boring
   (d.) arid
   e. fertile

3. **Unique** (line 4) most nearly means
   (a.) singular
   b. friendly
   c. aggressive
   d. commonplace
   e. docile

4. **Résumé** (line 11) is best defined as
   a. story
   b. experience
   (c.) job history
   d. regime change
   e. qualifications

5. **Customary** (line 15) most nearly means
   a. legal
   (b.) traditional
   c. untraditional
   d. reliable
   e. eccentric

6. **Trivial** (line 23) is best defined as
   (a.) trifling
   b. entertaining
   c. important
   d. profitable
   e. exceptional

7. From paragraphs 1 and 2 (lines 1–33), you can infer that a llama's usual work is
   a. to climb mountains
   b. to maintain hiking trails
   c. to carry golf bags
   d. to protect sheep
   (e.) to carry heavy burdens

8. From lines 34–36, you know that paragraph 3 contains several
   (a.) reasons
   b. contrasts
   c. comparisons
   d. descriptions
   e. explanations

9. The meaning of **vicious** (line 49) is
   a. hungry
   (b.) savage
   c. dangerous
   d. rabid
   e. natural

10. The author refers to an Iowa study (lines 58–64) in order to support the preceding sentence with
    a. an explanation
    b. a theory
    c. a description
    (d.) a statistic
    e. an anecdote

11. The tone of this passage is
    a. ironic
    b. frivolous
    (c.) informal
    d. biased
    e. philosophical

12. With which generalization would the author likely agree?
    a. Sheepdogs are the best protectors of sheep.
    (b.) Llamas protect sheep more effectively than sheepdogs.
    c. Coyotes are part of a natural plan and need no intervention.
    d. Coyotes are an endangered species and should be protected.
    e. Government efforts to destroy coyotes have proved useless.

CCSS Vocabulary: 4.a.; Reading (Informational Text): 2, 4, 6. (See pp. T14–15.)

Two-Word Completions

Select the pair of words that best completes the meaning of each of the following sentences.

1. Running our country is full of all kinds of hidden ________________ and traps for the unwary. For that reason, no president, no matter how alert or cautious, ever leaves office entirely ________________ by the experience.

a. regimes . . . lubricated
b. firebrands . . . poised
c. orations . . . animated
(d.) hazards . . . unscathed

2. Though crabmeat is the ________________ ingredient in the classic recipe for a New Orleans fish stew, it isn't always in season. Accordingly, professional chefs often replace it with whatever shellfish is ________________ at the time, without any noticeable damage to the dish.

a. humdrum . . . adjacent
b. unique . . . indispensable
(c.) customary . . . available
d. upright . . . transparent

3. The speaker showed complete ________________ to the record heat and heavy downpour. He was ________________, however, when hecklers interrupted his speech for the fourth time.

a. recompense . . . indispensable
(b.) indifference . . . indignant
c. constituent . . . poised
d. oration . . . literate

4. Winds fanned the flames, and the fire on the upper floors of the factory quickly spread to ________________ buildings. Though firefighters worked valiantly to ________________ its progress, the blaze soon engulfed the entire block.

a. available . . . goad
b. upright . . . germinate
c. miscellaneous . . . animate
(d.) adjacent . . . hinder

5. At one point in last night's hockey game, home-team fans became so angry with the referee that they began to ________________ him with refuse. Programs, paper cups, and even a dead fish ________________ through the air and landed at his feet.

(a.) pelt . . . hurtled
b. disrupt . . . droned
c. indulge . . . loomed
d. singe . . . trickled

6. When I was very young, I truly ________________ a life of excitement, adventure, and danger. But now that I'm a good deal older, I'm perfectly content with my rather ________________ existence.

a. brooded about . . . interminable
(b.) hankered for . . . humdrum
c. alighted on . . . trivial
d. indulged in . . . peevish

7. When the new ________________ took office, its first order of business was to pacify the country by arranging a ________________ with the rebel forces that had been waging all-out war against the previous administration.

a. dynasty . . . plague
b. drone . . . homicide
c. firebrand . . . résumé
(d.) regime . . . truce

CCSS Vocabulary: 4.a. (See pp. T14–15.)

In the passage "The Times of Zheng He" (see pages 12–13), the writer describes political unrest in fourteenth-century China by using the expression "a change was in the wind."

"A change in the wind" is an idiom that means a transformation of some kind will take place soon. An **idiom** is a figure of speech or an informal expression that is not meant literally. You learn idioms by hearing them used in daily conversation. Idioms can be fun to use in conversations, but because they are informal, use them sparingly in writing.

Choosing the Right Idiom

*Read each sentence. Use context clues to figure out the meaning of each idiom in **boldface** print. Then write the letter of the definition for the idiom in the sentence.*

1. You know that Katie will **raise a stink** if she thinks she's been treated unfairly. f
2. After an hour of his scrubbing and polishing, the bathroom is **as clean as a whistle**. c
3. The mayor signed a bill pledging to have all city buildings **go green** within the next two years. j
4. Because of obesity's bad health effects, I've vowed to quit **cold turkey** on chocolate and other sweets. e
5. After you graduate, what do you plan to do to **bring home the bacon**? a
6. Whatever you do, don't **upset the applecart** by telling Elena that you're quitting. g
7. Of all the dogs in the rescue shelter, only one, a black Scottish terrier, **caught my eye**. h
8. Marcus, who often speaks up without thinking, definitely needs to learn to **button his lip**. d
9. Marianela has been patient, but the next time you skip practice, she's going to **blow the whistle** on you. b
10. I forgot that the party was a surprise, so I **let the cat out of the bag** when I asked Austin if he was going to attend it. i

a. earn money; make a living
b. report misconduct or bad behavior
c. spotless
d. stop talking
e. immediately and completely stop a bad habit
f. complain in a forceful way; make something into a big issue
g. spoil someone's plans; cause trouble
h. attracted my attention
i. revealed something that's supposed to be secret
j. take steps to reduce pollution and save energy

CCSS Vocabulary: 5.a. (See pp. T14–15.)

Writing with Idioms

Find the meaning of each idiom. (Use a dictionary if necessary.) Then write a sentence for each idiom. **Answers will vary.**

1. it just goes to show **Sample answer: Terra has every advantage in life but is still dissatisfied; it just goes to show that money and status aren't everything.**
2. by the seat of my pants
3. shape up or ship out
4. put two and two together
5. play second fiddle
6. jump to conclusions 
7. down in the mouth
8. out in left field
9. put his foot in his mouth
10. down and out
11. wore a poker face
12. get carried away

CCSS Vocabulary: 5. (See pp. T14–15.)

Denotation and Connotation

Every word has a literal meaning that you can look up in a dictionary. This meaning is called its **denotation**.

Besides having a denotation, many words also have connotations. **Connotations** are emotional associations and implied meanings. They come from the ways people commonly use the word. Connotations are either positive or negative. Words that do not have strong connotations are considered neutral.

Consider these synonyms for the neutral word *question*.

interview *interrogate* *cross-examine* *grill*

Interview has a neutral connotation, but *interrogate*, *cross-examine*, and *grill* all have negative connotations.

> **Think:** You might be flattered to be interviewed, but would you enjoy being interrogated, cross-examined, or grilled for information?

Look at these examples of words that are similar in denotation but have different connotations.

NEUTRAL	POSITIVE	NEGATIVE
think	**ponder**	**brood**
ordinary	**normal**	**humdrum**
unusual	**unique**	**weird**

Be on the lookout for connotations when you read and write. For example, what is a journalist's attitude if she calls her subject *quirky*? What if she describes her subject as *peculiar*? The words' literal meanings are not so different, but their connotations are.

Shades of Meaning

Write a plus sign (+) in the box if the word has a positive connotation. Write a minus sign (–) if the word has a negative connotation. Put a zero (0) if the word is neutral.

1. unscathed +	**2.** mutual 0	**3.** interminable –	**4.** entrepreneur +
5. animated +	**6.** plague –	**7.** barren –	**8.** trivial –
9. adjacent 0	**10.** poised +	**11.** dynasty +	**12.** upright +
13. customary 0	**14.** indignant –	**15.** indifference –	**16.** luster +

CCSS Vocabulary: 5.c. (See pp. T14–15.)

Expressing the Connotation

Read each sentence. Select the word in parentheses that better expresses the connotation (positive, negative, or neutral) given at the beginning of the sentence.

positive	**1.** For her birthday, Emma received a(n) (**unusual, unique**) necklace that her Aunt Mara had beaded.
negative	**2.** The tennis player was (**indignant, surprised**) when he heard the judge's call.
neutral	**3.** After the principal's (**oration, speech**), some students had questions, but there was no time to answer them.
positive	**4.** After we gave our dog Molly a bath, her golden fur had a beautiful (**shine, luster**).
negative	**5.** Thoughts of what might happen in the future often (**plagued, troubled**) her.
neutral	**6.** I did not mean to (**insinuate, suggest**) that your friend is untrustworthy.
negative	**7.** Because of the years-long drought, the land was (**barren, dry**).
positive	**8.** Her presentation was a success because she was so (**calm, poised**) during her speech about energy conservation.

Challenge: Using Connotation

Choose vocabulary words from Units 1–3 to replace the highlighted words in the sentences below. Then explain how the connotation of the replacement word changes the tone of the sentence. **Answers will vary.**

dissuade	**animated**	**trivial**
peevish	**indifferent**	**goad**

1. Our boss likes to **urge** ____goad____ everyone to arrive a half hour early and stay late, but so far no one has complied.
Sample response: *Goad* darkens the tone of the sentence. It suggests a stronger, more controlling, and even bullying kind of urging.

2. Who would have thought that such close friends would end their relationship because of something so **unimportant** ____trivial____?
Sample response: *Trivial* is a stronger and more negative word than *unimportant*. It suggests that the friendship ended over something petty.

3. Jenna, who's often **cross** ____peevish____ when she's tired, complained about everything from the moment we began the rehearsal. **Sample response: *Peevish* has a more negative connotation than *cross*. It suggests that Jenna is often unpleasant and complaining, not just temporarily irritated.**

 CCSS Vocabulary: 5, 5.c. (See pp. T14–15.)

Classical Roots

pend, pens—to hang, weigh; to pay; to set aside

The Latin root *pens* appears in **indispensable** (page 25). That word's original meaning was "not able to be set aside or done away with," but now the word has come to mean "essential or necessary." Some other words based on the same root are listed below.

dependent	**dispense**	**expenditure**	**perpendicular**
dispensary	**expendable**	**pension**	**suspense**

From the list of words above, choose the one that corresponds to each of the brief definitions below. Write the word in the blank space in the illustrative sentence below the definition. Use a dictionary if necessary.

1. a fixed amount paid to retired employees or their families

   At age 65, he will receive a small ____**pension**____ from his company.

2. replaceable, nonessential

   It is difficult for some employees to realize that they are ____**expendable**____ and can be let go at any time.

3. a place where medicines are made or given out (*"place from which things are weighed out"*)

   The nurse obtained the medicine she needed in the hospital ____**dispensary**____.

4. relying on another for help or support; determined or conditioned by something else; a person who is supported by another

   A lion cub is ____**dependent**____ on its mother for nourishment.

5. the amount of money spent; spending, using up (*"paying out"*)

   Worrying is a needless ____**expenditure**____ of energy.

6. at right angles; exactly upright, vertical

   The wall is ____**perpendicular**____ to the floor.

7. to give out, distribute

   It is a judge's duty to ____**dispense**____ justice with an even hand.

8. the state of being uncertain or undecided; anxiety, nervous uncertainty

   The audience was kept in ____**suspense**____ until the winner of the singing contest was announced.

CCSS Vocabulary: 4.b. (See pp. T14–15.)

UNIT 4

Note that not all of the 20 Unit words are used in this passage. *Inflammable*, *malignant*, and *sodden* are not included.

*Read the following passage, taking note of the **boldface** words and their contexts. These words are among those you will be studying in Unit 4. As you complete the exercises in this Unit, it may help to refer to the way the words are used below.*

CCSS Vocabulary: 4; Reading (Informational Text): 4, 6. (See pp. T14–15.)

Coyotes in Legend and Myth

<Informational Essay>

In some of the most **spirited** Native American myths and legends, the main character is a trickster figure named Coyote. In these tales, Coyote is nearly always **controversial**, inspiring both admiration and disapproval. Sometimes he is wily and ingenious, while at other times he plays the **buffoon**. At first glance, such paradoxes may seem **bewildering**.

But Coyote's great achievement as a mythical figure is to break the **orthodox** mold. In the end, he cannot be easily classified. It is usually **fruitless** to predict how Coyote will behave in any given situation. He is a **virtual** bundle of contradictions. He is simultaneously a clown, a rebel, and a **wayward** troublemaker.

In myths and legends, the character Coyote displays some clear resemblances to the behavior of the animal known as *Canis latrans*. Like coyotes in real life, the story character is nearly always hungry. One of his primary concerns is to **procure** food to fill his belly. To this end, he **scurries** around, often in disguise and more than willing to cheat others.

One amusing tale about Coyote and cheating involves the challenge of a trader. This man dares Coyote to beat him in a deal. Far from being **disheartened**, Coyote accepts the challenge. He tells the man, though, that he needs to return home to collect his "cheating medicine." Coyote will need to borrow the trader's horse. Also, to make the horse comfortable, he will need to borrow the trader's clothes. Eagerly, the trader gives in to these requests. As Coyote rides off into the distance, the trader, who had hoped to **inflict** a defeat on Coyote, is left **mortified** and **wincing** with shame.

In another tale, an opponent turns the tables on Coyote, bearing out the truth of the old adage "set a thief to catch a thief." As often in trickster tales, Coyote has forged an **alliance** with his friend Iktome, or Spider. The two friends admire a beautiful rock named Iya. Coyote places his own blanket on the rock as a gift. When the weather turns colder, however, Coyote reclaims the blanket, despite Iktome's warnings. After Coyote refuses to return the blanket, Iya turns **hostile**. Rolling through the woods, he pursues the two friends. Finally, Iktome dashes down a hole to escape, abandoning Coyote. Iya then rolls over Coyote, flattening him out like a rug. The trickster has been beaten. At least, so it appears.

Coyote is never permanently defeated, however. In Native American legends and myths, he always has the power to return to life. In fact, many of these stories present Coyote as the creator of the world. In these tales, he fashions the universe from the **void** and makes people out of mud. Coyote is also featured as a culture hero who steals fire and gives it to human beings. This dimension of Coyote parallels the most famous deed of the Greek mythological hero Prometheus, who was punished by the gods for his theft of fire.

In fact, Coyote as a trickster resembles many of the best-known figures of world mythology, such as Loki in northern Europe, the fox Reynard in medieval France, the Japanese kitsune or seven-tailed fox, and the trickster/creator figure of Raven, who is also a hero in many Native American tales.

Audio

For iWords and audio passages, snap the code, or go to **vocabularyworkshop.com**.

Definitions

Note the spelling, pronunciation, part(s) of speech, and definition(s) of each of the following words. Then write the appropriate form of the word in the blank spaces in the illustrative sentence(s) following. Finally, study the lists of synonyms and antonyms.

1. alliance (ə lī′ əns)

(*n.*) a joining together for some common purpose

The two nations formed an **alliance** to defend each other in case of attack.

SYNONYMS: pact, league, coalition
ANTONYMS: rift, split

2. bewilder (bi wil′ dər)

(*v.*) to puzzle completely, confuse

The captain continues to **bewilder** his troops by giving contradictory orders.

SYNONYMS: perplex, confound; ANTONYMS: set straight, enlighten

3. buffoon (bə fün′)

(*n.*) a clown; a coarse, stupid person

Some students think that they need to play the **buffoon** in order to entertain their classmates and charm their teachers.

SYNONYMS: jester, dunce

4. controversial (kän trə vər′ shəl)

(*adj.*) arousing argument, dispute, or disagreement

The school board waited until all members were present before issuing the **controversial** proposal to ban after-school programs.

SYNONYMS: arguable, at issue

5. dishearten (dis härt′ ən)

(*v.*) to discourage

Do not let your low score on the math test **dishearten** you.

SYNONYMS: demoralize, dispirit; ANTONYMS: encourage, hearten

6. fruitless (früt′ ləs)

(*adj.*) not producing the desired results, unsuccessful

When their efforts to fight the infection with penicillin proved **fruitless**, the doctors tried a new antibiotic.

SYNONYMS: useless, vain, unproductive
ANTONYMS: productive, effective

7. hostile (häs′ təl)

(*adj.*) unfriendly; unfavorable; warlike, aggressive

Relations between the two nations have been **hostile** for decades.

ANTONYMS: friendly, cordial

CCSS Vocabulary: 4.c., 4.d. (See pp. T14–15.)

8. inflammable (in flam′ ə bəl)

(*adj.*) easily set on fire; easily angered or aroused

Always be cautious when using ____inflammable____ cleaning solvents.

SYNONYMS: flammable, excitable
ANTONYMS: fire-resistant, calm

9. inflict (in flikt′)

(*v.*) to give or cause something unpleasant, impose

Despite all the jokes, doctors do not like to ____inflict____ pain on their patients.

SYNONYMS: deal out, visit upon
ANTONYMS: suffer, undergo, sustain

10. malignant (mə lig′ nənt)

(*adj.*) deadly, extremely harmful, evil; spiteful, malicious

Much to the patient's relief, the x-ray revealed no ____malignant____ growth.

SYNONYMS: wicked, malevolent
ANTONYMS: wholesome, beneficial

11. mortify (môrt′ ə fī)

(*v.*) to hurt someone's feelings deeply; to cause embarrassment or humiliation; to subdue or discipline by self-denial or suffering

The teacher was ____mortified____ by the students' childish behavior on the field trip.

SYNONYMS: embarrass, abash

12. orthodox (ôr′ thə däks)

(*adj.*) in agreement with established or generally accepted beliefs or ways of doing things

Our principal, who believes in proven teaching methods, takes an ____orthodox____ approach to education.

SYNONYMS: traditional, standard, customary
ANTONYMS: unusual, unconventional, heretical

13. procure (prə kyür′)

(*v.*) to obtain through special effort; to bring about

The hospital held a raffle to ____procure____ the necessary funds for the new children's wing.

SYNONYMS: gain, achieve

14. scurry (skər′ ē)

(*v.*) to run quickly, scamper, hurry

The reappearance of the teacher caused the students in the class to ____scurry____ back to their seats.

SYNONYMS: rush, dash, scramble
ANTONYMS: trudge, plod, creep, crawl

CCSS Vocabulary: 4.c., 4.d. (See pp. T14–15.)

15. sodden (säd′ ən)

(*adj.*) soaked with liquid or moisture; expressionless, dull; spiritless, listless

All at once, and with much loud honking, the flock of geese rose from the **sodden** marshlands.

SYNONYMS: waterlogged, saturated
ANTONYMS: parched, arid

16. spirited (spir′ ə tid)

(*adj.*) full of life and vigor; courageous

The royal soldiers put up a **spirited** defense against the invading army.

SYNONYMS: lively, animated, gallant
ANTONYMS: lifeless, dull

17. virtual (vər′ chü əl)

(*adj.*) having a certain force or effect in fact but not in name; so close as to be equivalent to the real thing

To those who worked in the office, the bossy new manager was a **virtual** dictator.

SYNONYM: functioning as

18. void (void)

(*adj.*) completely empty; having no legal force or effect; (*n.*) empty or unfilled space; (*v.*) to cancel or nullify

I thought that poem was completely **void** of sense.

Grandmother's death left a great **void** in my grandfather's life.

Do you know how to **void** a check?

SYNONYMS: (*adj.*) invalid, vacant, bare
ANTONYMS: (*adj.*) in effect, teeming with; (*v.*) confirm

19. wayward (wā′ wərd)

(*adj.*) disobedient, willful; unpredictable, capricious

Tracking the **wayward** path of a comet is no easy matter.

SYNONYMS: insubordinate; rebellious; perverse
ANTONYMS: docile, well-behaved, predictable

20. wince (wins)

(*v.*) to draw back suddenly, as though in pain or fear; (*n.*) the act of drawing back in this way

The animal's bite made the child **wince** in pain.

The patient's **wince** told the doctor to press more gently.

SYNONYMS: (*v.*) flinch, shudder

CCSS Vocabulary: 4.c., 4.d. (See pp. T14–15.)

Choosing the Right Word

Select the ***boldface*** *word that better completes each sentence. You might refer to the passage on pages 50–51 to see how most of these words are used in context.*

On the night of December 25, 1776, Washington and his troops crossed the Delaware River into New Jersey to surprise the British forces.

1. When his army seemed (**virtually, soddenly**) defeated by the British, George Washington crossed the Delaware and won a victory.
2. A cold spell in December (**inflicted, bewildered**) heavy losses on the Florida citrus crop.
3. I still (**scurry, wince**) when I think of the two errors that cost us the championship.
4. I could see from the (**inflicted, bewildered**) expression on the child's face that he was lost.
5. Because I no longer go to high school, my student bus pass has been (**voided, disheartened**).
6. The scrappy coach's (**fruitless, spirited**) pep talk lifted the team out of its "losing-season blues."
7. "It's hard not to be a little (**procured, disheartened**) when your favorite team is in the cellar two weeks before the playoffs," I replied.
8. In high school, students should (**procure, void**) training in basic skills that they will need in order to get good jobs as adults.
9. We are going to form a broad (**void, alliance**) among all the groups that are working to improve life in our community.
10. (**Fruitless, Controversial**) political figures are likely to have as many outspoken critics as enthusiastic supporters.
11. Being scolded for my shortcomings in front of the entire basketball squad was a (**mortifying, wayward**) experience for me.
12. Instead of being (**wayward, hostile**), why don't you try to show some friendliness to those newcomers?
13. All our efforts to control pollution will be (**fruitless, inflammable**) unless we work out a careful, detailed plan in advance.
14. On the hottest night of the summer, the sheets on my bed became so (**sodden, malignant**) with perspiration that I had to change them.
15. Our supervisor acts calm most of the time, but we have learned that he has a very (**orthodox, inflammable**) temper.

CCSS Vocabulary: 4.d. (See pp. T14–15.)

16. From the deck of the starship, they gazed in awe at the empty black (**alliance, void**) of outer space.

17. (**Malignant, Virtual**) gossip has unjustly damaged their reputation.

18. I can understand that you want to be witty and amusing, but try not to make people think you're a mere (**alliance, buffoon**).

19. For this job, we hope to hire people who have a (**spirited, disheartened**) and upbeat attitude, not ones who are drab and dull.

20. Though her views about the role of women in society are far from (**hostile, orthodox**), even conservatives and traditionalists listen to them.

21. He plays computer games so much that he almost seems to live in a (**virtual, void**) world instead of in reality with the rest of us.

22. (**Controversial, Malignant**) growths need to be removed as soon as possible by an experienced surgeon.

23. Walking through the meadow at night, we could hear mice and other small animals (**scurrying, wincing**) in the grass.

24. "Whenever you find (**wayward, controversial**) children," the speaker said, "you also find ineffective parents."

25. That joke was so unfunny, even the comedian herself gave a (**buffoon, wince**).

Synonyms

*Choose the word from this Unit that is the same or most nearly the same in meaning as the **boldface** word or expression in the phrase. Write that word on the line. Use a dictionary if necessary.*

1. to **recoil** at the idea of getting up so early	wince
2. brought up the **debatable** issue on the Senate floor	controversial
3. made a **futile** effort to defeat the enemy	fruitless
4. persuaded lawmakers to **repeal** the law	void
5. **baffle** friends with his odd reaction	bewilder
6. walked on grass **drenched** with rain	sodden
7. would **humiliate** her parents with her crude behavior	mortify
8. used a highly **combustible** cleaning fluid	inflammable
9. became **dismayed** by the lack of money	disheartened
10. suffering from a **lethal** disease	malignant

CCSS Vocabulary: 5. (See pp. T14–15.)

Antonyms

*Choose the word from this Unit that is most nearly opposite in meaning to the **boldface** word or expression in the phrase. Write that word on the line. Use a dictionary if necessary.*

1. as **dry** as a desert during the summer months ___sodden___
2. gave a **lackluster** performance for the audience ___spirited___
3. got a **peaceful** response from the crowd ___hostile___
4. had a **benign** influence on other people ___malignant___
5. kept important papers in a **fireproof** safe ___inflammable___

Completing the Sentence

From the words in this Unit, choose the one that best completes each of the following sentences. Write the correct word form in the space provided.

1. If it is allowed to spread unchecked, the poison of racial prejudice will have a(n) ___malignant___ effect on our community.

2. Would it be a bad pun if I were to say that our attempts to set up an apple orchard have proved to be ___fruitless___?

3. When the Supreme Court finds a law unconstitutional, that law is said to be null and ___void___.

4. In 1949, the United States formed a(n) ___alliance___ with eleven other nations, calling it the North Atlantic Treaty Organization.

5. We ___inflicted___ such heavy casualties on the enemy that they were forced to break off the engagement and retreat.

6. After four days of steady rainfall, the ___sodden___ ground gurgled as we trudged wearily over it.

7. Before we set out on the camping trip, I was given sole responsibility for ___procuring___ all the equipment and supplies.

8. Because the gas did not burn when we brought a flame to it, the experiment showed that carbon dioxide is not ___inflammable___.

9. Some parts of the president's proposal were agreeable to everyone; others proved highly ___controversial___.

10. The frozen wastes of the Arctic may seem ___hostile___ to human life, but in fact thousands of people are able to survive there.

CCSS Vocabulary: 4.a., 5. (See pp. T14–15.)

11. I was thoroughly ____**mortified**____ when I suddenly stumbled and spilled punch all over the host's tuxedo.

12. Though the gallant defenders of the fort were hopelessly outnumbered, they put up a truly ____**spirited**____ fight.

13. Their behavior is so ____**wayward**____ and unpredictable that I never know what they are going to do next.

14. Even though you like to do things in your own way, I suggest that you first learn the ____**orthodox**____ method of batting.

15. Refusing to be ____**disheartened**____ by her failure to find a summer job, Lucy made up her mind to try again.

16. Despite the fact that she has no official title, she has become the ____**virtual**____ director of the company.

17. Even though I'm an adult, I still ____**wince**____ in discomfort at the thought of a trip to the dentist.

18. The often dreary courts of medieval kings were enlivened by the pranks and antics of jesters and ____**buffoons**____.

19. When the naughty children heard their mother's footsteps approaching, they quickly ____**scurried**____ back to bed.

20. The directions he gave us for driving to the beach were so complicated that I was completely ____**bewildered**____ by them.

Writing: Words in Action

Answers to both prompts will vary.

1. Look back at "Coyotes in Legend and Myth" (pages 50–51). Imagine that you are Coyote. You have spent your long life trying to trick others. You want to persuade your fellow mythical creatures that you are really doing good for the world. Write an argument using at least two details from the passage and three Unit words to support your claim.

2. Every culture on earth has its own myths. Although mythic events could not really happen, myths often contain powerful messages that relate to real life. Write a brief essay on the power of myth. Choose a myth that you know well, perhaps one from your own cultural background. Summarize the myth and explain what lesson about life the myth reveals. Support your ideas with your observations, studies, reading (refer to pages 50–51), or personal experience. Write at least three paragraphs, and use three or more words from this Unit.

Writing prompt #2 is modeled on that of standardized tests.

CCSS Vocabulary: 6; Writing: 1.c., 2.d., 3.d., 4. (See pp. T14–15.)

Vocabulary in Context: Informational Text for Unit 4 is available online at **vocabularyworkshop.com**.

Vocabulary in Context

Literary Text

The following excerpts are from Jack London's novel The Sea-Wolf. *Some of the words you have studied in this Unit appear in* ***boldface*** *type. Complete each statement below the excerpt by circling the letter of the correct answer.*

1. I had come to see a **malignant** devil in him which impelled him to hate all the world. I sometimes thought that he hated even himself, so grotesquely had life dealt with him, and so monstrously.

A **malignant** spirit is one that is

a. lonely	**c.** evil
b. friendly	**d.** mischievous

2. I ground my teeth in my anger and determination till the man I was attending **winced** under my hand.

If a person **winced**, then he or she was most likely feeling

a. pleasure	**c.** calm
b. pain	**d.** interest

3. "We must stand together, without appearing to do so, in secret **alliance**. I shall not be able to side with you openly, and, no matter what indignities may be put upon me, you are to remain likewise silent."

An **alliance** between two people

a. unites them	**c.** fools them
b. displeases them	**d.** harms them

The 1941 film version of *The Sea-Wolf* featured Edward G. Robinson, John Garfield, and Ida Lupino, well-known stars of the day.

4. That she was frightened and **bewildered**, and that she was bravely striving to hide it, was quite plain to me.

Someone who is **bewildered** is

a. focused	**c.** absent
b. confused	**d.** timid

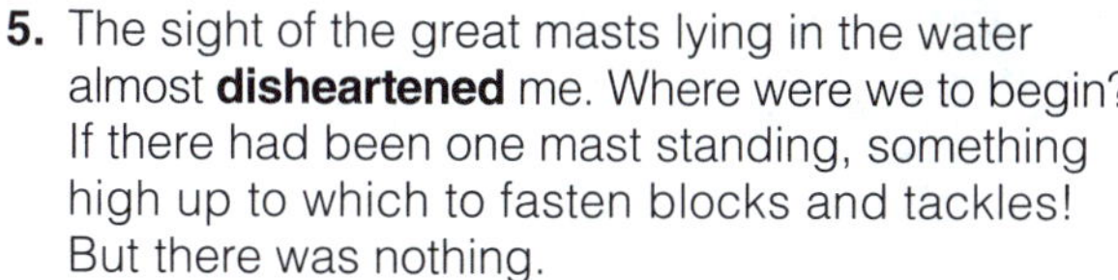

5. The sight of the great masts lying in the water almost **disheartened** me. Where were we to begin? If there had been one mast standing, something high up to which to fasten blocks and tackles! But there was nothing.

Someone who is **disheartened** is NOT

a. demoralized	**c.** clever
b. ordinary	**d.** enthusiastic

Snap the code, or go to **vocabularyworkshop.com**

CCSS Vocabulary: 4.d.; Reading (Literature): 4. (See pp. T14–15.)

UNIT 5

Note that not all of the 20 Unit words are used in this passage. *Consolidate*, *fickle*, *rural*, *tactful*, and *tamper* are not included.

*Read the following passage, taking note of the **boldface** words and their contexts. These words are among those you will be studying in Unit 5. As you complete the exercises in this Unit, it may help to refer to the way the words are used below.*

CCSS Vocabulary: 4; Reading (Informational Text): 4, 6. (See pp. T14–15.)

The "Elephant Man" is Dead

<Obituary>

Joseph Merrick, "The Elephant Man," Dies at 27

by Archibald Winsor Jorrocks for *The Sentinel*

Joseph Carey Merrick, known as the Elephant Man, died on April 11, 1890, in the London Hospital at age 27. He was cursed with extreme physical deformities caused by an unknown and incurable disease. The coroner's report lists the official cause of death as asphyxia. It was brought about by the **substantial** weight of his massive head.

Official versions, however, can be **fallible**. There is **uncertainty** surrounding this conclusion. His doctor and friend Frederick Treves believes Merrick's neck snapped as he attempted to sleep lying down. Because of his deformities, Merrick slept sitting up. Treves maintains that Merrick wanted to fulfill a simple wish to sleep like others—and that this wish cost him his life.

Joseph Merrick was born in Leicester on August 5, 1862, son of Joseph and Mary Jane Merrick. Although healthy at birth, young Joseph soon developed unsightly tumors. His lips swelled dramatically, and a large, bony lump formed on his forehead. Wart like growths resembling cauliflowers appeared on his head and body. His feet and right hand and arm ballooned to many times the normal size. (Measurements taken at the time of death indicate his head was 36 inches in circumference, while his right wrist was 12 inches around.)

Joseph Carey Merrick, known as the Elephant Man

Merrick's mother died when he was 11 years old, and his father remarried. His new stepmother **dominated** the household and showed Joseph not one **iota** of kindness. The boy was cast out to fend for himself. He became an unwilling **fugitive**, his life filled with loneliness. For a time, he lived in a **grimy** poorhouse. Because of his alarming appearance and unintelligible speech, Merrick was the **ultimate** outsider. But at age 20, he took advantage of the cruel fate bestowed upon him.

Merrick contacted a showman and offered to put himself on exhibit. Thus, "the Elephant Man—half-man, half-elephant," as he was billed, was put on display as a curiosity in a traveling freak show. According to a pamphlet put together by Merrick and his managers (which contained **counterfeit** autobiographical information), Merrick said his affliction was the result of his mother being knocked down by a fairground elephant while she was pregnant. This **anecdote** was told by his family to explain his disease, and Joseph held fast to this belief.

Merrick ended up in London on display at a shop set up to host cheap entertainment. Children and adults taunted him, and cruel onlookers **mauled** him. It was here that Frederick Treves discovered him and invited him to the London Hospital for an examination.

Because the hospital did not handle incurable cases, an administrator **entreated** other institutions to offer Merrick a safe haven. When this proved fruitless, a letter to *The Times* describing Merrick's plight brought an outpouring of sympathy and financial donations.

Merrick settled into a comfortable apartment at the London Hospital. And, finally, Joseph Merrick's **radiant** intelligence, gentle nature, and true **potential** were revealed. Beneath his startling exterior, the Elephant Man was a **docile**, compassionate, intelligent soul who loved art, music, and animals. He was drawn to beauty in all forms, and society patrons visited him and gave him gifts.

The world that treated Merrick so cruelly in life treated him with respect upon his death. A memorial service was attended by doctors, nurses, royalty, actors, and artists. A fitting epitaph might be: You'll never understand a person until you walk a mile in his shoes.

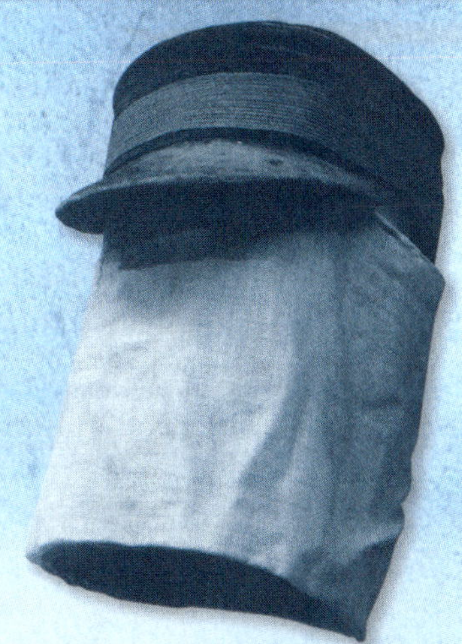

To protect himself from stares and scrutiny, Joseph Merrick often wore a hat and mask in public.

Audio

For iWords and audio passages, snap the code, or go to vocabularyworkshop.com.

Joseph Merrick made intricate models of churches and other buildings.

Definitions

Note the spelling, pronunciation, part(s) of speech, and definition(s) of each of the following words. Then write the appropriate form of the word in the blank spaces in the illustrative sentence(s) following. Finally, study the lists of synonyms and antonyms.

1. anecdote (an′ ek dōt)

(*n.*) a short account of an incident in someone's life

The governor told a humorous **anecdote** about her first day in office.

SYNONYMS: tale, sketch, vignette, yarn

2. consolidate (kən säl′ ə dāt)

(*v.*) to combine, unite; to make solid or firm

The generals agreed to **consolidate** their forces for the invasion.

SYNONYMS: strengthen, firm up, merge
ANTONYMS: scatter, disperse, dissipate

3. counterfeit (kau̇n′ tər fit)

(*n.*) an imitation designed to deceive; (*adj.*) not genuine, fake; (*v.*) to make an illegal copy

The painting was a **counterfeit** of Gainsborough's *Blue Boy*.

The forger was selling **counterfeit** postage stamps to his friends and neighbors.

It is a crime to **counterfeit** money.

SYNONYMS: (*adj.*) false, phony, bogus
ANTONYMS: (*adj.*) genuine, real, authentic

4. docile (däs′ əl)

(*adj.*) easily taught, led, or managed; obedient

She was a **docile** child, eager to learn and to please.

SYNONYMS: manageable, teachable, pliant
ANTONYMS: unruly, wayward, intractable, disobedient

5. dominate (däm′ ə nāt)

(*v.*) to rule over by strength or power, control; to tower over, command due to height

History shows that powerful nations tend to **dominate** weaker ones.

SYNONYMS: govern, overlook

6. entreat (en trēt′)

(*v.*) to beg, implore, ask earnestly

The dog's eyes seemed to **entreat** me for an extra helping of dinner.

SYNONYMS: plead, appeal to
ANTONYM: clamor for

CCSS Vocabulary: 4.c., 4.d. (See pp. T14–15.)

7. fallible (fal′ ə bəl)
(*adj.*) capable of being wrong, mistaken, or inaccurate

The researcher's ___**fallible**___ methods led to faulty conclusions.

SYNONYMS: errant, flawed; ANTONYMS: foolproof, unfailing, flawless

8. fickle (fik′ əl)
(*adj.*) liable to change very rapidly, erratic; marked by a lack of constancy or steadiness, inconsistent

My aunt's interests change with the weather, showing she is a truly ___**fickle**___ person.

SYNONYMS: inconstant, faithless; ANTONYMS: constant, steady

9. fugitive (fyü′ jə tiv)
(*n.*) one who flees or runs away; (*adj.*) fleeting, lasting a very short time; wandering; difficult to grasp

That thief is a ___**fugitive**___ from justice.

Mr. and Mrs. Hirsch had a few ___**fugitive**___ moments together before Mrs. Hirsch boarded the train.

SYNONYMS: (*n.*) deserter; (*adj.*) elusive
ANTONYMS: (*adj.*) lasting, enduring, permanent

10. grimy (grī′ mē)
(*adj.*) very dirty, covered with dirt or soot

The miners emerged from the pits with ___**grimy**___ hands and faces.

SYNONYMS: filthy, sooty, soiled, dirt-encrusted
ANTONYMS: spotless, spick-and-span, immaculate

11. iota (ī ō′ tə)
(*n.*) a very small part or quantity

The employer had not an ___**iota**___ of proof, but he blamed the new clerk for the theft anyway.

SYNONYMS: speck, dab, jot, bit, smidgen
ANTONYMS: flood, deluge, avalanche, glut

12. maul (môl)
(*v.*) to beat or knock about, handle roughly; to mangle; (*n.*) a heavy hammer

The tiger was about to ___**maul**___ its victim when the zookeeper stepped between them.

SYNONYMS: (*v.*) manhandle, batter

13. potential (pə ten′ chəl)
(*adj.*) possible, able to happen; (*n.*) something that can develop or become a reality

Hurricanes are a ___**potential**___ threat to this area.

They were a football team with ___**potential**___.

SYNONYMS: (*n.*) possibility, capability
ANTONYMS: (*adj.*) actual, real, unlikely, impossible

CCSS Vocabulary: 4.c., 4.d. (See pp. T14–15.)

14. radiant (rā′ dē ənt)

(*adj.*) shining, bright; giving forth light or energy

A model needs to have a **radiant** smile in order to advertise toothpaste.

SYNONYMS: glowing, brilliant, dazzling, resplendent
ANTONYMS: dull, tarnished, lackluster

15. rural (rür′ əl)

(*adj.*) relating to farm areas and life in the country

They settled in a **rural** community that was miles from the nearest large city.

SYNONYMS: countrified, pastoral
ANTONYMS: metropolitan, citified

16. substantial (səb stan′ shəl)

(*adj.*) large, important; major, significant; prosperous; not imaginary, material

Expecting a **substantial** raise in salary, the employee put a down payment on a new car.

SYNONYMS: considerable, tangible, big
ANTONYMS: minor, insignificant, negligible

17. tactful (takt′ fəl)

(*adj.*) skilled in handling difficult situations or people, polite

A **tactful** approach is usually the wisest one to take with coworkers.

SYNONYMS: skillful, discreet
ANTONYMS: clumsy, gauche, indiscreet

18. tamper (tam′ pər)

(*v.*) to interfere with; to handle in a secret and improper way

Please don't **tamper** with our baggage.

SYNONYMS: monkey with, fool with, mess with

19. ultimate (əl′ tə mət)

(*adj.*) last, final; most important or extreme; eventual; basic, fundamental

California is our **ultimate** destination on this cross-country trip.

SYNONYMS: farthest, furthest, terminal
ANTONYMS: first, initial, most immediate, nearest

20. uncertainty (ən sər′ tən tē)

(*n.*) doubt, the state of being unsure

Uncertainty about the future was the immigrants' greatest concern.

SYNONYMS: doubtfulness, unsureness
ANTONYMS: sureness, certainty, confidence

CCSS Vocabulary: 4.c., 4.d. (See pp. T14–15.)

Choosing the Right Word

*Select the **boldface** word that better completes each sentence. You might refer to the passage on pages 60–61 to see how most of these words are used in context.*

Since its dedication in 1886, the Statue of Liberty has symbolized America's willingness to welcome people from all lands.

1. Throughout the course of its history, the United States has opened its doors to (**fugitives, counterfeits**) from tyranny in other lands.
2. His (**anecdotes, entreaties**) were amusing, but what did they have to do with his central topic?
3. The mayor won't be reelected unless she can (**consolidate, maul**) the groups supporting her.
4. There, in the very heart of the noisy and (**grimy, fallible**) city, was a truly beautiful little park.
5. Although the ideals of my youth have been (**entreated, mauled**) by hard experience, they have not been totally destroyed.
6. Rarely in our history has one man so (**dominated, entreated**) the federal government as Franklin D. Roosevelt did during his four terms.
7. The (**ultimate, rural**) population of the United States is growing smaller, but farms are as important as ever to the nation.
8. The young man who seemed so quiet and (**docile, substantial**) turned out to be very well informed and to have strong opinions of his own.
9. Evidence showed that the lawyer had tried to (**consolidate, tamper**) with the witnesses by offering them bribes to change their testimony.
10. I suspected that his expression of happiness was (**potential, counterfeit**) and that he was really jealous of our success.
11. It wasn't very (**substantial, tactful**) of you to tell her that her new eyeglasses were out of style.
12. Imagine someone as changeable as George having the nerve to say that I'm the (**radiant, fickle**) one in the family!
13. Larry got good grades on the midterm tests, but he is headed for trouble because he hasn't done an (**anecdote, iota**) of work since then.
14. I know from personal experience how much harm smoking can do, and I (**dominate, entreat**) you not to get started on that miserable habit.
15. In modern hospitals, everything possible is done to prevent mistakes resulting from human (**fallibility, uncertainty**).

CCSS Vocabulary: 4.d. (See pp. T14–15.)

16. Alma is such a (**fickle, fallible**) fan that she starts rooting for the opposing teams when they start winning.

17. To make her finances easier to manage, Mrs. Bridges decided to (**entreat, consolidate**) her two bank accounts into one.

18. The Fire Department found that the wiring in our kitchen was a(n) (**potential, uncertain**) fire hazard.

19. If you want to see the (**iota, ultimate**) in shoe styles, ask Beth to show you the new sandals she bought for the spring dance.

20. The thief tried to (**tamper, counterfeit**) with the lock, but he couldn't get it to open.

21. How can we properly direct the (**iota, potential**) for good and evil in each of us into useful channels?

22. One of our best hopes of solving the energy problem lies in making direct use of (**radiant, fugitive**) energy from the sun.

23. One certain thing in life is that there will always be many (**fugitives, uncertainties**).

24. As soon as Horace opened his lunch bag, I realized he needed something more (**grimy, substantial**) to eat.

25. Marisa felt a (**rural, fugitive**) glow of happiness, but it was gone in an instant.

*Choose the word from this Unit that is the same or most nearly the same in meaning as the **boldface** word or expression in the phrase. Write that word on the line. Use a dictionary if necessary.*

1. a lovely, **rustic**, wooded landscape — rural
2. to **meddle with** the truth — tamper
3. made **remarkable** progress last week — substantial
4. made a **diplomatic** remark — tactful
5. is **changeable** in his moods — fickle
6. to **gather together** notes from different sources — consolidate
7. would **beseech** me to give them money — entreat
8. moved forward without **hesitation** — uncertainty
9. was a **runaway** from oppression — fugitive
10. shared a charming **story** from her childhood — anecdote

CCSS Vocabulary: 5. (See pp. T14–15.)

Antonyms

*Choose the word from this Unit that is most nearly opposite in meaning to the **boldface** word or expression in the phrase. Write that word on the line. Use a dictionary if necessary.*

1. a traffic jam in a crowded **urban** area ______ rural
2. a **boorish** person pushing to the head of the line ______ tactful
3. to **separate** the members of the two clubs ______ consolidate
4. a good idea to **leave it alone** ______ tamper
5. as **invariable** as an atomic clock ______ fickle

Completing the Sentence

From the words in this Unit, choose the one that best completes each of the following sentences. Write the correct word form in the space provided.

1. Since all our cashiers handle large sums of money, we have given them special training in recognizing ______ counterfeit ______ bills.
2. The wily old senator had such a forceful and aggressive personality that he soon came to ______ dominate ______ his entire party.
3. Though the United Nations has many lesser objectives, its ______ ultimate ______ goal is to achieve lasting world peace.
4. I took my car to a qualified repair shop, rather than run the risk of damaging it further by ______ tampering ______ with it myself.
5. The new book of presidential ______ anecdotes ______ contains many amusing stories involving our Chief Executives, both past and present.
6. Because I had expected the children to be hard to handle, I was pleasantly surprised by their ______ docile ______ behavior.
7. As she told us the good news, her face was ______ radiant ______ with joy.
8. To be ______ tactful ______ in everyday life means doing whatever you can to avoid hurting the feelings of other people.
9. Trying desperately to avoid the police, the ______ fugitive ______ hid in the cellar of the abandoned house.
10. The boat has been so badly ______ mauled ______ by the storm that it will have to be overhauled before it can be used again.

CCSS Vocabulary: 4.a., 5. (See pp. T14–15.)

11. Though Company A has very little chance of expanding in the near future, the **potential** growth rate of Company B is staggering.

12. Despite the doctor's best efforts, there has been no **substantial** change in the patient's condition for weeks.

13. The Board of Education believes it would save considerable money to **consolidate** three small schools into one big school.

14. The windows had become so **grimy** and spotted that it took me some time to get them clean.

15. There is an old saying that pencils are made with erasers because human beings are **fallible**.

16. "As a mother," the woman said to the judge, "I **entreat** you to show leniency toward my son."

17. Unwilling to bear the **uncertainty** any longer, I called the Dean of Admissions to find out if I had been admitted.

18. The taste of the public is so **fickle** that a TV performer who is a big hit one year may be forgotten the next.

19. After living so long in a large city, I was happy to spend a few weeks in those beautiful **rural** surroundings.

20. We discovered that there was not a(n) **iota** of truth in the rumors that they had spread so eagerly.

Writing: Words in Action

Answers to both prompts will vary.

1. Look back at "The 'Elephant Man' Is Dead" (pages 60–61). Suppose that you are Dr. Frederick Treves, Joseph Merrick's doctor and friend. A newspaper reporter is interviewing you about what Merrick was like. Write two or three questions and answers from the interview. Make each answer at least two sentences long. Use at least two details from the passage and three Unit words to give Dr. Treves's opinions about Merrick's life and character.

2. Joseph Merrick faced an unusually difficult challenge all through his life, and he met it with courage. All people face challenges, both large and small, throughout their lives. Write a brief essay on whether facing challenges makes people stronger. Choose your position on the issue, and defend it in at least two paragraphs. Give at least two reasons to support your position, and provide evidence from life, the reading passage (refer to pages 60–61), or your studies. Write at least three paragraphs, and use three or more Unit words.

Writing prompt #2 is modeled on that of standardized tests.

CCSS Vocabulary: 6; Writing: 1.c., 2.d., 3.d., 4. (See pp. T14–15.)

Vocabulary in Context: Informational Text for Unit 5 is available online at **vocabularyworkshop.com**.

Vocabulary in Context

Literary Text

The following excerpts are from Charles Dickens's novel Oliver Twist. *Some of the words you have studied in this Unit appear in* **boldface** *type. Complete each statement below the excerpt by circling the letter of the correct answer.*

1. Here, the clothesman, the shoe-vamper, and the rag-merchant, display their goods . . . here, stores of old iron and bones, and heaps of mildewy fragments of woollen-stuff and linen, rust and rot in the **grimy** cellars.

   A **grimy** cellar is

   a. dim
   b. dirty
   c. deep
   d. damp

2. And Mr. Sikes was right. By dint of alternate threats, promises, and bribes, the lady in question was **ultimately** prevailed upon to undertake the commission.

   Something that is done **ultimately** takes place

   a. soon
   b. at the start
   c. rarely
   d. in the end

3. The sun—the bright sun, that brings back, not light alone, but new life, and hope, and freshness to man—burst upon the crowded city in clear and **radiant** glory.

   When something is **radiant**, it is NOT

   a. bright
   b. warm
   c. dull
   d. funny

Like many of the novels of Charles Dickens, *Oliver Twist* examines the lives of the rich and poor in nineteenth-century England.

4. In a dreadful state of doubt and **uncertainty**, the agonized young woman staggered to the gate, and then, exchanging her faltering walk for a swift run, returned by the most devious and complicated route she could think of.

   Uncertainty is a state of

   a. despair
   b. hope
   c. grief
   d. confusion

5. They **entreated** to be made good, virtuous, contented, and obedient, and to be guarded from the sins and vices of Oliver Twist.

   When they **entreated**, they

   a. pleaded
   b. failed
   c. tried
   d. wished

Snap the code, or go to **vocabularyworkshop.com**

CCSS Vocabulary: 4.d.; Reading (Literature): 4. (See pp. T14–15.)

UNIT 6

Note that not all of the 20 Unit words are used in this passage. *Grim*, *scrimp*, *snare*, and *vengeance* are not included.

*Read the following passage, taking note of the **boldface** words and their contexts. These words are among those you will be studying in Unit 6. As you complete the exercises in this Unit, it may help to refer to the way the words are used below.*

CCSS Vocabulary: 4; Reading (Informational Text): 4, 6. (See pp. T14–15.)

Nazca Lines

<Persuasive Essay>

If one **browses** the list of more than 900 locations the United Nations has identified as World Heritage Sites, none remains more mysterious than the Nazca Lines of southwest Peru.

These lines, sometimes called geoglyphs, are giant ground drawings. They cover an area of nearly 200 square miles. In the dry, windless climate of the high desert plain, the drawings have survived for many centuries. The huge shapes, **prominent** from the air, first attracted world attention in the 1920s, when airplane pilots reported these unique and **inimitable** creations.

Some of the lines depict geometric shapes, such as trapezoids, triangles, and spirals. Others show gigantic animals and plants. One monkey, for example, measures 360 feet long, while a bird resembling a condor stretches 440 feet.

Who were the **anonymous** designers of these shapes? How were the geoglyphs made, and why? For nearly a century, experts have been in a lively, **dynamic** debate. They have done their **utmost** to explain a phenomenon that still **frustrates** rational explanation.

For many years, the German-born mathematician and archaeologist Maria Reiche **prescribed** the prevailing view on the Nazca Lines. Reiche argued that the lines were a giant sun calendar and astronomical observatory. Systematic investigation by the British astronomer Gerald Hawkins, however, dislodged this theory, even if it did not thoroughly **eradicate** it. Critics of Hawkins, in turn, have pointed out that he paid only **marginal** attention to the cultural context of the Nazca Lines. Hawkins has also been criticized for employing only a **makeshift** network of astronomical targets, a selection that would make more sense in England than in the Southern Hemisphere. Thus, Hawkins

A monkey depiction in the Nazca Lines is 360 feet long.

may have only scratched the surface of the astronomical significance of the Nazca Lines.

The Reiche-Hawkins debate, at least, has unfolded on a sober playing field. Some theorists of Nazca, however, have not been **reluctant** to offer explanations that may fairly be described as **quaint**.

Among the most eccentric theories is one that says the lines functioned as actual runways. One imaginative theorist, for example, was convinced that the drawings were meant to be seen from the air. He argued that the creators of the lines also managed to build hot-air balloons, which they used to admire their handiwork from aloft.

Another even more imaginative commentator has proposed that the "runways" of Nazca were not used for takeoffs, but for landings. According to this theory, the inbound passengers were space aliens. After they landed, they intermarried with earthlings. Was this theory deliberately intended to **dupe** the public? Perhaps it was, since its principal proponent **previewed** his ideas in a highly profitable best-selling book.

The puzzles of the Nazca Lines are far from being solved. Among the **pending** theories, perhaps the most persuasive claims that the lines had a religious purpose. According to this theory, ancient people walked the lines as pilgrims. These people worshipped mountain deities, largely because water came down from the mountains. For all cultures, water has a central role. The origin, movement, and function of water were subjects of fundamental importance. It may be, then, that the Nazca Lines, which are so much more visible from the air than from ground level, were designed to be pilgrimage routes for people worshipping the water-giving deities of the mountains. This is the most feasible and convincing answer to the puzzle of the Nazca Lines.

An aerial view of a bird representation in the Nazca Lines

Audio

For iWords and audio passages, snap the code, or go to **vocabularyworkshop.com**.

Definitions

Note the spelling, pronunciation, part(s) of speech, and definition(s) of each of the following words. Then write the appropriate form of the word in the blank spaces in the illustrative sentence(s) following. Finally, study the lists of synonyms and antonyms.

1. anonymous (ə nän′ ə məs)

(*adj.*) unnamed, without the name of the person involved (writer, composer, etc.); unknown; lacking individuality or character

The detective received an **anonymous** tip that helped to narrow the search for the thief.

SYNONYM: nameless

2. browse (braüz)

(*v.*) to nibble, graze; to read casually; to window-shop

I like to **browse** through a book before deciding to buy it.

SYNONYMS: scan, dip into
ANTONYMS: pore over, scrutinize

3. dupe (düp)

(*n.*) a person easily tricked or deceived; (*v.*) to deceive

He played the **dupe** in one of Shakespeare's comedies.

The villain in the play tried to **dupe** the hero out of his money.

SYNONYMS: (*v.*) mislead, hoodwink, delude
ANTONYMS: (*v.*) undeceive, disabuse

4. dynamic (dī nam′ ik)

(*adj.*) active, energetic, forceful

The social network was looking to hire a creative person with a **dynamic** personality.

SYNONYMS: high-powered, bold
ANTONYMS: lazy, lackadaisical, lethargic, sluggish

5. eradicate (i rad′ ə kāt)

(*v.*) to root out, get rid of, destroy completely

The team of doctors and researchers worked tirelessly to **eradicate** the disease.

SYNONYMS: uproot, abolish
ANTONYMS: implant, instill, foster, promote

6. frustrate (frəs′ trāt)

(*v.*) to prevent from accomplishing a purpose or fulfilling a desire; to cause feelings of discouragement

Nothing could **frustrate** our plans to storm the fort.

SYNONYMS: foil, baffle, disappoint
ANTONYMS: help, assist, abet

CCSS Vocabulary: 4.c., 4.d. (See pp. T14–15.)

7. grim (grim)

(*adj.*) stern, merciless; fierce, savage, cruel

Millions of poor people face the ____grim____ prospect of hunger.

SYNONYMS: dreadful, frightful; ANTONYMS: mild, merciful, delightful

8. inimitable (in im′ ə tə bəl)

(*adj.*) not capable of being copied or imitated

The young performer stole the show with her ____inimitable____ charm.

SYNONYMS: matchless, incomparable, unique

9. makeshift (māk′ shift)

(*n.*) a temporary substitute for something else; (*adj.*) crude, flimsy, or temporary

The boards and cinder blocks are only a ____makeshift____ until the bookcase arrives.

That army cot serves as a ____makeshift____ bed for guests.

SYNONYMS: (*n.*) stopgap, improvisation
ANTONYMS: (*adj.*) permanent, durable, solid, sturdy

10. marginal (märj′ ən əl)

(*adj.*) in, at, or near the edge or margin; only barely good, large, or important enough for the purpose

During times of economic hardship, many people have only a ____marginal____ standard of living.

SYNONYMS: borderline, peripheral; ANTONYMS: central, pivotal, focal

11. pending (pen′ diŋ)

(*adj.*) waiting to be settled; (*prep.*) until

Curiosity about the ____pending____ trial builds with each day.

Sentencing of the criminal was postponed ____pending____ the judge's decision.

SYNONYMS: (*adj.*) unsettled, unfinished
ANTONYMS: (*adj.*) settled, decided, resolved

12. prescribe (pri skrīb′)

(*v.*) to order as a rule or course to be followed; to order for medical purposes

The doctor was quick to ____prescribe____ complete bed rest.

SYNONYMS: specify, appoint

13. preview (prē′ vyü)

(*n.*) something seen in advance; (*v.*) to view beforehand

The critics saw a ____preview____ of the new movie.

The teacher decided to ____preview____ the video before showing it to the class.

SYNONYM: (*n.*) foretaste

CCSS Vocabulary: 4.c., 4.d. (See pp. T14–15.)

14. prominent
(präm′ ə nənt)

(*adj.*) standing out so as to be easily seen; important, well-known

Some famous authors are ____**prominent**____ figures in society.

SYNONYMS: conspicuous, noticeable
ANTONYMS: inconspicuous, unnoticeable, obscure

15. quaint
(kwānt)

(*adj.*) odd or old-fashioned in a pleasing way; clever, ingenious; skillfully made

My parents stayed at a ____**quaint**____ old inn in Stowe, Vermont.

SYNONYMS: picturesque, peculiar, strange, curious
ANTONYMS: familiar, commonplace, modern, contemporary

16. reluctant
(ri lək′ tənt)

(*adj.*) unwilling, holding back

The attorney called the ____**reluctant**____ witness to the stand.

SYNONYMS: hesitant, loath, disinclined
ANTONYMS: willing, eager, inclined

17. scrimp
(skrimp)

(*v.*) to handle very economically or stingily; to supply in a way that is small, short, or scanty

When the factory closed and other work was scarce, many people were forced to ____**scrimp**____.

SYNONYM: economize; ANTONYM: splurge

18. snare
(snâr)

(*v.*) to trap, catch; (*n.*) a trap or entanglement

They set a trap to ____**snare**____ the rodents that were getting into the garden.

The unsuspecting spy was caught in a ____**snare**____ set by the other side.

SYNONYMS: (*n.*) pitfall; (*v.*) entrap; ANTONYM: liberate

19. utmost
(ət′ most)

(*adj.*) greatest, highest, farthest; (*n.*) the extreme limit

The voters had the ____**utmost**____ regard for her ability as a leader.

SYNONYMS: (*adj.*, *n.*) supreme, best; ANTONYM: least

20. vengeance
(ven′ jəns)

(*n.*) punishment in return for an injury or a wrong; unusual force or violence

History is filled with examples of violent rulers taking ____**vengeance**____ on their enemies.

SYNONYMS: retaliation, reprisal
ANTONYMS: forgiveness, pardon

CCSS Vocabulary: 4.c., 4.d. (See pp. T14–15.)

Choosing the Right Word

*Select the **boldface** word that better completes each sentence. You might refer to the passage on pages 70–71 to see how most of these words are used in context.*

1. The exhibition at the fair was intended to give visitors a (**preview, dupe**) of what life might be like in twenty years.

2. The mistaken idea that the most important thing in life is to "have fun" is a (**snare, vengeance**) that leads to trouble for many people.

3. He still doesn't realize that he has been used as a (**dupe, makeshift**) by our opponents to do their dirty work for them.

4. As I was (**previewing, browsing**) my way lazily through the newspaper, I was shocked to see my own name in a headline!

5. We have many good musicians in our school orchestra, but they need a (**makeshift, dynamic**) conductor to make them play as a unit.

At the 1939 World's Fair, the Futurama exhibit modeled a view of "the America of 1960."

6. Although the announcement had promised us "a (**prominent, reluctant**) speaker," she turned out to be a minor public official.

7. I understand your (**reluctance, vengeance**) to be our candidate in the next election, but I think it is your duty to accept the nomination.

8. Although we cannot mention her by name, we want to express our heartfelt gratitude to the (**quaint, anonymous**) donor who gave us this generous gift.

9. (**Pending, Eradicating**) the outcome of the national election, none of the foreign governments is willing to take any definite action.

10. His reference to a "historic downfall" after I had failed the history test struck me as a rather (**dynamic, grim**) joke.

11. For months the winter was unusually mild, but when the cold weather finally came, it struck with a (**vengeance, prominence**).

12. The new parking regulations are only a (**snare, makeshift**) that will have to be replaced by a better plan within a few years.

13. The wily champion used every tennis trick she knew to (**frustrate, scrimp**) her opponent's attempt to come to the net and hit a winner.

14. To improve your unsatisfactory school record, I would (**browse, prescribe**) regular doses of study, to be taken every day for as long as is necessary.

15. It is very easy to say that our city government should (**scrimp, snare**) to balance its budget, but which departments should spend less?

CCSS Vocabulary: 4.d. (See pp. T14–15.)

16. "Try as they may, they will never (**eradicate, snare**) me!" said the thief just before he was caught.

17. Even before we saw Alice, we heard her (**inimitable, grim**) high-pitched giggle and knew she was at the party.

18. After the big hurricane destroyed our homes, many of us lived in (**pending, makeshift**) shelters.

19. The most effective advertising is honest advertising that does not try to (**browse, dupe**) the public.

20. Nothing can (**eradicate, scrimp**) the love of liberty from the hearts of a free people!

21. The (**anonymous, pending**) decision, once it is given, will be one of the most important of the year.

22. My job is only (**marginal, inimitable**); if business falls off a little, my employer might let me go.

23. Landing a man on the moon was a great achievement, but it is far from being the (**utmost, pending**) limit of our space program.

24. You must realize that, although we may find the customs of other lands (**anonymous, quaint**), they are just part of everyday life in those areas.

25. It is wise to (**dupe, preview**) the contents of a book before you buy it.

Synonyms

*Choose the word from this Unit that is the same or most nearly the same in meaning as the **boldface** word or expression in the phrase. Write that word on the line. Use a dictionary if necessary.*

1. the **harsh** terms delivered by the enemy ____grim____
2. got an **early glimpse** of the new spring clothing ____preview____
3. wanted to **wipe out** poverty ____eradicate____
4. was of **minimal** help to the team ____marginal____
5. is an issue that is still **undecided** ____pending____
6. tried to **save money** on unimportant items ____scrimp____
7. wanted to **capture** the rabbit ____snare____
8. waited to hear what the doctor would **recommend** ____prescribe____
9. gave a very **vigorous** effort ____dynamic____
10. will demand swift **revenge** ____vengeance____

CCSS Vocabulary: 5. (See pp. T14–15.)

The synonyms and antonyms here do not appear on the Definitions page.

Antonyms

*Choose the word from this Unit that is most nearly opposite in meaning to the **boldface** word or expression in the phrase. Write that word on the line. Use a dictionary if necessary.*

1. loved to **spend** money on food and clothing ____scrimp____
2. remained a **little-known** playwright ____prominent____
3. brought a spirit of **mercy** to the land ____vengeance____
4. decided to **release** the tiger ____snare____
5. heard the **pleasant** news on the radio ____grim____

Completing the Sentence

From the words in this Unit, choose the one that best completes each of the following sentences. Write the correct word form in the space provided.

1. Is there any sight in the world more restful than cows ____browsing____ in a meadow alongside a little brook?

2. When unexpected guests turned up on the doorstep, I hurriedly made a few ____makeshift____ arrangements to accommodate them.

3. After the angler ____snared____ the fish, he unhooked it from his line and threw it back into the stream.

4. When we visited Salem, Massachusetts, last year, we were charmed by the ____quaint____ eighteenth-century houses in the town.

5. I like to write ____marginal____ notes in a book alongside important material, but I never do so unless the book belongs to me.

6. Instead of seeking personal ____vengeance____ for the wrong that has been done to you, why don't you look for justice under the law?

7. After several unsuccessful attempts to catch the waiter's eye, I became more than a little ____frustrated____.

8. Safety measures are of the ____utmost____ importance when you are planning a canoe trip over rivers filled with dangerous rapids.

9. When we saw the ____grim____ expression on the poor man's face, we realized that the situation was indeed serious.

10. There is quite a contrast between the ____dynamic____ administration that now runs that country and the "do-nothing" regime that preceded it.

11. For months I **scrimped** on everything to save enough money to buy the replacement tires for my bicycle.

12. Many books have been written about boys, but none of them can match the **inimitable** qualities in the tales of Tom Sawyer and Huckleberry Finn.

13. We may not be able to **eradicate** crime in our community, but if we go about it in the right way, I am sure we can reduce it greatly.

14. I was **duped** into trusting him, and I have paid a heavy price for being misled so easily.

15. Although we know who wrote such famous epics as the *Aeneid* and the *Iliad*, the author of *Beowulf* remains **anonymous**.

16. The suspect was held in the local police station, **pending** the outcome of the investigation.

17. The eyewitness was **reluctant** to tell the police all that she had seen, but we convinced her that it was the only right thing to do.

18. It took the pharmacist about an hour to prepare the medicine that the doctor had **prescribed** for my illness.

19. Each unit in the textbook opens with a section that **previews** the chapter materials.

20. The most **prominent** feature of the skyline of that little town in Iowa is the four-story grain elevator.

Writing: Words in Action

Answers to both prompts will vary.

1. Look back at "Nazca Lines" (pages 70–71). Of the theories mentioned in the passage, which do you think is the most likely explanation of how the Nazca Lines came to be? In a detailed argument, state and support your opinion, using at least two details from the passage and three Unit words to support your claim.

2. The world is full of mysterious places. Some might be on a distant continent, while others might be in your own hometown. Write a brief essay in which you describe a mysterious place that you know of and explain what makes it strange and unusual. Suggest possible explanations for the characteristics that make the place "mysterious." Include specific examples from your observations, studies, reading (refer to pages 70–71), or personal experience. Write at least two paragraphs, and use three or more words from this Unit.

Writing prompt #2 is modeled on that of standardized tests.

CCSS Vocabulary: 6; Writing: 1.c., 2.d., 3.d., 4. (See pp. T14–15.)

Vocabulary in Context: Informational Text for Unit 6 is available online at **vocabularyworkshop.com**.

Vocabulary in Context

Literary Text

The following excerpts are from Sir Arthur Conan Doyle's The Adventures of Sherlock Holmes. *Some of the words you have studied in this Unit appear in* **boldface** *type. Complete each statement below the excerpt by circling the letter of the correct answer.*

1. I had never seen my friend's face so **grim** or his brow so dark as it was when we turned from the scene of this investigation. ("The Adventure of the Speckled Band")

A **grim** face is one that does NOT look

a. tired
b. dirty
c. pleasant
d. serious

2. "This, I take it, belongs to the room in which you used to sleep . . .?"

"Exactly so. But I am now sleeping in the middle one."

"**Pending** the alterations, as I understand. By the way, there does not seem to be any very pressing need for repairs at that end wall." ("The Adventure of the Speckled Band")

Pending the alterations means

a. once
b. until
c. still
d. before

3. "Again I laughed very heartily at the funny stories of which my employer had an immense repertoire, and which he told **inimitably**." ("The Adventure of the Copper Beeches")

A story told **inimitably** is told

a. with humor
b. with emotion
c. in an original way
d. in a dramatic way

Sherlock Holmes is perhaps the world's most famous and recognizable fictional detective.

4. "On the very day that I saw him last he cut himself in the bedroom, and yet I in the dining room rushed upstairs instantly with the **utmost** certainty that something had happened." ("The Man with the Twisted Lip")

Someone who feels the **utmost** certainty is

a. unsure
b. never sure
c. mostly sure
d. completely sure

5. "Had I been recognized in that den my life would not have been worth an hour's purchase; for I have used it before now for my own purposes, and the rascally Lascar who runs it has sworn to have **vengeance** upon me." ("The Man with the Twisted Lip")

The act of **vengeance** involves

a. friendship
b. punishment
c. argument
d. forgiveness

Interactive Quiz

Snap the code, or go to **vocabularyworkshop.com**

Vocabulary for Comprehension

*Read the following passage in which some of the words you have studied in Units 4–6 appear in **boldface** type. Then answer the questions on page 81.*

This passage discusses Nellie Bly (1864–1922), a groundbreaking American journalist whose stories often shocked her readers.

(Line)

Nellie Bly wasn't her real name; but when 18-year-old Elizabeth Cochrane, a **spirited** young woman from a small town in Pennsylvania, moved to Pittsburgh in 1885 to become a writer, the aspiring reporter knew she would need a catchy new name. She chose Nellie Bly, from the title of a popular Stephen Foster tune, and turned out stories on **controversial** subjects that would sell record numbers of newspapers.

Under the byline "Nellie Bly," the young woman wrote articles for the *Pittsburgh Dispatch* that were spiced with shocking **anecdotes** she heard from the older women living in her boardinghouse. Nellie's writing rang true; and soon she was exposing the **grim** conditions in Pittsburgh's slums, jails, and factories. When her stories became too sensational for her editors, Nellie left Pittsburgh for New York City. There she joined the staff of Joseph Pulitzer's *New York World*.

Once again, there was nothing typical about the topics Nellie chose to write about and nothing **orthodox** about the way she researched them. To expose the dreadful conditions in New York's insane asylum, Bellevue, she threw a fit and got admitted to the hospital. To test the capabilities of a ferry rescue crew, she jumped overboard into the Hudson River. To expose shameful prison conditions, Nellie framed herself on a robbery charge and landed in jail. Her stories both thrilled and embarrassed readers. Some of her work led to social reform. It also made her famous.

In the name of grabbing headlines, Nellie had her share of adventures. Yet a stunt she pulled in 1889 would be the greatest adventure of her career. Responding to the fame of Jules Verne's novel *Around the World in Eighty Days*, Nellie proposed to outdo the book's fictional character, Phileas Fogg, and circle the globe in less time. Pulitzer accepted her idea; and as readers breathlessly followed her course, Nellie made her way around the world. In the end, she bested Fogg. Her time: 72 days. People had said that it couldn't be done, but then Nellie Bly, still only 21, was used to beating the odds.

CCSS Vocabulary: 4.a.; Reading (Informational Text): 2, 4, 6. (See pp. T14–15.)

1. Which title best suits this passage?
a. "Around the World in Eighty Days"
b. "Elizabeth Cochrane vs. Nellie Bly"
c. "A Success Story"
d. "Nellie Bly: Investigative Reporter"
e. "Women Reporters in New York City"

2. The meaning of **spirited** (line 3) is
a. lively
b. psychic
c. good-natured
d. ambitious
e. atypical

3. **Controversial** (line 11) means
a. strange
b. patriotic
c. agreeable
d. depressing
e. debatable

4. The last sentence in paragraph 1 (lines 8–13)
a. restates the paragraph's main idea
b. summarizes paragraph 4
c. describes Nellie Bly's appearance
d. hints at Bly's trip around the world
e. provides a focus for the passage

5. **Anecdotes** (line 17) is best defined as
a. prescriptions
b. statistics
c. stories
d. disappointments
e. secrets

6. **Grim** (line 21) most nearly means
a. dreadful
b. predictable
c. dirty
d. humorless
e. benign

7. **Orthodox** (line 30) is best defined as
a. unusual
b. original
c. traditional
d. illegal
e. subtle

8. According to paragraph 3 (lines 28–44), one consequence of Nellie Bly's reporting was
a. the development of editorial pages
b. rising interest in the novels of Jules Verne
c. equal pay for women reporters
d. her successful movie career
e. social reforms related to her stories

9. From paragraph 3, you can conclude that Bly's methods primarily involved
a. interviewing older women in her boardinghouse
b. experiencing first-hand the situations she wrote about
c. imagining the details she included
d. depending on others to supply her with information
e. researching facts and details in library reference books

10. Which of the following best describes the writer's attitude toward Nellie Bly?
a. critical
b. skeptical
c. outraged
d. admiring
e. pitying

11. With which generalization would the author most likely agree?
a. Nellie Bly was a colorful reporter who wrote sensational stories.
b. Female reporters are more reliable than male reporters.
c. Male reporters are more imaginative than female reporters.
d. Nellie Bly was more interested in writing fiction than in reporting facts.
e. Nellie Bly was a second-rate reporter who accomplished little.

12. Which of the following best describes Nellie Bly's style of reporting?
a. subdued
b. self-promotional
c. modest
d. gullible
e. sympathetic

CCSS Vocabulary: 4.a.; Reading (Informational Text): 2, 4, 6. (See pp. T14–15.)

Two-Word Completions

Select the pair of words that best completes the meaning of each of the following sentences.

1. I know that an injection of novocaine doesn't normally ______________ a great deal of pain. Still, the mere thought of the dentist's sharp needle is enough to make me ______________ in imaginary discomfort.

(**a.**) inflict . . . wince
b. consolidate . . . scurry
c. eradicate . . . maul
d. procure . . . scrimp

2. The book is full of highly amusing stories involving many people who were ______________ at the time. One of these witty little ______________ tells how a famous director once used glue to get an actor to stand on his mark.

a. utmost . . . previews
b. inimitable . . . iotas
c. dominant . . . snares
(**d.**) prominent . . . anecdotes

3. "The president's new economic program has stirred up a good deal of ______________ on Capitol Hill," the reporter observed. "Some members of Congress favor the plan; others are definitely ______________ to it."

a. vengeance . . . anonymous
(**b.**) controversy . . . hostile
c. bewilderment . . . malignant
d. uncertainty . . . reluctant

4. Despite setbacks that would have ______________ a less determined or ambitious person, she continued to do her ______________ to become the top tennis player in the world. As she herself admitted, she knew that she wouldn't succeed unless she gave the task her "very best shot."

a. mortified . . . potential
b. entreated . . . ultimate
c. frustrated . . . virtual
(**d.**) disheartened . . . utmost

5. Come to my island, and you won't be sorry! It's a ______________ paradise, with clean air, clear blue water, ______________ blue skies, five miles of white sand beaches, and the friendliest people you'll ever meet.

a. fickle . . . substantial
(**b.**) virtual . . . radiant
c. fugitive . . . wayward
d. tactful . . . potential

6. "His methods are hardly what I'd call ______________, but they do get results," the sales manager remarked about her star salesperson. "If he took a more traditional approach when dealing with customers, the company's profits might not be so ______________."

a. dynamic . . . disheartening
b. quaint . . . marginal
(**c.**) orthodox . . . substantial
d. controversial . . . tactful

7. Two convicts escaped from the state prison last week. The police managed to recapture one of the ______________ in a matter of hours. Yet their efforts to catch the other have so far proved ______________.

a. buffoons . . . fallible
b. counterfeits . . . void
(**c.**) fugitives . . . fruitless
d. dupes . . . wayward

CCSS Vocabulary: 4.a. (See pp. T14–15.)

Proverbs

In the obituary for the Elephant Man (pages 60–61), the author concludes by saying, "You'll never understand a person until you walk a mile in his shoes."

"Walk a mile in another person's shoes" is a proverb that means that the best way to understand another person is to see the world from his or her perspective. A **proverb** is a memorable saying that expresses a truth about life. Because the meanings of proverbs are not always obvious, they must be learned, just like unfamiliar words.

Choosing the Right Proverb

*Read each sentence. Use context clues to figure out the meaning of each proverb in **boldface** print. Then write the letter of the definition for the proverb in the sentence.*

1. Since **all work and no play makes Jack a dull boy**, I'm going outside to shoot some baskets. __d__
2. I know you're disappointed that you didn't win the competition, but **don't give up the ship.** __c__
3. Whenever I'm tired and discouraged, I remind myself that **a journey of a thousand miles begins with a single step**. __g__
4. **Don't let the pot call the kettle black**; since you haven't cleaned your own room in months, is it fair to accuse your brother of being a slob? __h__
5. Grandpa wishes he could still work; **the old horse in the stable still yearns to run**. __j__
6. Apologize to him as soon as possible. It's best to **put out a fire while it is still small**. __i__
7. My Aunt Kim really believes that **when in Rome, do as the Romans do**. When she visited India, she wore saris, and she only ate local foods. __e__
8. After she broke up with her boyfriend, I tried to console my sister by telling her **there are other fish in the sea**, but that just made her cry harder. __b__
9. Of course you prefer Josh's bike, because **the grass is always greener on the other side**. __f__
10. Wait until you drive the car before you say whether you like it; after all, **the proof of the pudding is in the eating**. __a__

a. You can't know whether something is good until you try it.

b. That person wasn't the only one; there are many other people to choose from.

c. Hang in there.

d. People need time off now and then.

e. Visitors to a place should try to blend in and adopt the local customs.

f. We always want the things we don't have.

g. Every achievement has to start somewhere.

h. Don't criticize someone for something you too are guilty of.

i. Fix a small problem before it becomes a big one.

j. Age does not diminish passion and interest.

CCSS Vocabulary: 5.a. (See pp. T14–15.)

Writing with Proverbs

Find the meaning of each proverb. (Use a dictionary if necessary.) Then write a sentence for each proverb. **Answers will vary.**

1. Say "I can" or say "I can't," and you're right either way. **Sample response: I always believe in myself, because if you say "I can" or say "I can't," you're right either way.**

2. You can't make a silk purse out of a sow's ear.

3. If you can't beat them, join them.

4. You can lead a horse to water, but you can't make it drink.

5. A house divided against itself cannot stand.

6. A man's home is his castle.

7. A hyena cannot know its own stench.

8. A leopard doesn't change its spots.

9. A penny is a lot of money if you haven't got a penny.

10. You'll never plow a field by turning it over in your mind.

11. No wind, no waves.

12. People who live in glass houses shouldn't throw stones.

 CCSS Vocabulary: 5. (See pp. T14–15.)

Denotation and Connotation

A word's **denotation** is its dictionary meaning, which conveys a neutral tone. The **connotation** of a word is its emotional association. Connotations may be positive, negative, or neutral.

Connotations are informal, implied meanings. We know, for example, that there is a shade of difference in meaning between *worried* and *anxious*, even though the words have similar denotations. Consider these synonyms for the neutral word *country*:

rural *rustic* *backwoods* *countrified*

Rural and *rustic* have positive connotations, suggesting the peaceful countryside, while *backwoods* and *countrified* have negative connotations, suggesting roughness and a lack of sophistication.

> **Think:** If you live in the country, far away from cities and suburbs, you probably think of your home as rural or pleasantly rustic, but not as a backwoods or countrified.

Look at these examples of words that are similar in denotation but have different connotations.

NEUTRAL	POSITIVE	NEGATIVE
oversee	**govern**	**dominate**
important	**prominent**	**conspicuous**
economize	**save**	**scrimp**

When writers or speakers choose among synonyms, they select the word that contains the shade of meaning they want to express. Audiences who are aware of varying connotations understand the layers of meaning implied in spoken or written words.

Shades of Meaning

Write a plus sign (+) in the box if the word has a positive connotation. Write a minus sign (–) if the word has a negative connotation. Put a zero (0) if the word is neutral.

1. inflammable [–]	**2.** buffoon [–]	**3.** fugitive [–]	**4.** iota [0]
5. spirited [+]	**6.** orthodox [0]	**7.** dupe [–]	**8.** fickle [–]
9. tactful [+]	**10.** grim [–]	**11.** preview [0]	**12.** malignant [–]
13. wince [–]	**14.** alliance [+]	**15.** docile [+]	**16.** radiant [+]

CCSS Vocabulary: 5.c. (See pp. T14–15.)

Expressing the Connotation

Read each sentence. Select the word in parentheses that better expresses the connotation (positive, negative, or neutral) given at the beginning of the sentence.

positive 1. Willie is so (**easygoing, docile**) that anyone can convince him to do his or her bidding.

positive 2. My parents ate at a (**quaint, strange**) old restaurant where there was no written menu.

negative 3. Mr. Jacobs likes to tell (**anecdotes, tales**) about his adventures.

negative 4. After two inches of rain, the golf course was (**wet, sodden**).

neutral 5. A (**changeable, fickle**) friend is often not there when you need help.

negative 6. Turning the corner, we came face-to-face with a crowd of people wearing (**serious, grim**) expressions.

neutral 7. The third-graders built a (**rickety, makeshift**) fort out of branches.

positive 8. The speaker's use of video and audio made for a(n) (**interesting, dynamic**) presentation.

Challenge: Using Connotation

Choose vocabulary words from Units 4–6 to replace the highlighted words in the sentences below. Then explain how the connotation of the replacement word changes the tone of the sentence. Answers will vary.

anecdote	**buffoon**	**tactful**
voiding	**dynamic**	**mauling**

1. Even as a child, Susie wanted to be a **comedian** buffoon and make crowds of people laugh.
Sample response: *Buffoon* is a more extreme, negative word than *comedian*; it makes Susie sound foolish instead of clever.

2. The orchestra played at a **frantic** dynamic pace that was quite a bit faster than most listeners were used to.
Sample response: *Frantic* implies excessive excitement or anxiety, whereas *dynamic* implies that the orchestra played energetically.

3. We didn't go far into the woods, because we had heard stories of bears **attacking** mauling campers.
Sample response: *Mauling* is more specific than *attacking* and connotes more violence, making the description more terrifying.

 CCSS Vocabulary: 5, 5.c. (See pp. T14–15.)

Classical Roots

scrib, scribe, script—
to write

This Latin root appears in **prescribe** (page 73). Literally "to write before," *prescribe* means "to set down as a rule, order for medical treatment, or give medical advice." Some other words based on the same root are listed below.

circumscribe	**inscription**	**proscribe**	**subscribe**
indescribable	**postscript**	**script**	**transcribe**

From the list of words above, choose the one that corresponds to each of the brief definitions below. Write the word in the blank space in the illustrative sentence below the definition. Use a dictionary if necessary.

1. handwriting; a manuscript of a play or movie
The actor read the ___**script**___ before he agreed to star in the new action movie.

2. to write out or make a typewritten copy of; to write in another alphabet
The assistant will need to ___**transcribe**___ her shorthand notes before inputting the information in her computer.

3. to outlaw, forbid, prohibit; to banish
Building codes ___**proscribe**___ that type of flimsy construction.

4. that which is written on a monument, coin, building; a dedication in a book
The ___**inscription**___ on the monument is short and to the point.

5. to draw a line around, encircle; to confine within limits, restrict
After major surgery, patients may need to ___**circumscribe**___ their physical activities for a while.

6. an addition to a letter written after the writer's name has been signed
The ___**postscript**___ she added to her letter was so long that it took up an entire page.

7. to sign one's name; to express agreement or approval; to promise to take or to pay for
My parents ___**subscribe**___ to several newspapers and magazines.

8. beyond description
The joy the winning team felt was ___**indescribable**___.

CCSS Vocabulary: 4.b. (See pp. T14–15.)

UNIT 7

Note that not all of the 20 Unit words are used in this passage. *Amiss*, *fledgling*, *notable*, *perjury*, and *prior* are not included.

Read the following passage, taking note of the ***boldface*** *words and their contexts. These words are among those you will be studying in Unit 7. As you complete the exercises in this Unit, it may help to refer to the way the words are used below.*

CCSS Vocabulary: 4; Reading (Informational Text): 4, 6. (See pp. T14–15.)

Everything That Happens, Happens as It Should

<First-Person Narrative>

What a day! I am shivering and my feet are swollen from our long, grueling march, yet I must first attend to the needs of my master, Emperor Marcus Aurelius. We are on the northern frontier, on a campaign to put down an uprising of a rogue Germanic tribe. These barbarians fired the first **salvo** yesterday, raining arrows down on a number of our brave legionnaires. Today we moved to higher ground to gain **momentum** for an attack.

My master is exhausted and takes his dinner alone this evening, without his generals. I am starving but would not **presume** to eat. At least I got to taste a little beef and wine, as I sample everything first in case a foe tries to poison him. I am ever **vigilant** to possible plots against his life, and I trust no one, although I know my master trusts me. As well he should, for I was sold into slavery before birth to pay off my father's debts and have been in the Imperial household all my life.

We have been gone from Rome many months. Life is hard for all of us, from emperor and general to foot soldier and slave. But our monarch is benevolent, and **foremost** a devoted thinker and philosopher. Perhaps that is why he is rarely **flustered**, even when facing misfortune and suffering. For if Marcus is not putting down uprisings from uncouth savages, he is placating unruly senators prone to fighting and **brawling**. To me, these men display a **flagrant** disregard for the respect due an emperor. It's appalling!

The Stoic philosophy Marcus Aurelius subscribes to declares that all men are by nature equal. "Blasius," he said to me the other day, "you are cold. Go to the provisions tent and get warmer clothes." My master has **nurtured** my education, and so I have grown **proficient** in reading, writing, and music. Sometimes I play the lute while he converses with me. I pretend we are friends and equals instead of master and slave. I long for our days at the Imperial palace or at one of the country villas, with the many luxuries. Oh, what I would give for the taste of a honey-drenched fig! I also miss my dear friend, Grumio; I rarely see him even in Rome, for he is a **domestic** slave in the house of a rich merchant on the other side of the city.

Still, questioning my lot in life will get me nowhere. Marcus **detests** complaining and has told me many times that things are as they are and as they are meant to be, so I won't incur his **wrath** by appearing ungrateful. My friend Gaius, a freed slave, chose to fight as a gladiator for fame and fortune. Gaius is still alive, but just barely. Whereas I live a charmed life in comparison, thanks to my master.

Marcus Aurelius often reminds me that no man is given more hardship than he can endure. Even out here, in the midst of battle, he writes daily of life's **paradoxes** and how to accept the idea that what looks like contradiction may be true. He says he is **flawed**, like all men, but he has had a long reign over an unruly empire and is strong and unbowed. As for me, I wish that I had one-quarter of his fortitude and courage!

Audio

For iWords and audio passages, snap the code, or go to vocabularyworkshop.com.

Definitions

Note the spelling, pronunciation, part(s) of speech, and definition(s) of each of the following words. Then write the appropriate form of the word in the blank spaces in the illustrative sentence(s) following. Finally, study the lists of synonyms and antonyms.

1. amiss (ə mis′)

(*adj.*) faulty, imperfect, not as it should be; (*adv.*) in a mistaken or improper way, wrongly

Under the circumstances it would not be **amiss** to offer our congratulations.

SYNONYM: (*adj.*, *adv.*) awry
ANTONYM: (*adv.*) properly

2. brawl (brôl)

(*n.*) a noisy quarrel or fight; (*v.*) to quarrel or fight noisily

The noise coming from the classroom sounded more like a **brawl** than a debate.

SYNONYMS: (*n.*) scuffle, donnybrook; (*v.*) spar, scrap

3. detest (di test′)

(*v.*) to hate, dislike very much, loathe

Children who dislike green vegetables often **detest** spinach.

SYNONYMS: despise, abhor
ANTONYMS: relish, love, admire, esteem

4. domestic (də mes′ tik)

(*adj.*) native to a country, not foreign; relating to the life or affairs of a household; (*n.*) a household servant

The newspaper is filled with information about our country's **domestic** affairs.

When my grandmother first came to this country, she took a job as a **domestic**.

SYNONYMS: (*adj.*) native; (*n.*) servant
ANTONYMS: (*adj.*) foreign, alien

5. flagrant (flā′ grənt)

(*adj.*) extremely bad, glaring; scandalous, notorious

Crossing against the light shows a **flagrant** disregard for the law.

SYNONYMS: blatant, gross, outrageous
ANTONYMS: petty, piddling, trifling, inconsequential

6. flaw (flô)

(*n.*) a slight fault, defect, crack

We noticed a **flaw** in the plan to start building the house before the spring rains.

SYNONYMS: imperfection, blemish
ANTONYMS: faultlessness, perfection

CCSS Vocabulary: 4.c., 4.d. (See pp. T14–15.)

7. fledgling (flej′ liŋ)

(*n.*) an inexperienced person, beginner; a young bird about to leave the nest; (*adj.*) inexperienced, budding

We placed the **fledgling** back in its nest.

A **fledgling** police officer appeared on the scene and wisely called for assistance.

SYNONYMS: (*n.*) novice, tyro, neophyte
ANTONYMS: (*n.*) pro, expert, veteran

8. fluster (fləs′ tər)

(*v.*) to make or become confused, agitated, or nervous; (*n.*) a state of confusion or agitation

During the trial, the judge told the attorney not to **fluster** the witness.

SYNONYMS: (*v.*) agitate, disconcert
ANTONYMS: (*v.*) reassure, soothe, quiet

9. foremost (fôr′ mōst)

(*adj.*) chief, most important, primary; (*adv.*) in the first place

Among my interests, music is **foremost**.

First and **foremost**, you must call home to let your family know you'll be late.

SYNONYMS: (*adj.*) leading, principal, paramount
ANTONYMS: (*adj.*) hindmost, last, secondary

10. momentum (mō ment′ əm)

(*n.*) the force or speed with which something moves

The presidential campaign gained **momentum** once the first primary was over.

SYNONYMS: drive, thrust, impetus

11. notable (nōt′ ə bəl)

(*adj.*) striking, remarkable; (*n.*) a person who is well known, distinguished, or outstanding in some way

Being chosen for the team was a **notable** event in our lives.

The party was attended by **notables** from the film world.

SYNONYMS: (*adj.*) noteworthy, exceptional
ANTONYMS: (*adj.*) undistinguished, unremarkable; (*n.*) unknown

12. nurture (nər′ chər)

(*v.*) to bring up, care for, train, nourish; (*n.*) rearing, training, upbringing

It is wonderful to watch chimpanzees **nurture** their young.

The **nurture** they received as children served them well as they grew into adulthood.

SYNONYMS: (*v.*) raise, rear, foster
ANTONYMS: (*v.*) neglect, ignore, discourage, hinder

13. paradox (par′ ə däks)

(*n.*) a self-contradictory statement that on closer examination proves true; a person or thing with seemingly contradictory qualities

It is a ___**paradox**___ to say that youth is wasted on the young.

SYNONYMS: riddle, enigma, anomaly, absurdity

14. perjury (pər′ jə rē)

(*n.*) the act of swearing to a lie

The witness was convicted of ___**perjury**___ and was sentenced to serve two years in prison.

SYNONYM: false witness

15. presume (pri züm′)

(*v.*) to take for granted, assume or suppose; to dare, take upon oneself, take liberties

The counselors ___**presume**___ that the jobs they had last summer will be theirs this summer as well.

SYNONYMS: surmise, trespass, infringe

16. prior (prī′ ər)

(*adj.*) earlier, former

Unfortunately, the governor had a ___**prior**___ appointment and could not meet with the class.

SYNONYMS: anterior, preceding; ANTONYMS: later, ensuing, following

17. proficient (prə fish′ ənt)

(*adj.*) skilled, expert, or capable in any field or activity

Dad knows his way around the kitchen and is quite a ___**proficient**___ cook.

SYNONYMS: competent, adept
ANTONYMS: incompetent, inept, unskilled, ignorant

18. salvo (sal′ vō)

(*n.*) a burst of gunfire or cannon shot, often as a tribute or salute; a sudden burst of anything; a spirited verbal attack

The audience erupted in a ___**salvo**___ of laughter.

SYNONYMS: barrage, volley

19. vigilant (vij′ ə lənt)

(*adj.*) wide-awake, alert, watchful

The ___**vigilant**___ guards paced back and forth in front of the barracks.

SYNONYM: attentive; ANTONYMS: sleepy, inattentive, unobservant

20. wrath (rath)

(*n.*) intense anger

In Greek and Roman myths, characters fear the ___**wrath**___ of the gods.

SYNONYMS: rage, ire, choler, indignation
ANTONYMS: favor, approval, pleasure, blessing

CCSS Vocabulary: 4.c., 4.d. (See pp. T14–15.)

Choosing the Right Word

*Select the **boldface** word that better completes each sentence. You might refer to the passage on pages 88–89 to see how most of these words are used in context.*

The story of Romeo and Juliet's ill-fated love has captivated audiences for centuries.

1. To say that the U.S. Constitution is one of the greatest documents of all time does not mean that it is entirely without (**momentum, flaws**).

2. *Romeo and Juliet* opens with members of the rival houses of Montague and Capulet (**brawling, perjuring**) in the streets of Verona.

3. She may have given wrong information in court, but this was an honest mistake and certainly does not make her guilty of (**perjury, wrath**).

4. How can you expect the court to excuse your repeated and (**flagrant, vigilant**) violations of the traffic laws?

5. Though I hadn't expected to be treated quite so unkindly by the audience, I didn't become (**flustered, nurtured**) or lose my professional cool.

6. As support for our candidate continued to gain (**momentum, salvo**), it soon became clear that she would win the election by a landslide.

7. Nowadays (**domestics, fledglings**) are seen more often in old books and movies than in real life.

8. No parent can ever be (**vigilant, amiss**) enough to prevent a small child from taking many a painful tumble.

9. Under the American system of justice, any person accused of a crime is (**presumed, flawed**) to be innocent until proven guilty.

10. I am disturbed by the (**momentum, paradox**) of impoverished people in the richest land on earth.

11. Because there had been no (**prior, proficient**) notice of the scholarship competition, we had practically no time to prepare for it.

12. "Something is (**foremost, amiss**) in this room," said the detective, peering over the back of the sofa, "and I intend to discover what it is."

13. Abraham Lincoln had very little formal schooling, but his mind was (**nurtured, flawed**) by such great literary works as the Bible and the plays of Shakespeare.

14. It was an error only a (**flaw, fledgling**), not a more experienced officer, could have committed.

15. I can forgive an honest mistake, but I (**presume, detest**) any attempt to cover up errors by lying.

CCSS Vocabulary: 4.d. (See pp. T14–15.)

16. The struggle against terrorism has been one of the (**notable, proficient**) features of our time.

17. The easternmost tip of Cuba was the first populated area in the region to feel the (**paradox, wrath**) of Hurricane Zelda.

18. The charges of incompetence the candidate leveled at her opponent were but the opening (**brawl, salvo**) in her campaign to become mayor.

19. The rather skinny boy whom we had noticed only two years before as a (**prior, fledgling**) quarterback was now an all-American!

20. (**Foremost, Flagrant**) among the reasons that so many millions of immigrants have come to the United States is the desire for freedom.

21. A happy (**domestic, nurture**) life can afford an executive a great deal of relief from the everyday strains of running a large company.

22. It was hard to believe that the small, rather ordinary-looking person who was standing before us was a world-famous (**notable, fledgling**).

23. Please don't take it (**amiss, notably**) if I suggest that your French accent sounds more like Paris, Texas, than Paris, France.

24. She worked so easily and quietly that at first we did not realize how remarkably (**proficient, amiss**) she was in the laboratory.

25. The unexpected award left me in a confused but thrilling (**fluster, wrath**).

Synonyms

Choose the word from this Unit that is the same or most nearly the same in meaning as the ***boldface*** *word or expression in the phrase. Write that word on the line. Use a dictionary if necessary.*

1. felt his enemy's **fury** wrath
2. witnessed a violent street **battle** brawl
3. did not **rattle** the experienced pilot fluster
4. was responsible for a variety of **household** chores domestic
5. committed **false oath** during the trial perjury
6. a really **impressive** effort notable
7. became an **able** gymnast after much practice proficient
8. not trust the script to **apprentice** screenwriters fledgling
9. had been involved in a **previous** arrest prior
10. suspected that something had gone **off target** amiss

 CCSS Vocabulary: 5. (See pp. T14–15.)

Antonyms

*Choose the word from this Unit that is most nearly opposite in meaning to the **boldface** word or expression in the phrase. Write that word on the line. Use a dictionary if necessary.*

1. a real **old-timer** at the game of chess ___fledgling___
2. had no **subsequent** arrests ___prior___
3. an **ordinary** person without any striking qualities ___notable___
4. almost nothing **correct** in her homework ___amiss___
5. the witness's **honesty** on the stand ___perjury___

Completing the Sentence

From the words in this Unit, choose the one that best completes each of the following sentences. Write the correct word form in the space provided.

1. I must warn you once again that if you fail to tell the truth, you may lay yourself open to a charge of ___perjury___.
2. Her parents ___nurtured___ her musical talents by hiring the finest teachers and taking her to hear the performances of great musicians.
3. I have no way of knowing for sure why she left, but I ___presume___ that she had a good reason for doing so.
4. In most respects she is a fine person, but excessive stubbornness is the one important ___flaw___ in her character.
5. It's a fact that some important battles of the American Revolution occurred ___prior___ to the signing of the Declaration of Independence.
6. Some people truly love the music of such modern composers as Arnold Schoenberg or Igor Stravinsky; others absolutely ___detest___ it.
7. How do you explain the fact that some students who do poorly in math are highly ___proficient___ in figuring out batting averages?
8. We must be ___vigilant___ in recognizing the early signs of decay in our community and move quickly to improve conditions.
9. I wouldn't call such a(n) ___flagrant___ and premeditated lie merely a "minor lapse of memory."
10. I well remember how often during my childhood I felt the full force of my parents' ___wrath___ when I had done something wrong.

CCSS Vocabulary: 4.a., 5. (See pp. T14–15.)

11. We suspected that something was ___amiss___ when he did not return home from school at the usual time.

12. At what point does a spinning top lose sufficient ___momentum___ to topple over?

13. ___Foremost___ among her many outstanding qualities is her ability to understand the points of view of other people.

14. Like a(n) ___fledgling___ eagle about to leave the nest for the first time, our son is preparing to spend his first summer away from home.

15. When two players suddenly started to throw punches at each other during last night's game, an ugly bench-clearing ___brawl___ ensued.

16. In the old days, wooden battleships saluted their victorious admiral by repeatedly firing ___salvos___ of cannon shot from their decks.

17. The speaker went right on with his speech, in no way ___flustered___ or disturbed by the jeers and catcalls of a few rowdy hecklers.

18. Though his career as a whole was not particularly distinguished, he did score one ___notable___ success on Broadway a few years ago.

19. That terrible instruments of war should in fact prove useful as guardians of the peace is one of the ___paradoxes___ of modern life.

20. The minister saw from the statistics that imported goods were cutting into the ___domestic___ market.

Writing: Words in Action

Answers to both prompts will vary.

1. Look back at "Everything That Happens, Happens as It Should" (pages 88–89). Think about the title, and relate it to what you learned about Blasius and his circumstances. Do you agree that everything that happens in Blasius's world has happened as it should? Write an argument stating and defending your opinion. Write two or three paragraphs, and use at least three details from the passage and three Unit words.

2. In the reading "Everything That Happens, Happens as It Should," the Roman slave Blasius says that Emperor Marcus Aurelius believes that "no man is given more hardship than he can endure." Do you agree with this statement? In a brief essay, support your opinion with specific examples from your observations, studies, reading (refer to pages 88–89), or personal experience. Write at least three paragraphs, and use three or more words from this Unit.

Writing prompt #2 is modeled on that of standardized tests.

CCSS Vocabulary: 6; Writing: 1.c., 2.d., 3.d., 4. (See pp. T14–15.)

Vocabulary in Context: Informational Text for Unit 7 is available online at **vocabularyworkshop.com**.

Vocabulary in Context

Literary Text

The following excerpts are from Mark Twain's novel A Connecticut Yankee in King Arthur's Court. *Some of the words you have studied in this Unit appear in* ***boldface*** *type. Complete each statement below the excerpt by circling the letter of the correct answer.*

1. The woman paled slightly, but quite perceptibly, and the man looked **flustered** and irresolute.

Someone who is **flustered** is NOT

a. steady
b. agitated
c. confused
d. tired

2. "Take a rest, child; the way you are using up all the **domestic** air, the kingdom will have to go to importing it by to-morrow, and it's a low enough treasury without that."

Air that is **domestic** is

a. neat and tidy
b. unlikely to cause trouble
c. native to a place
d. from a distant location

3. They are full of admiration of his vast bulk and his prodigious strength; they speak with pride of the fact that he can do a hundred marvels which are far and away beyond their own powers; and they speak with the same pride of the fact that in his **wrath** he is able to drive a thousand men before him.

Someone who feels **wrath** is

a. careful
b. mighty
c. brave
d. angry

Mark Twain was one of the greatest humor writers in American literature. In *A Connecticut Yankee*, his main character goes back in time to the era of knights in armor.

4. Ah, Sandy, what a right heart she had, how simple, and genuine, and good she was! She was a **flawless** wife and mother.

A **flawless** person is

a. impatient
b. hasty
c. perfect
d. tired

5. The saving in expense was a **notable** economy. You will see that by these figures: . . . at former rates, this would have cost the government about $240; at the new rate we pulled through for about $35, thus saving upward of $200 at one swoop.

A **notable** economy is

a. impressive
b. ordinary
c. indifferent
d. declining

Interactive Quiz

Snap the code, or go to **vocabularyworkshop.com**

UNIT 8

Note that not all of the 20 Unit words are used in this passage. *Evict*, *legible*, *pervade*, *ordain,* and *quench* are not included.

*Read the following passage, taking note of the **boldface** words and their contexts. These words are among those you will be studying in Unit 8. As you complete the exercises in this Unit, it may help to refer to the way the words are used below.*

CCSS Vocabulary: 4; Reading (Informational Text): 4, 6. (See pp. T14–15.)

A Fish That Fishes

<Magazine Article>

by Laverne J. Cambalda, Ph.D.

A fish that fishes? Can such a creature really exist in the natural order of things? One might at first be inclined to deny the possibility, but at the risk of being **disputatious**, the answer is yes. The creature that appears to use rod and lure to capture its prey is known as the anglerfish. One glance at this bizarre denizen of the deep suffices to establish its appearance as **abnormal** in the extreme.

The old adage points out that "it takes one to know one." But human observers of this creature do not even need to be anglers themselves to recognize the uncanny resemblance of the anglerfish's projecting spine to a fishing rod.

By the same token, the fleshy **nub** at the end of the spine, called the esca, resembles a lure. Even more strangely, the esca sometimes appears lit up in the murky ocean depths due to a phenomenon known as bioluminescence—this shining in the dark is, in fact, caused by clusters of bacteria.

Such a setup often spells **catastrophe** for the anglerfish's prey: skatefish, haddock, cod, whiting, and sand eels. An offensive **onslaught** by an anglerfish is formidable. The angler's head is enormous, with a huge mouth ringed with needle-sharp teeth. If a potential victim succumbs to the **incentive** of the lure, the contest is almost always over. The anglerfish comes equipped with a remarkable triggering mechanism; any external contact with its spinelike tentacle will trigger a virtually **simultaneous**, immediate rapid-fire bite. This swiftness almost invariably **outstrips** any defensive actions by the prey.

The cavernous size of the angler's mouth means that it can capture even cautious, **prudent** prey by making even the slightest **swerve** in any direction. Sometimes, moreover, the prey can be twice the angler's own size. Indeed, anglerfish are said to possess the fastest biting action of any vertebrate.

Reassuringly, boaters who **capsize** are unlikely to encounter an anglerfish when they hit the water. Anglers are deep-sea residents, living a mile or more below the surface. Anglerfish occur worldwide, and they are generally divided into four groups: batfish, frogfish,

deep-sea anglerfish, and goosefish. Of the 200 species of anglerfish, some can be tiny, measuring only one-fourth of an inch, while others may stretch up to six feet long. Scientists agree that thanks to their remote habitat and effective "fishing" techniques, anglerfish are **flourishing**. In this respect, as in so many others, they differ from other marine species, many of which are in decline.

Some curious differences separate male anglerfish from females. Only the female angler, for example, comes armed for fishing with the spine and the esca. Males, overall, are much smaller than females. In fact, throughout their lives males actually **decrease** in size. A male attaches itself to a female's body, becoming completely dependent on her. One can only imagine the consequences of any **insubordination** on his part!

Ultimately, the male's body dwindles to a mere **remnant**. He has become merely a fertilizing mechanism for the female.

Such is the remarkable world of the anglerfish—both intriguing and demanding but perfectly suited for the anglerfish.

Laverne J. Cambalda, Ph.D., has been fascinated by marine life since she first saw the ocean. A native of Nebraska, Cambalda moved to Monterey, California, after she went to graduate school to study marine biology. This is her first article for Ocean Seven *magazine.*

Audio

For iWords and audio passages, snap the code, or go to **vocabularyworkshop.com**.

Definitions

Note the spelling, pronunciation, part(s) of speech, and definition(s) of each of the following words. Then write the appropriate form of the word in the blank spaces in the illustrative sentence(s) following. Finally, study the lists of synonyms and antonyms.

1. abnormal
(ab nôr′ məl)

(*adj.*) not usual, not typical, strange

For my sister, who is always late, being early for class would be an **abnormal** situation.

SYNONYMS: freakish, unnatural, irregular, anomalous
ANTONYMS: normal, usual, regular, typical

2. capsize
(kap′ sīz)

(*v.*) to turn bottom side up, upset

Anyone watching could see that it was our inexperience that caused us to **capsize** the canoe.

SYNONYMS: upend, tip over

3. catastrophe
(kə tas′ trə fē)

(*n.*) a large-scale disaster, misfortune, or failure

During the Cold War, the United States did everything possible to avoid a nuclear **catastrophe**.

SYNONYMS: tragedy, cataclysm
ANTONYMS: triumph, victory, success

4. decrease
(*v.*, di krēs′; *n.*, dē′ krēs)

(*v.*) to become or make less; (*n.*) a lessening

The manager hopes that theft will **decrease** once the new security system is installed.

Because of a sharp **decrease** in sales, the company had to lay off two-thirds of its workers.

SYNONYMS: (*v.*) lessen, reduce, dwindle, diminish
ANTONYMS: (*v.*) increase, grow, develop, wax

5. disputatious
(dis pyü ta′ shəs)

(*adj.*) inclined to argue or debate; provoking debate

The **disputatious** senator had engaged in filibusters to block the passage of many a bill.

SYNONYMS: argumentative, quarrelsome, contentious
ANTONYMS: nonargumentative, peaceable, pacific

6. evict
(i vikt′)

(*v.*) to force out from a property, eject

The landlord reluctantly decided to **evict** the tenants who fell on hard times and had not paid their rent in six months.

SYNONYMS: oust, expel, kick out
ANTONYMS: admit, insert

CCSS Vocabulary: 4.c., 4.d. (See pp. T14–15.)

7. flourish (flər′ ish)

(*v.*) to grow, thrive, be prosperous; to wave in the air; (*n.*) a dramatic gesture; a fanfare of horns

It is fortunate for lovers of the arts that painting and opera still ___**flourish**___ in Italy.

Actors often enter the stage with a ___**flourish**___.

SYNONYMS: (*v.*) prosper, burgeon, increase
ANTONYMS: (*v.*) wither, die, fade, shrivel up

8. incentive (in sen′ tiv)

(*n.*) a reason for doing something; something that stimulates action

Because career advancement is such a strong ___**incentive**___, adults are usually eager and hard-working students.

SYNONYMS: stimulus, spur, motive, inducement
ANTONYMS: curb, check, restraint, hindrance

9. insubordinate (in sə bôrd′ ən ət)

(*adj.*) disobedient, rebellious

The ___**insubordinate**___ soldier repeatedly interrupted his commanding officer.

SYNONYMS: defiant, unruly, mutinous
ANTONYMS: obedient, submissive, docile, tractable

10. legible (lej′ ə bəl)

(*adj.*) easily read

In keeping with the jokes, pharmacists will tell you that most doctors' handwriting is barely ___**legible**___.

SYNONYMS: clear, decipherable
ANTONYMS: unreadable, indecipherable

11. nub (nəb)

(*n.*) the central point or heart of a matter; a knob

After seemingly endless digressions, the speaker finally got to the ___**nub**___ of his argument.

SYNONYMS: kernel, nucleus, crux
ANTONYMS: fringe, periphery, edge

12. onslaught (än′ slôt)

(*n.*) a violent attack; a sudden rush of something

To prepare for the ___**onslaught**___ of winter, we replenished our supply of firewood and rock salt.

SYNONYMS: assault, charge, foray, onset

13. ordain (ôr dān′)

(*v.*) to establish by law; to order or command; to appoint as a priest or minister; to destine

Ancient astrologers believed that the stars could ___**ordain**___ one's future.

SYNONYMS: anoint, consecrate, enact, decree
ANTONYMS: forbid, veto, cancel

14. outstrip (au̇t strip′)

(*v.*) to get ahead of, do better than, exceed

By offering customers low prices and good terms, the new store hopes to ____**outstrip**____ the competition.

SYNONYMS: outdo, outperform, outdistance, surpass
ANTONYMS: trail, lag behind

15. pervade (pər vād′)

(*v.*) to spread throughout

Pollutants ____**pervade**____ the atmosphere of many of our nation's large cities.

SYNONYMS: permeate, diffuse, imbue

16. prudent (prüd′ ənt)

(*adj.*) cautious, careful, showing good sense

It pays to make ____**prudent**____ investments.

SYNONYMS: wary, judicious
ANTONYMS: foolish, unwise, rash

17. quench (kwench)

(*v.*) to put out, extinguish, end

The firefighters will ____**quench**____ the flames with water.

SYNONYMS: douse, stifle
ANTONYMS: ignite, kindle

18. remnant (rem′ nənt)

(*n.*) a small part remaining behind

By the end of the war, the rebels had but a ____**remnant**____ of their former strength.

SYNONYMS: remainder, residue, leftover

19. simultaneous (si məl tā′ nē əs)

(*adj.*) happening or existing at the same time

The diplomats put on headphones so that they could listen to a ____**simultaneous**____ translation of the speech.

SYNONYMS: occurring at the same time, concurrent
ANTONYM: occurring at different times

20. swerve (swərv)

(*v.*) to turn aside sharply; (*n.*) a sharp or sudden turn

Be aware that if you ____**swerve**____ too sharply, you may lose control of the car.

The sudden ____**swerve**____ of the bus caused some passengers to fall out of their seats.

SYNONYMS: (*v.*) digress, sheer off

CCSS Vocabulary: 4.c., 4.d. (See pp. T14–15.)

Choosing the Right Word

*Select the **boldface** word that better completes each sentence. You might refer to the passage on pages 98–99 to see how most of these words are used in context.*

1. After finishing the painting, the artist signed his name in big letters with a playful (**flourish, incentive**).

2. The only advice I can give you is to take the problems one at a time and deal with each in a sensible and (**prudent, disputatious**) way.

3. We have made some progress in cleaning up our community, but that is certainly no reason to (**decrease, evict**) our efforts.

Spanish painter Francisco Goya (1746–1828) signed his name with a distinctive flourish.

4. To get a good grade, make sure that your composition is interesting in content, correct in grammar and spelling, and (**abnormal, legible**).

5. There's nothing like pure water to (**quench, evict**) your thirst.

6. Two of the more (**abnormal, disputatious**) members of the committee soon got into an argument about where to build the new facility.

7. After the protesters had been sleeping in the building for two months, the police finally (**evicted, ordained**) them.

8. As we returned to the dressing room after that terrible first half, the whole atmosphere seemed to be (**pervaded, capsized**) by defeat.

9. The train and the car approached the crossing almost (**simultaneously, prudently**), and a terrible accident seemed unavoidable.

10. "We have become so engrossed in the minor details of the situation that we have left no time to consider the (**nub, incentive**) of the matter," I said.

11. When the musicians failed to arrive and the air-conditioning conked out, we realized that the party was becoming a (**remnant, catastrophe**).

12. The possibility of getting a summer job in an office is all the (**incentive, onslaught**) I need to improve my computer skills.

13. All our hopes and plans were (**capsized, outstripped**) when we learned that we would not be able to attend the music festival.

14. Experts predict a (**remnant, decrease**) in the number of medical school applicants this year due to rising costs of tuition.

15. The first (**onslaught, remnant**) of the disease is marked by a severe fever and the appearance of an ugly rash all over the body.

CCSS Vocabulary: 4.d. (See pp. T14–15.)

16. With eager students and able teachers, learning will (**flourish, outstrip**), even though the school building may be old and shabby.

17. As (**ordained, flourished**) in the U.S. Constitution, the President must be a native-born American at least 35 years old when he or she takes office.

18. Months after the fire, a strong scent of charred wood (**pervaded, outstripped**) the forest.

19. When the elderly pianist began to play, we were saddened to observe that he had only a(n) (**incentive, remnant**) of his once great skill.

20. Doesn't it seem (**abnormal, insubordinate**) for a bright young person to show no interest in taking part in any school activities?

21. The high spirits with which we had begun the hike were soon (**pervaded, quenched**) when it began to rain.

22. I'm following a very strict study schedule, but I must admit that I (**swerved, flourished**) from it when the play-offs were televised.

23. Has the ability of human beings to produce new inventions (**quenched, outstripped**) our ability to use them wisely?

24. Even though you may think your supervisor is wrong, you won't be able to hold your job if you act (**simultaneously, insubordinately**).

25. Be careful when you come to the sudden (**capsize, swerve**) in the road ahead!

Synonyms

Choose the word from this Unit that is the same or most nearly the same in meaning as the ***boldface*** *word or expression in the phrase. Write that word on the line. Use a dictionary if necessary.*

1. finally got to the **core** of the matter ____nub____
2. was forced to **veer** to the right ____swerve____
3. wants to **throw out** the guests ____evict____
4. had to **appoint** a minister ____ordain____
5. witnessed the **calamity** of war ____catastrophe____
6. has **readable** handwriting ____legible____
7. tried to **slake** her thirst with water ____quench____
8. winds that could **overturn** the boat ____capsize____
9. left with only a **fragment** of her pride ____remnant____
10. clothing **saturated** with the liquid ____pervaded____

CCSS Vocabulary: 5. (See pp. T14–15.)

Antonyms

*Choose the word from this Unit that is most nearly opposite in meaning to the **boldface** word or expression in the phrase. Write that word on the line. Use a dictionary if necessary.*

1. to **activate** a powerful force ______quench______
2. unbearably **messy** handwriting ______legible______
3. had to **disestablish** his appointment ______ordain______
4. **to restrict** the spread of pollution ______pervade______
5. wished they could **take in** more pets ______evict______

Completing the Sentence

From the words in this Unit, choose the one that best completes each of the following sentences. Write the correct word form in the space provided.

1. American farms continue to produce more and more food, even though the number of people working on them has actually ______decreased______.

2. Do you really believe that making money is the only ______incentive______ that leads people to work hard and try to excel?

3. By landing the damaged plane in an open field, the pilot prevented a major ______catastrophe______ from occurring.

4. When that land is developed into a mall, the city will ______evict______ any illegal squatters and offer them other alternatives for living situations.

5. "If that ______insubordinate______ young hothead had followed my orders to the letter," the general remarked sourly, "we wouldn't be in this fix!"

6. Let's ignore minor side issues and get to the ______nub______ of the problem as quickly as possible.

7. As the holidays approached, a feeling of excitement and anticipation seemed to ______pervade______ the entire school.

8. My brother was ______ordained______ a priest after he had completed his studies at the seminary.

9. Though we are still the leading producers of various industrial products, other countries are catching up fast and may soon ______outstrip______ us.

10. The secret of the trick is to remove the first card and pick up the second so quickly that the two actions seem to be ______simultaneous______.

CCSS Vocabulary: 4.a., 5. (See pp. T14–15.)

11. Trying to avoid an argument with that ___disputatious___ fellow is like trying to nail oatmeal to the wall.

12. When my canoe unexpectedly hit a tree stump and ___capsized___, I suddenly found myself neck-deep in some very cold and dirty water.

13. Even the most ___prudent___ businessperson knows that there are times when it is necessary to take chances.

14. The only thing that ever really ___quenches___ my thirst on a stifling summer afternoon is a glass of ice-cold lemonade.

15. After I had eaten my fill, I threw the ___remnants___ of my dinner into the dog's bowl.

16. After our team won the last big game of the season, we all ran out onto the field, ___flourishing___ our pennants and banners jubilantly.

17. Although we are used to severe winters, a heavy snowfall this early in the season is quite ___abnormal___.

18. At the first shock of the enemy's ___onslaught___, our lines wavered a bit, but they soon recovered and held firm.

19. When a deer suddenly ran onto the road, the car ___swerved___ quickly to avoid hitting it.

20. The writing on the curious old document had faded badly, but it was still perfectly ___legible___ when held up to the light.

Writing: Words in Action

Answers to both prompts will vary.

1. Look back at "A Fish That Fishes" (pages 98–99). Write a summary of the article. Your summary should be no more than half the length of Dr. Cambalda's original text and should use your own words. Include all the key facts in the article, and omit minor details. Use at least three Unit words in your summary.

2. In her article on the anglerfish, Dr. Cambalda notes that climate change, overfishing, and pollution are often cited as key reasons for the decline of fish populations in the world's oceans. Write an essay in which you examine the consequences of a decline in the population of fish species and suggest one or more possible solutions to the problem. Support your points with examples from your observations, studies, reading (refer to pages 98–99), or personal experience. Write at least three paragraphs, and use three or more Unit words.

Writing prompt #2 is modeled on that of standardized tests.

CCSS Vocabulary: 6; Writing: 1.c., 2.d., 3.d., 4. (See pp. T14–15.)

Vocabulary in Context: Informational Text for Unit 8 is available online at **vocabularyworkshop.com**.

Vocabulary in Context
Literary Text

The following excerpts are from Jules Verne's novel A Journey to the Center of the Earth. *Some of the words you have studied in this Unit appear in* **boldface** *type. Complete each statement below the excerpt by circling the letter of the correct answer.*

1. Our thirst was so intense that to **quench** it we would have dug below the bed of old Ocean itself.

When you **quench** your thirst, you

a. discover it **c.** satisfy it
b. worsen it **d.** enjoy it

2. If the degree of heat increased instead of **decreasing**, as we approached the surface of the earth, it was simply because the causes were local and solely due to volcanic influence.

When something is **decreasing**, it is NOT

a. growing **c.** shrinking
b. melting **d.** drying out

3. My companions, doubtless, felt the same horrible tortures, but neither of them would touch the wretched morsel of meat that remained. It lay there, a last **remnant** of all our great preparations for the mad and senseless journey!

A **remnant** is something that is

a. forgotten **c.** final
b. horrible **d.** left over

In the 1959 film based on Verne's novel, a group of adventurers discovers a strange world at Earth's core, complete with dinosaurs, lakes, and even a sun.

4. In many doubtful or dangerous places, it became necessary for us to be tied together by a long rope in order that should any one of us be unfortunate enough to slip, he would be supported by his companions. This connecting link was doubtless a **prudent** precaution.

A **prudent** precaution is

a. wise **c.** indifferent
b. reckless **d.** useless

5. An invincible dread had taken possession of my brain and soul. I could only look forward to an immediate **catastrophe**, such a catastrophe as not even the most vivid imagination could have thought of.

One example of a **catastrophe** is

a. a long journey **c.** a new experience
b. a shipwreck **d.** a bad dream

Snap the code, or go to **vocabularyworkshop.com**

CCSS Vocabulary: 4.d.; Reading (Literature): 4. (See pp. T14–15.)

UNIT 9

Note that not all of the 20 Unit words are used in this passage. *Canvass*, *casual*, *parch*, *quibble*, and *ratify* are not included.

*Read the following passage, taking note of the **boldface** words and their contexts. These words are among those you will be studying in Unit 9. As you complete the exercises in this Unit, it may help to refer to the way the words are used below.*

C CCSS Vocabulary: 4; Reading (Informational Text): 4, 6. (See pp. T14–15.)

Marc Chagall

<Biographical Sketch>

Marc Chagall (1887–1985) was one of the most celebrated and prolific artists of the twentieth century. He was born Moishe Shagal, eldest of nine children, to an oppessed and **downtrodden** but proud Orthodox Jewish family in Vitebsk, a port city in Russia. His father, Khatskel, labored in a herring factory. His mother, Feiga-Ita, ran a small grocery shop.

Shagal exhibited impressive artistic talent early on. But money was tight, and his father tried to **stifle** his son's ambition. Why couldn't his son devote himself fully to his faith and family? And how could he support himself on an artist's **puny** income?

But Shagal had far-reaching dreams. He was not going to be a humble **bystander** in the world. He believed he saw things that "regular" people did not see. He represented people, animals, flowers, religious symbols, and his own dreams in **vital**, lively paintings. People flew in the sky, and size and scale were often ignored.

Shagal **persisted** with his dreams, and in 1907, with his mother's help, he went to St. Petersburg, then the capital of Russia and a cultural center, to study art. While he learned valuable skills and techniques, he **floundered** and struggled for a time. Many of his days in the cosmopolitan city were an **ordeal**. He had to work as a servant to pay bills, and he was jailed once for not having working papers.

Chagall in front of his stained glass window at the United Nations, 1964

Poverty and struggle followed him, but his confidence in his talent never **eroded**. Shagal moved to Paris in 1910, changing his name to the more French-sounding Marc Chagall. He enrolled in an art academy. He befriended other artists and spent hours studying those he admired.

It was in Paris that his vivid, **graphic** images took shape, and his distinctive way of depicting his worldview **accelerated**. He said, "My art needed Paris like a tree needs water." Chagall invented his own style. In spite of his **melancholy** childhood and tough times, his family, his early village life, his faith and belief in tradition were mainstays of

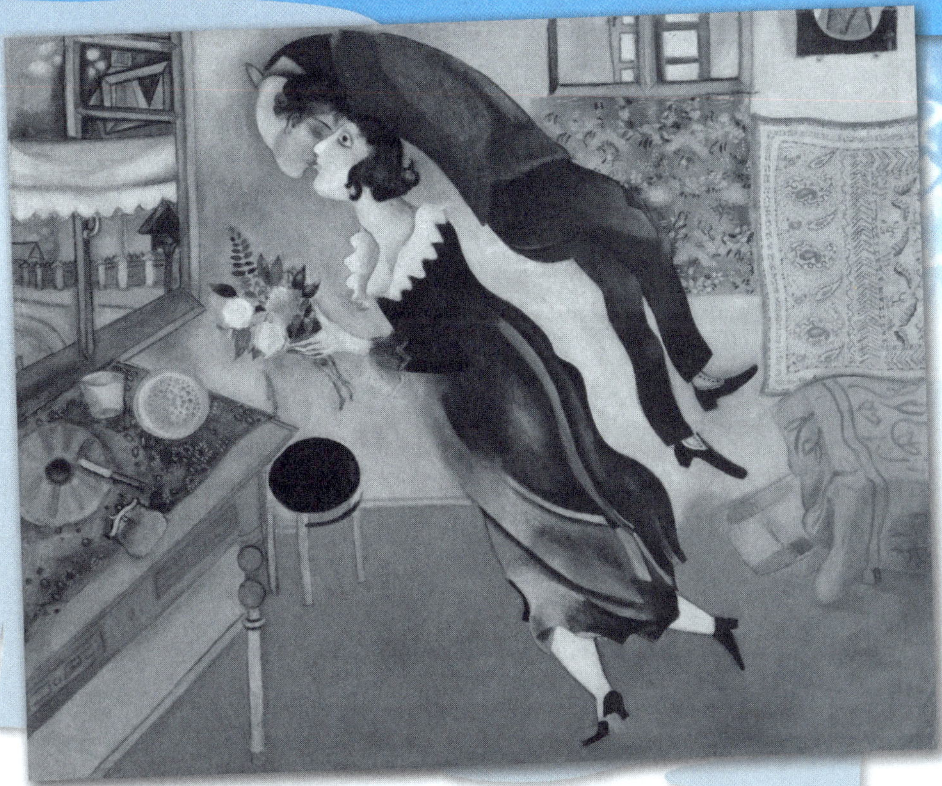

"Birthday" ("L'Anniversaire"), 1915. Digital Image © The Museum of Modern Art/Licensed by SCALA/Art Resource, NY.

his enchanting paintings. Chagall stayed close to his humble origins, for one sees great things from the valley and only small things from the peak.

In 1914, Chagall returned to Vitebsk, **enticed** by his fiancée, Bella Rosenfeld, a **regal**, cultured woman and his muse. He stayed in Russia after the outbreak of World War I and during the 1917 Russian Revolution. He and Bella eventually returned to Paris in 1923, and Chagall became a French citizen. Then World War II broke out in 1939, and he was swept up in the **gruesome** horror of war, the persecution of the Jews, revolutions, and personal tragedy. Chagall fled to the United States in 1941. He and his family took whatever paintings they could save as he went into exile. Chagall spent seven happy and productive years in the United States. He then returned to France for the remainder of his life.

During Chagall's long career, he experimented with many different art forms, from painting to tapestries to theatrical set designs to stained glass. His stained-glass commissions include a series of Biblical windows for a synagogue in Jerusalem. He also created the famous "Peace" window at the United Nations building in New York. The lobby of the Metropolitan Opera House at Lincoln Center, in midtown Manhattan, is the venue for one of his most beloved works, immense murals called "The Triumph of Music" and "The Sources of Music."

Definitions

Note the spelling, pronunciation, part(s) of speech, and definition(s) of each of the following words. Then write the appropriate form of the word in the blank spaces in the illustrative sentence(s) following. Finally, study the lists of synonyms and antonyms.

1. accelerate (ak sel′ ə rāt)

(*v.*) to speed up, cause to move faster; to bring about more quickly

The hikers needed to **accelerate** their pace once it became clear that it would soon rain.

SYNONYMS: step up, quicken, hasten
ANTONYMS: slow down, decelerate

2. bystander (bī′ stan dər)

(*n.*) one who looks on or observes, a person present but not taking part

The **bystander** who had witnessed the collision gave his statement to the police.

SYNONYMS: observer, onlooker
ANTONYM: active participant

3. canvass (kan′ vəs)

(*v.*) to go through an area in order to procure votes, sales, or opinions; to go over in detail; to discuss

The students volunteered to **canvass** the neighborhood for our candidate.

SYNONYMS: survey, solicit

4. casual (kazh′ ə wəl)

(*adj.*) happening by chance or on an irregular basis; showing little concern; informal

A **casual** remark made by the mayor was taken out of context and used against him by the press.

SYNONYMS: haphazard, offhand
ANTONYMS: formal, serious, premeditated

5. downtrodden (daůn′ träd ən)

(*adj.*) treated unfairly and cruelly, oppressed

Most of the immigrants at Ellis Island represented the **downtrodden** masses yearning to be free.

SYNONYMS: mistreated, ground underfoot
ANTONYMS: uplifted, liberated

6. entice (en tīs′)

(*v.*) to attract, tempt

To **entice** shoppers into the store, salespersons were giving away coupons for free gifts.

SYNONYMS: lure, lead on
ANTONYMS: nauseate, sicken, revolt, repel

CCSS Vocabulary: 4.c., 4.d. (See pp. T14–15.)

7. erode (i rōd′)

(*v.*) to wear away gradually, eat away

Storms and mudslides **eroded** the road so that eventually it became impassable.

SYNONYMS: corrode, abrade
ANTONYMS: nurture, promote, encourage

8. flounder (flaůn′ dər)

(*v.*) to thrash about in a clumsy or ineffective way

After suffering much damage in the storm, the small craft was left to **flounder** about helplessly.

SYNONYMS: wallow, struggle

9. graphic (graf′ ik)

(*adj.*) lifelike, vivid; relating to the pictorial arts

A witness gave the reporter a **graphic** account of the destruction caused by the tornado.

SYNONYMS: colorful, descriptive
ANTONYMS: dull, boring, unrealistic, colorless

10. gruesome (grü′ səm)

(*adj.*) horrible, revolting, ghastly

The **gruesome** crime rocked the ordinarily quiet neighborhood.

SYNONYMS: gory, hideous
ANTONYMS: pleasant, delightful, appealing

11. melancholy (mel′ ən käl ē)

(*adj.*) sad, gloomy, unhappy; (*n.*) sadness, gloominess

It must have been the gloom of the house and the steady rain that made me feel so **melancholy**.

The tune and the lyrics of the song were filled with **melancholy**.

SYNONYMS: (*adj.*) depressed, dejected; (*n.*) dejection, depression
ANTONYMS: (*adj.*) merry, happy, cheerful; (*n.*) joy, elation

12. ordeal (ôr dēl′)

(*n.*) a difficult or painful experience, a trial

The climbers were exhausted by their **ordeal** and quickly fell asleep.

SYNONYMS: hardship, trauma
ANTONYMS: pleasure, cinch

13. parch (pärch)

(*v.*) to make dry and thirsty; to shrivel with heat

The fields of Oklahoma were **parched** by drought in the 1930s.

SYNONYMS: dry up, dehydrate
ANTONYMS: soak, drench, saturate

CCSS Vocabulary: 4.c., 4.d. (See pp. T14–15.)

14. persist (pər sist′)

(*v.*) to continue steadily in a course of action, refuse to stop or be changed; to last, remain

Despite stern warnings from their doctor, the brothers __**persist**__ in their bad habits.

SYNONYMS: persevere, keep at it, endure
ANTONYMS: give up, discontinue

15. puny (pyü′ nē)

(*adj.*) of less than normal strength or size; of no importance

The wrestler let out a coarse burst of laughter when his __**puny**__ opponent entered the ring.

SYNONYMS: undersized, pint-size, small, weak
ANTONYMS: robust, brawny, mammoth, gigantic

16. quibble (kwib′ əl)

(*v.*) to evade or belittle a point by twisting words or raising minor objections; (*n.*) a petty objection

Let's not __**quibble**__ over details.

The buyer's __**quibble**__ notwithstanding, the parties soon came to an agreement.

SYNONYMS: (*v.*) split hairs, cavil; (*n.*) squabble

17. ratify (rat′ ə fī)

(*v.*) to approve, give formal approval to, confirm

The legislatures of three-fourths of the states must __**ratify**__ an amendment to the Constitution.

SYNONYMS: endorse, sanction
ANTONYMS: cancel, annul, veto

18. regal (rē′ gəl)

(*adj.*) royal, kinglike; fit for a king

The two families pooled their resources to give the bride and groom a truly __**regal**__ wedding.

SYNONYMS: majestic, stately, princely, august
ANTONYMS: lowly, humble, abject, servile

19. stifle (stī′ fəl)

(*v.*) to smother, prevent from breathing; to hold back or choke off

Unable to __**stifle**__ her anger, the sculptor lashed out at her harshest critic.

SYNONYMS: strangle, suppress, snuff
ANTONYMS: nurture, promote, encourage

20. vital (vīt′ əl)

(*adj.*) having life, living; necessary to life, essential; key, crucial

The treaty is of __**vital**__ importance to the security of our nation.

SYNONYMS: indispensable, fundamental
ANTONYMS: nonessential, unnecessary

CCSS Vocabulary: 4.c., 4.d. (See pp. T14–15.)

Choosing the Right Word

*Select the **boldface** word that better completes each sentence. You might refer to the passage on pages 108–109 to see how most of these words are used in context.*

For more than 200 years, Americans have participated in public affairs by voting and by getting involved in issues.

1. In a democracy, the average citizen should be an active participant in public affairs, not just a quiet (**bystander, enticer**).
2. After weeks of no rain, the (**parched, graphic**) earth turned to dust that was blown away by the strong winds.
3. The soundness of the basic ideas of the U.S. Constitution has been (**ratified, enticed**) by the experience of more than 200 years.
4. In spite of all the setbacks we have had, we must (**persist, quibble**) in our efforts to achieve the goal we have set for ourselves.
5. "How can you compare a union employee," the factory owner asked, "to the (**downtrodden, melancholy**) serfs and slaves of earlier times?"
6. Aided by diagrams on the chalkboard, she gave a summary of her plan so clear and (**graphic, regal**) that it won the full support of the audience.
7. It is hard to believe that this sturdy, six-foot basketball star was a (**vital, puny**) 100-pounder only a few years ago.
8. If you press the gas pedal just a little, this car will (**erode, accelerate**) like a racing vehicle.
9. Wearing that thick scarf and ski mask, as well as a heavy coat over layers of clothing, he must have felt hot and (**stifled, enticed**) even in the chilly air.
10. I think it showed bad judgment on your part to tell such a (**gruesome, puny**) story to a child who is so easily frightened.
11. With her (**regal, graphic**) bearing and imperious manner, Elizabeth I looked every inch the queen she in fact was.
12. Instead of continuing to (**flounder, accelerate**), we must decide on a goal and start to move toward it.
13. You will never do well in school as long as your attitude toward your studies remains (**downtrodden, casual**) and unconcerned.
14. In the heat of the desert afternoon, we felt (**parched, regal**) despite drinking from our canteens every few minutes.
15. The assistant principal (**canvassed, quibbled**) the faculty for ways of improving the educational standards of the school.

CCSS Vocabulary: 4.d. (See pp. T14–15.)

16. If you have prepared properly for the exams, there will be no reason to regard them as a terrible (**quibble, ordeal**).

17. No doubt he has our best interests at heart, but my faith in him has been (**eroded, downtrodden**) by repeated evidence of his poor judgment.

18. She made what proved to be a (**vital, parched**) mistake when she gave the job to one of the applicants without checking his references first.

19. In spite of the bright sunshine and the happy crowds, a strange mood of (**ordeal, melancholy**) seemed to take possession of me.

20. "This case is much more than a mere (**canvass, quibble**) between former friends," said the lawyer during the closing remarks.

21. Do her efforts to (**accelerate, flounder**) our departure mean that she is trying to help us, or just get rid of us?

22. I find your offer most (**gruesome, enticing**), but my better judgment tells me to have nothing to do with it.

23. The dictator used fear and violence to (**stifle, canvass**) discontent among the people he ruled.

24. When I asked you what you meant by those words, I wasn't (**quibbling, ratifying**) but trying to discover what the problem was.

25. Sunset on a cold autumn day can be a wistful, (**melancholy, casual**) sight.

Synonyms

*Choose the word from this Unit that is the same or most nearly the same in meaning as the **boldface** word or expression in the phrase. Write that word on the line. Use a dictionary if necessary.*

1. described the devastation in **realistic** detail — graphic
2. land **desiccated** by a blistering sun — parched
3. a meeting that seemed **accidental** — casual
4. horrified by the **grisly** sight — gruesome
5. the Supreme Court will **uphold** the law — ratify
6. would **beguile** them with homemade treats — entice
7. standing among the crowd of **spectators** — bystanders
8. would **nitpick** over the smallest details — quibble
9. to **poll** voters for their opinion — canvass
10. survived the painful **test** — ordeal

CCSS Vocabulary: 5. (See pp. T14–15.)

Antonyms

Choose the word from this Unit that is most nearly opposite in meaning to the ***boldface*** *word or expression in the phrase. Write that word on the line. Use a dictionary if necessary.*

1. **ignore** all the possible witnesses	canvass
2. expected Congress to **repeal** the legislation	ratify
3. dislike playing on a **waterlogged** field	parched
4. gave their full attention to a **serious matter**	quibble
5. every **intentional** detail of his design	casual

Completing the Sentence

From the words in this Unit, choose the one that best completes each of the following sentences. Write the correct word form in the space provided.

1. After an hour of trudging along the dusty road under the hot sun, we were so ____parched____ that all we could think of was cold water.

2. He now claims that he was just an innocent ____bystander____, but I saw him actually taking part in the fight.

3. Though the new halfback looked a little ____puny____ to us, he managed to hold his own against players twice his size and build.

4. How can he ____persist____ in denying that he was at the scene of the crime when several people saw him there?

5. If you were spending your own money, rather than mine, you would be more inclined to ____quibble____ over the price of the repairs.

6. Regular visits to the dentist are ____vital____ if you wish to have healthy, good-looking teeth.

7. Since the twins' birthday party is by no means a formal affair, I feel assured in saying that ____casual____ clothing is in order.

8. At that tender age, I was so shy that I found it a(n) ____ordeal____ to be introduced to people I'd never met before.

9. Although these workers were ____downtrodden____ in their native land, in the United States they are entitled to a fair wage and safe working conditions.

10. The sled ____accelerated____ with alarming speed as it went down the steep slope.

CCSS Vocabulary: 4.a., 5. (See pp. T14–15.)

11. When the inexperienced swimmer realized that he was in very deep water, he panicked and began to ___flounder___ about wildly.

12. According to Greek mythology, the Sirens used their remarkable singing voices to ___entice___ unwary sailors to watery graves.

13. A group of reporters from the local TV station ___canvassed___ our district for reactions to the proposed changes in the law.

14. The ___gruesome___ sight that greeted my eyes at the scene of that awful traffic accident gave me nightmares for weeks.

15. She gave us a clear, detailed, and ___graphic___ picture of what is likely to happen if we fail to come to grips with the pollution problem.

16. In our environment class, we learned that in much of the United States, the topsoil has been badly ___eroded___ by natural forces.

17. Some poets write best about happy events, while others seem to prefer the more ___melancholy___ side of life.

18. As we fought the forest fire, we were practically ___stifled___ by the extreme heat and heavy smoke.

19. As soon as he learned that he was to play the king in the play, his whole personality took on an almost ___regal___ air.

20. The president's powers in foreign affairs are limited by the fact that any treaty he may negotiate must be ___ratified___ by a two-thirds vote of the Senate.

Writing: Words in Action

Answers to both prompts will vary.

1. Look back at "Marc Chagall" (pages 108–109). Suppose that you are Marc Chagall and you are writing a memoir about your life. Choose a period from your life that is covered in the passage, and tell about the experiences and feelings you had at that time. You may invent details, but be sure they are convincing and serious. Write at least two paragraphs, and use at least three Unit words in your memoir.

2. Marc Chagall defied his father's wishes and moved away from his home country in order to fulfill his dream of becoming an artist. For Chagall, this decision brought great success. But should everyone follow his example? Is it necessary to "leave home" in order to find success? In a brief essay, support your opinion with specific examples from your observations, studies, reading (refer to pages 108–109), or personal experience. Write at least three paragraphs, and use three or more words from this Unit.

Writing prompt #2 is modeled on that of standardized tests.

CCSS Vocabulary: 6; Writing: 1.c., 2.d., 3.d., 4. (See pp. T14–15.)

Vocabulary in Context: Informational Text for Unit 9 is available online at **vocabularyworkshop.com**.

Vocabulary in Context

Literary Text

The following excerpts are from Bram Stoker's novel Dracula. *Some of the words you have studied in this Unit appear in* **boldface** *type. Complete each statement below the excerpt by circling the letter of the correct answer.*

1. The tomb in the daytime, and when wreathed with fresh flowers, had looked grim and **gruesome** enough, but now, some days afterwards, when the flowers hung lank and dead . . . the effect was more miserable and sordid than could have been imagined.

If something looks **gruesome**, it appears

a. limp **c.** dull
b. faded **d.** ghastly

2. [He] sank into a sort of **melancholy**, in which state he has remained up to now. . . . It is now after the dinner hour of the asylum, and as yet my patient sits in a corner brooding, with a dull, sullen, woebegone look in his face.

A person in a state of **melancholy** feels

a. pleasant **c.** unhappy
b. wrathful **d.** excited

Dracula, the fearsome vampire, is one of the most familiar villains in all of fiction

3. After another hour Lucy waked from her sleep, fresh and bright and seemingly not much the worse for her terrible **ordeal**.

An **ordeal** is a

a. vision **c.** mistake
b. test **d.** nightmare

4. She had been restless all the morning, so that we were at first glad to know that she was sleeping. When, however, her husband mentioned **casually** that she was sleeping so soundly that he could not wake her, we went to her room to see for ourselves.

To mention something **casually** is to say it

a. offhandedly **c.** humorously
b. solemnly **d.** delicately

5. As he heard the voice his face brightened, through its mutilation, and he said, "That is Dr. Van Helsing. How good it is of you to be here. Give me some water, my lips are dry, and I shall try to tell you. I dreamed. . . ." He stopped and seemed fainting. We moistened the **parched** lips, and the patient quickly revived.

Parched lips are NOT

a. dry **c.** moist
b. rough **d.** thin

Snap the code, or go to **vocabularyworkshop.com**

 CCSS Vocabulary: 4.d.; Reading (Literature): 4. (See pp. T14–15.)

Vocabulary for Comprehension

Read the following passage in which some of the words you have studied in Units 7–9 appear in ***boldface*** *type. Then answer the questions on page 119.*

This passage discusses the significant impact of the Civilian Conservation Corps on America's landscape and economy during the Great Depression.

During the Great Depression of the 1930s, the **domestic** economy was all but destroyed. Joblessness was widespread, and millions of Americans were hungry. In an effort to address the economic **catastrophe** gripping the nation, President Franklin D. Roosevelt created several ambitious programs under a policy known as the New Deal. These programs were aimed not only at building the nation's economy but also at uplifting the American spirit.

Although the New Deal provided help to banks, farmers, and failing businesses, perhaps its most **notable** achievement was in the creation of programs to **decrease** the number of the nation's unemployed. By 1932, twelve million people were jobless, and Roosevelt knew he had to put Americans back to work. Promising "direct, vigorous action" in his Inaugural Address, the President created a variety of programs to help the jobless and **downtrodden**.

One of the first and most successful of these programs was the Civilian Conservation Corps, or CCC, which operated from 1933 to 1942. This was a massive public works project that addressed two of the President's interests: promoting conservation and providing jobs for the nation's unemployed youths. Calling the CCC a civilian "tree army," Roosevelt put the program under the Army's control. Guided by engineers and experts in forestry and agriculture, nearly 3 million young men between the ages of 17 and 28 went to work. They planted trees, dug canals, conserved soil, cleared beaches and campgrounds, stocked lakes and rivers with fish, and even restored historic battlefields. And they did it for just thirty dollars a month, warm clothing, and three meals a day.

Although the CCC proved an **ordeal** for some, it gave others a lifeline. Unexpectedly, it also proved to be a boon for the nation. As the future would show, it gave the Army much-needed experience in managing large numbers of recruits, while it also prepared the nation's young men for the military discipline they would soon face in the Second World War.

CCSS Vocabulary: 4.a.; Reading (Informational Text): 2, 4, 6. (See pp. T14–15.)

1. Which is the best title for this passage?
   a. "Saving the Environment"
   b. "FDR's New Deal Programs"
   c. "$30 and Three Meals a Day"
   d. "High Marks for the CCC"
   e. "A History of the Great Depression"

2. The meaning of **domestic** (line 2) is
   a. household
   b. foreign
   c. industrial
   d. national
   e. agricultural

3. **Catastrophe** (line 7) means
   a. disaster
   b. debate
   c. problem
   d. instability
   e. success

4. **Notable** (line 18) is best defined as
   a. mammoth
   b. impressive
   c. competent
   d. well-known
   e. attentive

5. **Decrease** (line 19) most nearly means
   a. assist
   b. employ
   c. increase
   d. reduce
   e. recruit

6. **Downtrodden** (line 28) is best defined as
   a. needy
   b. uplifted
   c. homeless
   d. sickly
   e. oppressed

7. The function of paragraphs 1 and 2 (lines 1–28) is to provide
   a. biographical information about Franklin D. Roosevelt
   b. detailed information about the CCC
   c. historical context for the CCC
   d. the history of the Great Depression
   e. an analysis of Roosevelt's New Deal

8. The CCC was founded to benefit
   a. women and men in rural areas
   b. engineers and experts in forestry
   c. unemployed young men
   d. out-of-work fathers
   e. college students needing a job

9. From paragraph 3 (lines 29–51), you can infer that the main reason for joining the CCC was
   a. to join the army
   b. to leave home
   c. to see the country
   d. to be outdoors
   e. to have a job

10. The meaning of **ordeal** (line 53) is
   a. challenging game
   b. easy time
   c. new adventure
   d. hardship
   e. pleasant experience

11. The writer's attitude toward the subject can best be described as
   a. respectful
   b. ironic
   c. disinterested
   d. sarcastic
   e. critical

12. The CCC had all of the following beneficial effects EXCEPT
   a. promoting conservation
   b. creating several new national parks
   c. giving the U.S. Army experience managing large numbers of recruits
   d. providing jobs for unemployed young men
   e. giving young men experience with military discipline

CCSS Vocabulary: 4.a.; Reading (Informational Text): 2, 4, 6. (See pp. T14–15.)

Two-Word Completions

Select the pair of words that best completes the meaning of each of the following sentences.

1. My throat became so ______________ during that long trek over dusty trails on the hottest day of summer that I firmly believed nothing would ever ______________ my thirst!

   a. flawed . . . nurture
   b. puny . . . decrease
   (c.) parched . . . quench
   d. flagrant . . . pervade

2. "There's nothing ______________ about feeling a bit ______________ after you've been through a disappointment, such as not getting picked for a team," my teacher assured me.

   a. gruesome . . . domestic
   (b.) abnormal . . . melancholy
   c. prudent . . . casual
   d. puny . . . regal

3. If you want to stop your automobile, apply the brakes. If you want it to gain ______________, step on the ______________.

   (a.) momentum . . . accelerator
   b. salvo . . . nub
   c. wrath . . . flaw
   d. incentive . . . paradox

4. As we ______________ violently to the right to avoid some rocks that suddenly sprang into view, our canoe ______________ and pitched us headlong into the churning waters of the river.

   a. flourished . . . flustered
   b. canvassed . . . evicted
   (c.) swerved . . . capsized
   d. brawled . . . nurtured

5. When prices go up, the value of our money ______________. As the cost of living rises, the more deeply inflation ______________ the purchasing power of the dollar.

   a. accelerates . . . entices
   (b.) decreases . . . erodes
   c. persists . . . perjures
   d. flourishes . . . parches

6. "It isn't ______________ to spend more than you make," I observed. "Only a fool would allow expenses to ______________ income."

   a. vital . . . fluster
   b. amiss . . . stifle
   c. abnormal . . . nurture
   (d.) prudent . . . outstrip

7. "An experienced worker doesn't usually have trouble handling a new job with ______________," the personnel manager observed. "A beginner, however, will normally ______________ around until he or she learns the ropes."

   a. prudence . . . quibble
   (b.) proficiency . . . flounder
   c. incentive . . . flourish
   d. vigilance . . . swerve

 CCSS Vocabulary: 4.a. (See pp. T14–15.)

In the passage about anglerfish (see pages 98–99), a bizarre-looking creature, the author uses the expression, "It takes one to know one."

"It takes one to know one" is an adage that means, "We recognize others who are like ourselves." An **adage** is a short, wise saying that reveals a commonly understood truth about life. The meanings of adages often go beyond the literal meanings of the words. As a result, adages must be learned as if they were unfamiliar words.

Choosing the Right Adage

*Read each sentence. Use context clues to figure out the meaning of each adage in **boldface** print. Then write the letter of the definition for the adage in the sentence.*

1. "**First thing's first**," Mom said, "so finish your homework before you go outside." __f__
2. The best way to deal with people who have insulted you is to **kill them with kindness**. __j__
3. I don't mind being short on cash; **a good name is better than riches**. __e__
4. **A word to the wise is enough**, so Alma cleaned her room without being told twice. __a__
5. Granddad's success was based on the belief that **fortune favors the bold**. __g__
6. I told Eva and her husband not to be so worried about being out of work; **they'll land on their feet.** __d__
7. "**Share and share alike**," I thought, giving Jeremy half my sandwich. __b__
8. As **slow help is no help**, you need to be on time for the cleanup. __i__
9. Kim was going to buy an expensive new phone, until she remembered, "**Waste not, want not**." __h__
10. **Don't rock the boat**; even if you disagree with the team's decision, it's better to go along with it. __c__

a. Good advice doesn't have to be repeated.

b. Give equal portions.

c. Avoid causing problems in a group.

d. People can do well after going through a difficult time.

e. Good character is more important than money.

f. Take care of the most important thing first.

g. Success requires taking risks.

h. Don't spend money foolishly.

i. You're no help if you come late.

j. People who try to hurt you will be bewildered if you act pleasantly toward them.

CCSS Vocabulary: 5.a. (See pp. T14–15.)

Writing with Adages

Find the meaning of each adage. (Use a dictionary if necessary.) Then write a sentence for each adage. **Answers will vary.**

1. Charity begins at home. **Sample response: In our family, we forgive each other for our mistakes, because charity begins at home.**

2. Beauty is in the eye of the beholder.

3. If at first you don't succeed, try and try again.

4. Good things come to those who wait.

5. A man is known by his friends.

6. Life is a bowl of cherries.

7. Life is ten percent what happens to you and ninety percent how you react to it.

8. He who lives by the sword, dies by the sword.

9. If you chase two rabbits, you will not catch either.

10. Knowledge is power.

11. If you play with fire, you get burned.

12. Don't throw the baby out with the bathwater.

 CCSS Vocabulary: 5. (See pp. T14–15.)

Denotation and Connotation

A **denotation** is a word's literal meaning. It is the formal meaning of the word found in a dictionary. A denotation conveys a neutral tone.

A **connotation** is an association or feeling that readers and listeners make to a word. A word's connotation may carry positive or negative associations.

Consider these synonyms for the word *beginner*:

fledgling *novice* *tyro* *greenhorn*

Fledgling and *novice* are words with positive connotations, but *tyro* and *greenhorn* have negative connotations.

Think: A fledgling or novice has an aura of youth and promise, but a tyro or a greenhorn gives the impression of inexperience and incompetence.

Look at these examples of words that are similar in denotation but have different connotations.

NEUTRAL	POSITIVE	NEGATIVE
different	**special**	**abnormal**
casual	**leisurely**	**unconcerned**
notable	**famous**	**notorious**

Whether you are reading a text or writing one, you will do a better job if you understand the connotations of words. As a reader, you will sense the feelings behind the words. As a writer, you will know which word to choose to express exactly what you mean.

Shades of Meaning

Write a plus sign (+) in the box if the word has a positive connotation. Write a minus sign (–) if the word has a negative connotation. Put a zero (0) if the word is neutral.

1. amiss –	**2.** flourish +	**3.** quench +	**4.** prior 0
5. wrath –	**6.** canvass 0	**7.** domestic 0	**8.** foremost +
9. proficient +	**10.** catastrophe –	**11.** gruesome –	**12.** legible +
13. insubordinate –	**14.** momentum +	**15.** nurture +	**16.** simultaneous 0

CCSS Vocabulary: 5.c. (See pp. T14–15.)

WORD STUDY

Expressing the Connotation

Read each sentence. Select the word in parentheses that better expresses the connotation (positive, negative, or neutral) given at the beginning of the sentence.

positive **1.** I think Tuan is going to become one of the (**foremost, known**) musicians of our time.

negative **2.** Shannon experienced a (**mishap, catastrophe**) when her bicycle chain came off as she was riding fast.

negative **3.** The second attack of that terrible day was a furious (**onslaught, approach**) on our eastern flank.

neutral **4.** Before we knew it, the driver made a sharp (**swerve, turn**) to avoid a bump in the road.

positive **5.** Her posture was proud and (**regal, formal**), befitting the great actor that she was.

neutral **6.** The best way to persuade people to work hard is to give them a(n) (**incentive, motive**) that really matters to them.

negative **7.** Committing (**perjury, falsehood**) is one of the worst mistakes a person can make in the courtroom.

positive **8.** His contribution to the project is so (**vital, important**) that we could not possibly finish without him.

Challenge: Using Connotation

Choose vocabulary words from Units 7–9 to replace the highlighted words in the sentences below. Then explain how the connotation of the replacement word changes the tone of the sentence. Answers will vary.

erode	**capsize**	**entice**
wrath	**flounder**	**brawl**

1. Sometimes, if the soldiers are slow to obey orders, the sergeant's **irritation** ____wrath____ can be very intimidating.
Sample response: *Wrath* makes the tone of the sentence more negative and extreme; irritation is far less powerful and threatening than wrath.

2. Most young people must **search** ____flounder____ for a few years after they finish school before they figure out what they want to do in life.
Sample response: *Flounder* has a negative connotation, and it suggests a much more painful struggle for meaning than *search*.

3. Over the centuries, wind and rain will **destroy** ____erode____ even a stone monument made of granite.
Sample response: *Erode* has a less negative connotation than *destroy*. An eroded surface changes gradually over time; a destroyed surface is ruined.

 CCSS Vocabulary: 5, 5.c. (See pp. T14–15.)

Classical Roots

graph, graphy—to write

This Greek root appears in **graphic** (page 111), which literally means "having to do with writing." The word now means "lifelike or vivid," "relating to graphs or diagrams," "representation," or "having to do with the visual arts." Some other words based on the same root are listed below.

autobiography	**biography**	**graphite**	**pictograph**
autograph	**geography**	**graphology**	**seismograph**

From the list of words above, choose the one that corresponds to each of the brief definitions below. Write the word in the blank space in the illustrative sentence below the definition. Use a dictionary if necessary.

1. the study of handwriting
   Police investigators often rely on ___**graphology**___ to help them unlock clues to a criminal's personality.

2. the study of Earth's surface, climate, plants, animals, natural resources, people, and industries; the physical features of a place or region
   Maps are important tools in the study of ___**geography**___.

3. an instrument that records the direction, force, and duration of earthquakes and other earth tremors
   A(n) ___**seismograph**___ measures the intensity of an earthquake.

4. an account of a person's life written by another person; such writings, collectively
   Carl Sandburg wrote a famous ___**biography**___ of Abraham Lincoln.

5. a picture or symbol used to represent an idea in a system of picture writing; a diagram using pictures to represent data
   The Lakota used ___**pictographs**___ to record important events from their past.

6. to write in one's own handwriting; to write one's signature on or in; a signature
   Fans hounded the actor for his ___**autograph**___.

7. a soft, black form of carbon
   The "lead" in lead pencils is actually ___**graphite**___.

8. the story of one's own life written by oneself
   Helen Keller's ___**autobiography**___ is entitled *The Story of My Life.*

CCSS Vocabulary: 4.b. (See pp. T14–15.)

UNIT 10

Note that not all of the 20 Unit words are used in this passage. *Farce*, *lair*, *parasite*, *shirk*, and *veto* are not included.

*Read the following passage, taking note of the **boldface** words and their contexts. These words are among those you will be studying in Unit 10. As you complete the exercises in this Unit, it may help to refer to the way the words are used below.*

CCSS Vocabulary: 4; Reading (Informational Text): 4, 6. (See pp. T14–15.)

The Straight History of Orthodontics

<Historical Nonfiction>

Some people look forward to getting braces on their teeth, thinking they look cool. Other people grow **morbid** at the idea. These unwilling patients avoid visiting the orthodontist until resistance becomes **futile**. But anyone who benefits from the orthodontist's trade today should be thankful for the progress this science has made over the centuries. In bygone days, many a butcher **botched** an attempt to remedy a problem that's now easily cured. The pain that once made dental work **notorious** has been minimized by anesthesia. But it took some time for orthodontics to reach its present state.

Fossil remains of crooked human teeth and **cluttered** mouths date back tens of thousands of years. Greek and Roman texts describing the treatment of irregular teeth by the application of pressure date back as far as the fifth century BCE (Before Common Era). Archaeological evidence indicates even earlier use of orthodontic appliances, including artifacts found in rich, **lavish** burial sites in ancient Italy. Another early attempt at braces may have been discovered on Egyptian mummies with **dilapidated** but recognizable metal bands around their teeth. The metal bands may have anchored elastic strings made of catgut. Thus, from at least 1000 BCE, it was known that teeth move in response to pressure.

Techniques for correcting dental irregularities did not advance much until the eighteenth century. French dentists led the way to building orthodontic practice on scientific foundations from which it has not been **dismantled**. The greatest contribution came from Pierre Fauchard. In 1728, Fauchard published the first general study of dentistry. In it, he described the

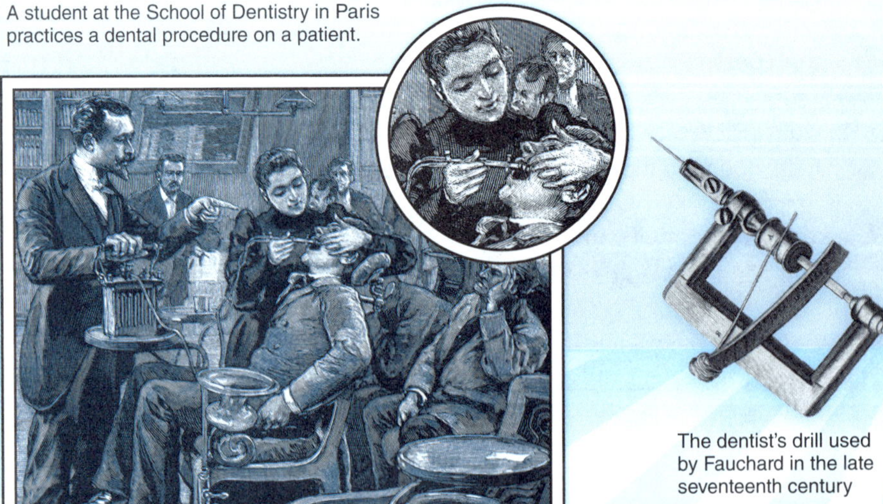

A student at the School of Dentistry in Paris practices a dental procedure on a patient.

The dentist's drill used by Fauchard in the late seventeenth century

bandeau. It was used to expand the arch and correct crowded and crooked teeth. Fauchard described another process of straightening. He filed down a crooked tooth to create **surplus** space around it. Then he repositioned the tooth using a device called a "pelican," a kind of pliers. With the tooth in its proper position, he bound it to its neighbors and let it set. French and English dentists improved on Fauchard's work through the eighteenth century. **Beneficiaries** of Fauchard's treatment may have been grateful when the work was complete. But no doubt many of them faced the prospect of treatment with fearful **timidity** and **bellowed** during the procedures. Indeed, these treatments must have been **grueling** without anesthesia. But evidently there were many Frenchmen who knew that you can't make an omelet without breaking some eggs. Hundreds of patients flocked to Fauchard to **pamper** themselves and improve their looks with dental work.

Pioneering European orthodontists introduced new techniques and instruments in the nineteenth century. Among them were the wire crib, the lever and screw, the chin strap, the use of rubber bands, and plaster models of patients' teeth. By midcentury, the American economy was quite **hospitable** to innovation. American dentists began to take the lead in research and invention. Electricity revolutionized the operating room, and anesthesia made surgery less painful. Norman Kingsley pioneered treatments for cross-bites and cleft palates. John Farrar developed guidelines for using screws to move teeth by applying force in short doses at regular intervals.

The twentieth century saw refinement in the materials and methods of orthodontics. But the fundamental principles of the science were developed during the days of Fauchard. The research performed between then and now has established orthodontics as a profession and opened the way for everyone to benefit from straighter teeth.

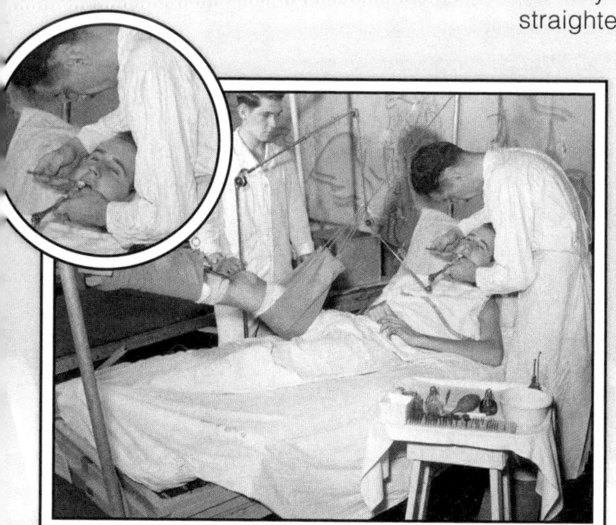

Dental procedures improved a great deal over the twentieth century.

Audio

For Words and audio passages, snap the code, or go to vocabularyworkshop.com.

Definitions

Note the spelling, pronunciation, part(s) of speech, and definition(s) of each of the following words. Then write the appropriate form of the word in the blank spaces in the illustrative sentence(s) following. Finally, study the lists of synonyms and antonyms.

1. bellow (bel′ ō)

(*v.*) to make a sound similar to that of a bull, roar; (*n.*) a loud, angry roar

The wounded buffalo began to **bellow** in pain.

The troop commander's **bellow** could be heard a mile away.

SYNONYMS: (*v.*) yell, bawl, holler; (*n.*) howl
ANTONYMS: (*v.*) whisper; (*n.*) murmur

2. beneficiary (ben ə fish′ ē er ē)

(*n.*) one who benefits from something; a person who is left money or other property in a will or the like

The **beneficiary** of the dead man's will was the main suspect in the murder case.

SYNONYMS: recipient, heir

3. botch (bäch)

(*v.*) to repair or patch poorly; make a mess of; (*n.*) a hopelessly bungled job

The unsupervised laborers proceeded to **botch** the job badly.

SYNONYMS: (*v.*) foul up, mangle

4. clutter (klət′ ər)

(*v.*) to fill or cover in a disorderly way; (*n.*) a state of disorder, mess

When we moved into our new house, we unloaded the truck and began to **clutter** up the dining room with boxes.

Attics are often filled with **clutter**.

SYNONYMS: (*v.*) litter; (*n.*) confusion
ANTONYMS: (*n.*) order, tidiness, neatness

5. dilapidated (də lap′ ə dā tid)

(*adj.*) falling apart or ruined, run-down

The old house had become so **dilapidated** that no one could live in it anymore.

SYNONYMS: in disrepair, deteriorated, gone to seed
ANTONYMS: shipshape, trim

6. dismantle (dis man′ təl)

(*v.*) to take apart; to strip of something

After the final performance, all the actors worked with the stagehands to **dismantle** the set.

SYNONYM: disassemble
ANTONYMS: put together, assemble, construct

CCSS Vocabulary: 4.c., 4.d. (See pp. T14–15.)

7. farce (färs)

(*n.*) a play filled with ridiculous or absurd happenings; broad or far-fetched humor; a ridiculous sham

The humor in the play was so broad and the plot so ridiculous that the critic termed the play a **farce**.

SYNONYMS: buffoonery, travesty; ANTONYMS: tragedy, melodrama

8. futile (fyüt′ əl)

(*adj.*) not successful, failing to have any result; useless; unimportant, frivolous

After several **futile** attempts to save it, the captain ordered the ship abandoned.

SYNONYMS: fruitless, vain, ineffective
ANTONYMS: successful, effective

9. grueling (grü′ liŋ)

(*adj.*) very tiring, calling for an extreme effort

After the **grueling** climb, two of the mountaineers collapsed from exhaustion.

SYNONYMS: exhausting, punishing, taxing
ANTONYMS: easy, effortless

10. hospitable (häs pit′ ə bəl)

(*adj.*) offering friendly or generous treatment to guests; open to anything new or strange

Known for their generosity to strangers, the local inhabitants offered a **hospitable** welcome to our tour group.

SYNONYMS: gracious, cordial, courteous
ANTONYMS: unfriendly, cold, icy, chilly

11. lair (lâr)

(*n.*) the home or den of a wild animal; any hideout

The police were making careful preparations to trap the smugglers in their **lair**.

SYNONYMS: nest, burrow, hideaway

12. lavish (lav′ ish)

(*adj.*) overly generous, extravagant; abundant; (*v.*) to spend or give freely or without limit

The couple received **lavish** wedding gifts from their closest friends.

SYNONYMS: (*adj.*) excessive, profuse
ANTONYMS: (*adj.*) stingy, meager; (*v.*) begrudge, stint, deny

13. morbid (môr′ bid)

(*adj.*) in an unhealthy mental state, extremely gloomy; caused by or related to disease, unwholesome

The police captain was afraid that the officer was taking a **morbid** interest in the crime.

SYNONYMS: depressed, unsound, "sick"
ANTONYMS: wholesome, healthy, cheerful, blithe

CCSS Vocabulary: 4.c., 4.d. (See pp. T14–15.)

14. notorious
(nō tôr′ ē əs)

(*adj.*) widely known because of bad conduct

Chicago had its share of ____**notorious**____ gangsters in the 1930s.

SYNONYMS: disgraceful, infamous, disreputable
ANTONYMS: unknown, obscure, respectable

15. pamper
(pam′ pər)

(*v.*) to allow too many privileges, be too generous and easygoing toward

If my aunt continues to ____**pamper**____ that child, he may grow into an irresponsible adult.

SYNONYMS: cater to, indulge
ANTONYMS: abuse, maltreat, mistreat, discipline

16. parasite
(par′ ə sīt)

(*n.*) an organism that lives in or on another organism; one who lives off another person

Uninvited, he hung around with the players so much that the team considered him a real ____**parasite**____.

SYNONYMS: sponger, freeloader

17. shirk
(shərk)

(*v.*) to avoid or get out of doing work, neglect a duty; to sneak, slink

People who tend to ____**shirk**____ their responsibilities are not to be relied upon.

SYNONYMS: duck, dodge; ANTONYMS: fulfill, perform, shoulder

18. surplus
(sər′ pləs)

(*n.*) an amount beyond what is required, excess; (*adj.*) more than what is needed or expected

Dad was relieved to find that his business had a ____**surplus**____ at the end of the year.

The Army decided to sell its ____**surplus**____ goods to a group of manufacturers.

SYNONYMS: (*n.*) glut, surfeit, overage
ANTONYMS: (*n.*) shortage, lack, dearth, paucity

19. timidity
(tə mid′ ə tē)

(*n.*) the state of being easily frightened

The shy child's natural ____**timidity**____ had made her afraid to try out for the team.

SYNONYMS: faintheartedness, shyness
ANTONYMS: fearlessness, boldness, intrepidity

20. veto
(vē′ tō)

(*n.*) the power to forbid or prevent; (*v.*) to prohibit, reject

The president decided to ____**veto**____ the bill presented to him by Congress.

SYNONYMS: (*v.*) turn down, nix
ANTONYMS: (*v.*) approve, endorse, ratify

CCSS Vocabulary: 4.c., 4.d. (See pp. T14–15.)

Choosing the Right Word

*Select the **boldface** word that better completes each sentence. You might refer to the passage on pages 126–127 to see how most of these words are used in context.*

1. The modern TV sitcom developed from the type of broad (**surplus, farce**) that slapstick comedians served up in the 1920s and 1930s.

2. Since I was led to believe that she would approve my proposal, I was very much taken aback when it was (**lavished, vetoed**) out of hand.

3. Beneath the (**dismantled, dilapidated**) body of the getaway car, there was a powerful, finely tuned motor, capable of reaching high speeds.

4. After winning the award for best actress, she joyously (**lavished, dismantled**) praise on everyone who had worked with her on the movie.

5. The campaign to eliminate pollution will prove (**futile, grueling**) unless it has full public support.

Lucille Ball starred in the television comedy *I Love Lucy* from 1951–1957.

6. He amazed us by reaching into the pile of (**clutter, lair**) on his desk and pulling out the exact the piece of paper he wanted.

7. "I discovered a really cool store with all kinds of (**morbid, surplus**) army and navy equipment," Joel told his friends excitedly.

8. I sometimes think that he enjoys being sick and having everyone wait on him, sympathize with him, and (**shirk, pamper**) him.

9. When he said he would "beard the lion in his (**lair, bellow**)," he merely meant that he was going to have it out with the boss.

10. What a difference between the (**timidity, farce**) of the typical freshman and the know-it-all confidence of a senior!

11. He is (**hospitable, notorious**) for his habit of taking small loans from his best friends and then conveniently forgetting about them.

12. Even the toughest critics have been (**lavish, dilapidated**) in their praise of the new movie.

13. The first thing Rick and Maria do when they enter a room is to (**clutter, shirk**) it with their jackets, shoes, backpacks, books, electronic equipment, and pencils.

14. When I think back to my days of basic training, I can almost hear the drill sergeant (**pampering, bellowing**) commands across the field.

15. It would be impossible to (**pamper, dismantle**) our system of governmental checks and balances without destroying American democracy.

CCSS Vocabulary: 4.d. (See pp. T14–15.)

16. The courts of many Renaissance princes were jammed with (**parasites, lairs**), toadies, and other idle hangers-on.

17. The sudden thunderstorm made a (**morbid, botch**) of the picnic, forcing us to flee for cover and soaking most of our food.

18. After buying all the supplies for the club party, we were delighted to find that we had a grand (**surplus, veto**) of 65 cents.

19. The best way to avoid those (**grueling, bellowing**) cram sessions just before the exams is to do your work steadily all term long.

20. Their record is 100% consistent—they have managed to (**botch, clutter**) every job they have undertaken.

21. My experience has been that people who cut corners on small matters will also (**shirk, botch**) their obligations.

22. We who live in the United States today are the chief (**beneficiaries, parasites**) of the rich heritage of freedom left to us by the framers of the Constitution.

23. Ever since I was bitten by a stray mutt years ago, I have had a (**morbid, lavish**) fear of all dogs.

24. She was indeed fortunate to find herself working under a person who was (**notorious, hospitable**) to her novel ideas.

25. Most presidents don't like to exercise their (**veto, beneficiary**) power often.

*Choose the word from this Unit that is the same or most nearly the same in meaning as the **boldface** word or expression in the phrase. Write that word on the line. Use a dictionary if necessary.*

1. cautiously inspected the **decayed** old building — dilapidated
2. took up acting to overcome their **fearfulness** — timidity
3. may **fumble** the assignment if not careful — botch
4. was reluctant to **coddle** the spoiled child any further — pamper
5. cleaned up the **tangle** of tools in Dad's workroom — clutter
6. a meeting that turned into a **mockery** — farce
7. saw that the wolf had returned to its **hiding place** — lair
8. will attempt to **halt** the passing of the law — veto
9. trying to **sidestep** her responsibilities — shirk
10. would hang on like a **leech** — parasite

CCSS Vocabulary: 5. (See pp. T14–15.)

Antonyms

*Choose the word from this Unit that is most nearly opposite in meaning to the **boldface** word or expression in the phrase. Write that word on the line. Use a dictionary if necessary.*

1. the decision to **confirm** the anti-pollution bill ____veto____
2. saw a **tearjerker** of a play ____farce____
3. a younger sibling who was a real **helper** ____parasite____
4. resting on the ground **out in the open** ____lair____
5. not one to **take on** extra chores ____shirk____

Completing the Sentence

From the words in this Unit, choose the one that best completes each of the following sentences. Write the correct word form in the space provided.

1. A sitting president can ____veto____ a measure passed by a majority of Congress, but lawmakers can overrule his decision.

2. Since the defendant was never given a chance to prove his innocence, his so-called "trial" was nothing more than a ____farce____.

3. I know what it is that I have to do, and you may be certain that I will not ____shirk____ my duty.

4. It is a curious fact of nature that most ____parasites____ are unable to survive when they are separated from the organisms they feed on.

5. The practice session was so ____grueling____ that we scarcely had the strength to get to the dressing room and take our showers.

6. Ever since the new tax laws went into effect, there has been speculation as to who the real ____beneficiaries____ of the changes will be.

7. All the members of that family are such ____hospitable____ people that we are always completely at ease whenever we visit them.

8. The ____surplus____ of food produced each year in the United States is desperately needed to feed hungry people all over the world.

9. Many people both here and abroad seem to have a ____morbid____ fascination with the tragic fate of the Russian royal family.

10. It is hard to believe that a teenager so courageous and able on a camping trip can show so much ____timidity____ when invited to a dance.

CCSS Vocabulary: 4.a., 5. (See pp. T14–15.)

11. Though the cabin was a little **dilapidated** when we bought it, we were able to spruce it up without going to a great deal of expense.

12. Why must you **clutter** up your mind with so many trivial and useless scraps of information?

13. When he realized that he had been tricked by his opponent, he let out a **bellow** of rage that could be heard all over the gym.

14. They gave me so **lavish** a helping of dinner that for the first time in my life I was unable to polish off the food on my plate.

15. Unfortunately, the brave lifeguard's valiant attempts to rescue the drowning swimmer proved **futile**.

16. The inexperienced assistant **botched** the business letter he was trying to compose and had to rewrite it.

17. He is such a **notorious** liar that no one takes anything he says seriously anymore.

18. When I accepted the invitation to join them on the vessel, I didn't realize that I had agreed to help **dismantle** the ship.

19. The animals in the zoo are kept in quarters that are designed to imitate their **lairs** in the wild.

20. As a child she was so **pampered** by her parents that she still seems to think that her wishes should be instantly granted.

Writing: Words in Action

Answers to both prompts will vary.

1. Look back at "The Straight History of Orthodontics" (pages 126–127). The passage discusses how, for thousands of years, people have used orthodontics to improve their appearance, often suffering great pain to do so. Do people care too much about their appearance, or is the quest for physical improvement a healthy impulse? Consider both sides of the issue. Then write at least two paragraphs for each side. Include at least one passage detail for each side, and use at least three Unit words.

2. The subject of "The Straight History of Orthodontics" is one that anyone who has visited the dentist can identify with. Write a one-page personal narrative about your experiences with an orthodontist or dentist. Your narrative may be humorous or serious. Include specific examples from your experiences, readings (refer to pages 126–127), and observations. Write at least three paragraphs, and use three or more words from this Unit.

Writing prompt #2 is modeled on that of standardized tests.

 CCSS Vocabulary: 6; Writing: 1.c., 2.d., 3.d., 4. (See pp. T14–15.)

Vocabulary in Context: Informational Text for Unit 10 is available online at **vocabularyworkshop.com**.

Vocabulary in Context

Literary Text

The following excerpts are from Victor Hugo's novel The Hunchback of Notre Dame. *Some of the words you have studied in this Unit appear in* **boldface** *type. Complete each statement below the excerpt by circling the letter of the correct answer.*

1. Claude Frollo groped about for several moments in the dark **lair** into which the captain had bolted him . . . there was neither window nor air-hole, and the slope of the roof prevented one from standing upright.

A **lair** is a place where one usually feels

a. bright
b. beautiful
c. hidden
d. known

2. "But do say something," said Madame Aloise, suddenly giving his shoulder a push; "you have grown very timid."

We can assure our readers that **timidity** was neither the captain's virtue nor his defect. But he made an effort to do what was demanded of him.

Another word for **timidity** is

a. humor
b. curiosity
c. stubbornness
d. shyness

3. Among other things, she had a pair of little shoes, the like of which King Louis XI certainly never had! Her mother had stitched and embroidered them herself; she had **lavished** on them all the delicacies of her art of embroideress.

One who has **lavished** has

a. taken back
b. given fully
c. chosen wisely
d. felt inadequate

Actor Charles Laughton played Quasimodo, the hunchback, in the 1939 film of Hugo's novel.

4. The interior of the den was no less **dilapidated**. . . . [T]here were chalk walls, blackened beams in the ceiling, a dismantled chimney-piece, spiders' webs in all the corners, in the middle a staggering herd of tables and lame stools, a dirty child among the ashes, and at the back a staircase.

A **dilapidated** building must be

a. in bad condition
b. hidden from sight
c. in a large city
d. at least fifty years old

5. [A]s he plunged deeper into the street . . . blind men and lame men swarmed about him . . . from the air-holes of cellars, howling, **bellowing**, yelping, all limping and halting, all flinging themselves towards the light.

Someone who is **bellowing** is NOT

a. angry
b. loud
c. alert
d. quiet

Snap the code, or go to **vocabularyworkshop.com**

UNIT 11

Note that not all of the 20 Unit words are used in this passage. *Emblem*, *hearth*, *misdemeanor*, *overture*, and *vindictive* are not included.

*Read the following passage, taking note of the **boldface** words and their contexts. These words are among those you will be studying in Unit 11. As you complete the exercises in this Unit, it may help to refer to the way the words are used below.*

 CCSS Vocabulary: 4; Reading (Informational Text): 4, 6. (See pp. T14–15.)

The Babe Is Here

<Magazine Article>

September 17, 1954
By Mitch P. J. Cunningham IV for *Sport and Game* magazine

You can hear a pin drop. It's almost a **stalemate** among several long-time rivals. Can Babe pull it off? She eyes the eighteenth hole, extends her arms for the downswing and—it's a hole in one! Babe Didrikson Zaharias, queen of the fairway, has triumphed, and the crowd goes wild. Her fans rush forward, and there's confusion and **havoc** on the greens.

There's a poignancy to this win because Babe, a co-founder of the LPGA (Ladies Professional Golf Association), was diagnosed with cancer at the height of her fame. Doctors said she'd never play again, but they should have known not to bet against this indomitable woman. After **mulling** it over for about a split second, she figured she wasn't going to let a little thing like a serious illness **mar** her remarkable athletic career. She had other fish to fry. She made a **pact** with her husband and manager, former pro wrestler George Zaharias, after undergoing surgery. She swore she'd keep the door **ajar** to return, and return she did. Friends **implored** her to slow down. What did she have to prove? But Babe wasn't buying it. She won the Serbin Women's Open Tournament less than a year after surgery. As she's been heard to say before a tournament: "The Babe's here. Who's coming in second?"

It seems as if Port Arthur, Texas, native Mildred "Babe" Didrikson has the Midas touch when it comes to athletics. Is there any sport at which she doesn't excel? Her many talents are legendary and practically **innumerable**. Most agree she's the best woman athlete alive. In fact, in 1949 the Associated Press voted her the greatest female athlete of the half-century, and she's won a gaggle of other awards and lifetime achievement honors. No one comes close to this lady with the incredible gifts and **gigantic** heart of a champion.

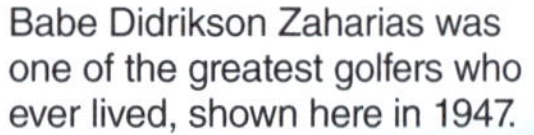

Babe Didrikson Zaharias was one of the greatest golfers who ever lived, shown here in 1947.

The **narrative** of Babe's life reads like something out of a Hollywood movie script, complete with brash **dialogue** between Babe and whoever tries to get in her way. Born in 1911 to Norwegian immigrants, she displayed exceptional physical prowess at a tender age. She excelled in baseball, swimming, diving, tennis, and bowling. Friends started calling her Babe—as in Babe Ruth—after she hit five home runs in one baseball game. She was an All-American high school basketball player. Then she became a bona fide star at the 1932 Summer Olympics, taking home two gold medals in track and field. (Some say she should have won a third for the high jump, but her **infamous** and illegal style of diving shoulders-first over the bar cost her first place.) Many would have **wilted** under the pressure, but Babe never weakened. At this point, she could have rested on her laurels. Any of these accomplishments would have been more than **adequate** for the average woman (or man, come to think of it).

But Babe is no average woman. She was introduced to golf in 1935—and golf has never been the same since! She started winning titles in 1940, continued her unparalleled run, and completed the Grand Slam for women's golf in 1950, winning the U.S. Open, the Titleholders Championship, and the Women's Western Open. We'd be **lax** if we didn't mention that Babe is working on her autobiography, due out next year. The little girl from Port Arthur has done plenty to advance the ideals of women's sports and win the admiration of millions.

Babe Didrikson Zaharias was a champion in many different sports, here seen winning the hurdle event at the 1932 Olympics in Los Angeles.

Babe Didrikson Zaharias won 82 tournaments in her golfing career.

Audio

For iWords and audio passages, snap the code, or go to vocabularyworkshop.com.

Definitions

Note the spelling, pronunciation, part(s) of speech, and definition(s) of each of the following words. Then write the appropriate form of the word in the blank spaces in the illustrative sentence(s) following. Finally, study the lists of synonyms and antonyms.

1. adequate (ad′ ə kwət)

(*adj.*) sufficient, enough

Be sure to allow ___**adequate**___ time to check in at the airport.

SYNONYMS: satisfactory, sufficing
ANTONYM: insufficient

2. ajar (ə jär′)

(*adj.*, *adv.*) partly open

That night, the children foolishly left the back gate ___**ajar**___, and the dog escaped.

ANTONYMS: (*adj.*, *adv.*) closed tight, shut, open wide

3. dialogue (dī′ ə läg)

(*n.*) a conversation between two or more people; an interchange of opinions and ideas, free discussion

The witty ___**dialogue**___ in the play kept the audience amused.

SYNONYM: exchange of ideas
ANTONYMS: monologue, soliloquy

4. emblem (em′ bləm)

(*n.*) a symbol, sign, token

Like the heart, the red rose is an ___**emblem**___ of love.

SYNONYMS: badge, crest

5. gigantic (jī gan′ tik)

(*adj.*) huge, giant, immense

When it fell to Earth, the meteorite made a ___**gigantic**___ hole in the ground.

SYNONYMS: enormous, colossal, mammoth
ANTONYMS: tiny, infinitesimal, diminutive

6. havoc (hav′ ək)

(*n.*) very great destruction, ruin; great confusion and disorder

The monkey created ___**havoc**___ at the fair as soon as it broke from its leash.

SYNONYMS: devastation, harm, disarray
ANTONYMS: peace and quiet, calm, order

7. hearth (härth)

(*n.*) the floor of a fireplace; the fireside as a symbol of the home and family

It was our custom to sit by the ___**hearth**___ and listen to my grandfather's stories.

SYNONYM: chimney corner

CCSS Vocabulary: 4.c., 4.d. (See pp. T14–15.)

8. implore
(im plôr′)

(*v.*) to beg earnestly for

The attorney proceeded to **implore** the judge to show his client mercy.

SYNONYMS: entreat, beseech, pray
ANTONYMS: demand forcefully, clamor for

9. infamous
(in′ fə məs)

(*adj.*) very wicked; disgraceful, shameful

Because of the outlaw's **infamous** deeds, the town was offering a large bounty for his capture.

SYNONYMS: scandalous, villainous, flagrant, heinous
ANTONYMS: glorious, splendid, illustrious, praiseworthy

10. innumerable
(i nüm′ ə rə bəl)

(*adj.*) too many to count, without number

The landlord heard **innumerable** complaints about the noisy new tenant.

SYNONYMS: countless, beyond reckoning
ANTONYMS: countable, few in number

11. lax
(laks)

(*adj.*) not strict, careless; lacking discipline; not tense, relaxed

Some players took advantage of the new coach's somewhat **lax** control of the team.

SYNONYMS: slack, remiss
ANTONYMS: strict, vigilant, conscientious, scrupulous

12. mar
(mär)

(*v.*) to spoil, damage, injure

Spilled cleaning fluid will surely **mar** the wooden tabletop.

SYNONYMS: scar, disfigure
ANTONYMS: beautify, embellish, repair

13. misdemeanor
(mis di mē′ nər)

(*n.*) a crime or offense that is less serious than a felony; any minor misbehavior or misconduct

He was not only fined for the **misdemeanor** but also sentenced to serve 30 days in jail.

SYNONYMS: misdeed, petty offense or transgression
ANTONYMS: felony, serious crime

14. mull
(məl)

(*v.*) to think about, ponder; to grind or mix; to heat and flavor with spices

The governor had some time to **mull** over the bill before signing it into law.

SYNONYMS: consider, reflect on

CCSS Vocabulary: 4.c., 4.d. (See pp. T14–15.)

15. narrative (nar′ ə tiv)

(*n.*) a story, detailed report; (*adj.*) having the quality or the nature of a story

The ___**narrative**___ of the West African captive gives us a vivid picture of the horrors aboard a slave ship.

Henry Wadsworth Longfellow is considered a ___**narrative**___ poet because of the stories he tells in his poems.

SYNONYMS: (*n.*) tale, chronicle

16. overture (o′ vər chůr)

(*n.*) an opening move toward negotiation or action; a proposal or offer; an introductory section or part

Our family enjoyed the ___**overture**___ to the opera better than the rest of it.

SYNONYMS: prelude, tender
ANTONYMS: finale, postlude

17. pact (pakt)

(*n.*) an agreement, treaty

All the nations signed the ___**pact**___ after the war in an effort to ensure world peace.

SYNONYMS: compact, alliance, deal

18. stalemate (stāl′ māt)

(*n.*) a situation in which further action by either of two opponents is impossible; (*v.*) to bring to a standstill

The negotiations ended in ___**stalemate**___, as both sides refused to budge on the main issue.

Recent aggression on the part of one nation threatened to ___**stalemate**___ the peace talks.

SYNONYMS: (*n.*) standoff, draw; (*v.*) deadlock
ANTONYMS: (*n.*) victory; (*v.*) defeat

19. vindictive (vin dik′ tiv)

(*adj.*) bearing a grudge, feeling or showing a strong tendency toward revenge

The mayor was so ___**vindictive**___ that he threatened to sue the newspaper for its unflattering remarks about his administration.

SYNONYMS: spiteful, malicious
ANTONYMS: forgiving, relenting

20. wilt (wilt)

(*v.*) to become limp and drooping (as a flower), wither; to lose strength and vigor

Intense heat or lack of water will ___**wilt**___ the flowers.

SYNONYMS: sag, weaken, shrivel up
ANTONYMS: flourish, bloom, sprout, perk up, revive

CCSS Vocabulary: 4.c., 4.d. (See pp. T14–15.)

Choosing the Right Word

*Select the **boldface** word that better completes each sentence. You might refer to the passage on pages 136–137 to see how most of these words are used in context.*

Enlistment posters appeal to citizens' sense of honor and duty.

1. British enlistment posters in World War I assured young men that they would be fighting for "king and country, (**hearth, havoc**) and home."

2. The blustery winds on that cold November day played (**havoc, pact**) with my hair.

3. As long as the door to compromise is even slightly (**ajar, vindictive**), there is a chance that we will be able to reach an understanding.

4. The wonders of nature are as (**innumerable, adequate**) as the grains of sand on the seashore.

5. Jorge and Louise both want to be friends again, but somehow their sincere efforts have been (**stalemated, wilted**).

6. Instead of resorting at once to armed force, the two nations resolved the conflict by entering into a diplomatic (**dialogue, havoc**).

7. In spite of all the criticism, our flag still stands throughout most of the world as a(n) (**pact, emblem**) of justice and freedom.

8. After World War II, the United States was not (**vindictive, lax**) toward its former enemies but tried to help them recover and rebuild.

9. For many years Benedict Arnold served his country faithfully, but then he disgraced his name for all time by an (**ajar, infamous**) act of treason.

10. Contract talks have been stalled for weeks, and nothing either side has suggested can seem to break the (**stalemate, dialogue**).

11. "(**Adequate, innumerable**) is simply not good enough," the company president said. "We want to be the best in our field."

12. The facts of history cannot always be arranged in the form of a smooth and logical (**pact, narrative**).

13. The man has such a (**vindictive, gigantic**) ego that absolutely nothing ever seems to fluster, faze, or deflate him.

14. "I (**stalemate, implore**) you not to take this reckless action," the city council president pleaded with the mayor.

15. I wish you had (**marred, mulled**) over all the pros and cons before you made your final decision.

16. I was a little miffed when my polite (**stalemates, overtures**) of friendship were so rudely and nastily rejected.

17. Though jaywalking may be considered a(n) (**misdemeanor, overture**), murder is definitely not!

18. Some parents are quite strict with their children; others are somewhat (**lax, adequate**) and permissive.

19. Instead of continuing to (**mull, implore**) over the injustices that people have done to you, forget about the past and concentrate on the future.

20. Our high hopes for an easy victory (**wilted, mulled**) away to nothing as we watched our opponents steadily increase their lead over us.

21. As I look over your record, I get the impression that your background in math and science is not (**adequate, ajar**) for an engineering course.

22. Since I am willing to contribute to any worthy cause, there is no need to (**wilt, implore**) me for aid in such an emotional way.

23. Her insistence on studying the terms of our tutoring agreement made me think that I'd signed a (**pact, hearth**) with a lawyer.

24. I will not allow our long and much cherished friendship to be (**marred, implored**) by this unfortunate misunderstanding.

25. I prefer (**narrative, dialogue**) fiction to drama or poetry.

Synonyms

*Choose the word from this Unit that is the same or most nearly the same in meaning as the **boldface** word or expression in the phrase. Write that word on the line. Use a dictionary if necessary.*

1. committed a **vengeful** crime against his accuser	vindictive
2. a peaceful scene by the **home fire**	hearth
3. a trash heap that would **deface** the view	mar
4. began to **hang downward** in the extreme heat	wilt
5. wears an **insignia** on his collar	emblem
6. refused to make the first **advance**	overture
7. signed the **accord** that would end the fighting	pact
8. so **negligent** in her duties	lax
9. to treat the crime as a **little mishap**	misdemeanor
10. picked up where the **anecdote** left off	narrative

CCSS Vocabulary: 5. (See pp. T14–15.)

Antonyms

*Choose the word from this Unit that is most nearly opposite in meaning to the **boldface** word or expression in the phrase. Write that word on the line. Use a dictionary if necessary.*

1. had committed **a violent criminal act** misdemeanor
2. the lovely **conclusion** of the symphony overture
3. a house with a working **air conditioner** hearth
4. a completely **meaningless gesture** emblem
5. a wonderfully **merciful** person vindictive

Completing the Sentence

From the words in this Unit, choose the one that best completes each of the following sentences. Write the correct word form in the space provided.

1. She implored the doctor to tell her frankly how badly her son had been hurt.
2. On our trip to northern California, we felt very small and unimportant as we stood beside the gigantic redwood trees.
3. The smoke from the logs burning on the hearth curled slowly upward into the chimney.
4. Because the front door was ajar, the cat strolled into the living room.
5. As you will learn, in most operettas, the musical numbers are connected to one another by spoken dialogue.
6. One careless mistake can seriously mar an otherwise perfect record.
7. You cannot expect to discipline a group of teenagers by making a capital offense of every misdemeanor.
8. By entering into World War I, the United States broke the stalemate on the Western Front and tipped the balance in favor of an Allied victory.
9. "The Highwayman" by Alfred Noyes is a(n) narrative poem that tells the story of a woman who sacrifices her life for her sweetheart.
10. Though Hitler's Germany and Stalin's Russia were bitter enemies, the two countries signed a nonaggression pact in 1939.

CCSS Vocabulary: 4.a., 5. (See pp. T14–15.)

11. Who has not gazed with awe at the **innumerable** stars that fill the sky on a clear summer night!

12. Can any punishment be too severe for someone who has been guilty of such a(n) **infamous** crime?

13. The flood had wrought such **havoc** that the governor of the state declared the stricken region a disaster area.

14. Since I have never done him any harm, I don't understand why he should take such a(n) **vindictive** attitude toward me.

15. Let me have some time to **mull** over your proposal before I give you a definite answer.

16. Though some of Verdi's operas begin with short preludes, for others he composed full-length **overtures**.

17. Before you leave, be absolutely sure that your supplies of food and water are **adequate** for an eight-day journey across the desert.

18. A white dove holding an olive branch in its beak is often used as a(n) **emblem** of peace.

19. No one questions the honesty and good intentions of the mayor, but he has been criticized for being **lax** in carrying out his duties.

20. Though my sister started out looking as fresh as a daisy, she began to **wilt** noticeably after only five minutes in that humidity.

Writing: Words in Action

Answers to both prompts will vary.

1. Look back at "The Babe Is Here" (pages 136–137). What trait do you think was most important in making Babe Didrikson Zaharias a champion? State your opinion and support it in a brief argument of two paragraphs or more. Include at least two details from the passage, and use at least three Unit words.

2. Babe Didrikson Zaharias's domination of several sports made her a cultural icon. Why do you think that sports heroes are so important to Americans? Write a brief essay in which you state your opinion and support it with examples from your observations, studies, reading (refer to pages 136–137), or personal experience. Write at least three paragraphs, and use three or more words from this Unit.

Writing prompt #2 is modeled on that of standardized tests.

 CCSS Vocabulary: 6; Writing: 1.c., 2.d., 3.d., 4. (See pp. T14–15.)

Vocabulary in Context: Informational Text for Unit 11 is available online at **vocabularyworkshop.com**.

Vocabulary in Context

Literary Text

The following excerpts are from Mary Wollstonecraft Shelley's novel Frankenstein. *Some of the words you have studied in this Unit appear in* **boldface** *type. Complete each statement below the excerpt by circling the letter of the correct answer.*

1. He then told me that he would commence his **narrative** the next day when I should be at leisure. This promise drew from me the warmest thanks. I have resolved every night, when I am not imperatively occupied by my duties, to record, as nearly as possible in his own words, what he has related during the day.

   To tell a **narrative** is to share a(n)

   a. essay　　**c.** letter
   (b.) story　　**d.** poem

2. No distinct ideas occupied my mind; all was confused. I felt light, and hunger, and thirst, and darkness; **innumerable** sounds rang in my ears, and on all sides various scents saluted me.

   Sounds that are **innumerable** may NOT be

   a. infinite　　**c.** limitless
   b. recorded　　**(d.)** counted

3. What a miserable night I passed! The cold stars shone in mockery, and the bare trees waved their branches above me. . . . I, like the arch-fiend, bore a hell within me, and . . . wished to tear up the trees, spread **havoc** and destruction around me, and then to have sat down and enjoyed the ruin.

   Havoc is a state of

   a. reason and calm　　**(c.)** noise and confusion
   b. pride and fear　　**d.** darkness and silence

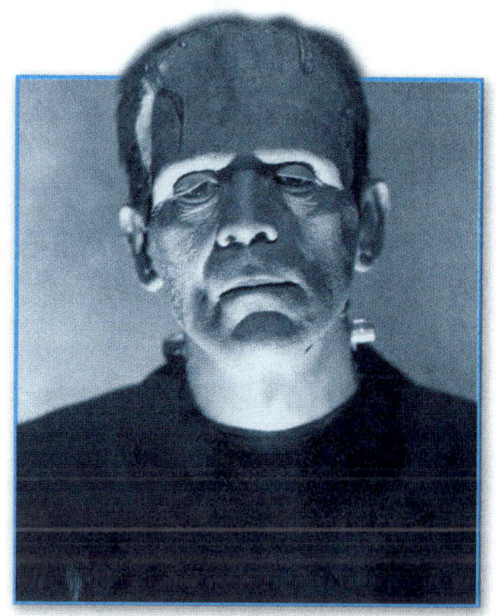

Boris Karloff played Frankenstein's monster in several films, including *Bride of Frankenstein* in 1935.

4. A **gigantic** monster, they said, had arrived the night before, armed with a gun and many pistols, putting to flight the inhabitants of a solitary cottage through fear of his terrific appearance.

   A **gigantic** monster has great

   a. ugliness　　**c.** strength
   b. wildness　　**(d.)** size

5. I doubted at first whether I should attempt the creation of a being like myself. . . . The materials at present within my command hardly appeared **adequate** . . . but I doubted not that I should ultimately succeed.

   An **adequate** supply is

   (a.) enough　　**c.** too little
   b. the wrong kind　　**d.** too much

Snap the code, or go to **vocabularyworkshop.com**

UNIT 12

Note that not all of the 20 Unit words are used in this passage. *Clarification*, *embezzle*, *piecemeal*, *random*, and *rant* are not included.

*Read the following passage, taking note of the **boldface** words and their contexts. These words are among those you will be studying in Unit 12. As you complete the exercises in this Unit, it may help to refer to the way the words are used below.*

CCSS Vocabulary: 4; Reading (Informational Text): 4, 6. (See pp. T14–15.)

Hero From the Wrong Side of the Track Retires

<Profile>

by Chester Byron Langdon
November 11, 1940

The Great Depression had darkened almost every door in this country, and war clouds were gathering on the European horizon. America was hungry for a hero. Then came a horse named Seabiscuit, whose looks hid the champion he would become. He was knobby-kneed and undersized, and had a laid-back, **leisurely** demeanor. But he hadn't a trace of a **malady** where it counts in a champion—his heart. His heart **abounded** in courage and overflowed with determination.

Foaled in 1933, Seabiscuit grew up in Kentucky. His performance in his first races was mediocre—hard work at a young age had made him **lethargic**, and in 1936, his owners sold the tired colt to Charles S. Howard. Howard, a wealthy businessman, had pioneered the sale of automobiles in California. Howard formed an unorthodox team: Seabiscuit's new trainer was Tom Smith, known for his reluctance to speak, and Johnny "Red" Pollard was Seabiscuit's jockey. Most people in the racing world did not know that Pollard was blind in one eye, thus depriving him of bifocal vision and depth perception.

From left to right: Tom Smith, George Woolf, Seabiscuit, and C.S. Howard

The team led a **nomadic** existence, escorting their horse to races in the eastern states, the Midwest, and California. Against the odds, Seabiscuit's record improved, and he quickly gathered increasing attention in the racing community. Howard was a born marketer, a Western-bred underdog challenging the East Coast racing establishment. It was just the role that millions of Americans wanted a winning horse to play. Amid the

turmoil and confusion of the Depression, down and out and starved for hope, Seabiscuit's fans saw in him a gritty fighter. The horse became a celebrity almost overnight: "Seabiscuit-itis" swept the nation. A huge **cache** of press clippings devoted to the thoroughbred showed that Seabiscuit, at one point, enjoyed more publicity than President Franklin D. Roosevelt.

But, as the saying goes, trouble rides a fast horse, and it caught up with this racing team. In early 1938, jockey Pollard fell from another horse and shattered his collarbone in a **heartrending** accident that kept him from riding. The same year, with Pollard sidelined, the **quest** for a match-race against War Admiral, a scion of the Eastern horseracing establishment, came to an exciting end. Pimlico Racecourse, near Baltimore, announced it would host the "match of the century" on November 1, 1938. A new jockey, George Woolf, would pilot Seabiscuit in the most important contest of both of their careers.

The outcome was sensational. Seabiscuit beat the favorite by four lengths—about 11 yards—to the delight of 40,000 fans at the track and an estimated radio audience of 40 million people. Never a **braggart**, Pollard drily remarked from his hospital bed that his horse had turned War Admiral into a rear admiral.

Seabiscuit makes a rear admiral out of War Admiral in their famous match race.

In the winner's circle after the match of the century

In early 1940, Seabiscuit pulled a ligament and left the track to rest in the quiet **seclusion** of Howard's ranch. It was said he would never race again. Howard and Smith, however, did not become **despondent**; they believed in their horse. And Seabiscuit had one more race to claim: the coveted Santa Anita Derby in California, with its $100,000 prize. Seabiscuit, with Pollard back in the saddle, came from behind to win, setting a record track time and **reinforcing** his **status** as the country's greatest racehorse. No wonder Seabiscuit had become an American legend. Now he will retire permanently at Howard's ranch to enjoy the lazy, **mellow** life he deserves.

Audio

For iWords and audio passages, snap the code, or go to **vocabularyworkshop.com**.

Definitions

Note the spelling, pronunciation, part(s) of speech, and definition(s) of each of the following words. Then write the appropriate form of the word in the blank spaces in the illustrative sentence(s) following. Finally, study the lists of synonyms and antonyms.

1. abound (ə baůnd′)

(*v.*) to be plentiful, be filled

Lush fruit trees **abound** in the orchards of central California.

SYNONYMS: burst with, overflow with, teem with
ANTONYMS: lack, want

2. braggart (brag′ ərt)

(*n.*) a boaster; (*adj.*) boastful in a loud, annoying way

There seems to be a **braggart** in every family, who boasts about his or her achievements and worth.

Greek mythology is filled with **braggart** gods and heroes who take great pride in their deeds and skills.

SYNONYMS: (*n.*) bigmouth, blowhard

3. cache (kash)

(*n.*) a hiding place; something hidden or stored

We found a **cache** of canned food hidden under the stairs in the cellar.

SYNONYMS: stockpile, hoard, store

4. clarification (klar ə fə kā′ shən)

(*n.*) the act of making clear or understandable, an explanation

Reporters asked for a **clarification** of the politician's statement so that they could accurately report her position.

SYNONYM: elucidation

5. despondent (di spän′ dənt)

(*adj.*) sad, without hope, discouraged

The doctor was **despondent** over the loss of his patient and dear friend.

SYNONYMS: dejected, depressed, forlorn
ANTONYMS: jubilant, elated

6. embezzle (em bez′ əl)

(*v.*) to steal property entrusted to one's care

The senator's aide lost his job when he was caught trying to **embezzle** campaign funds.

SYNONYMS: swindle, defraud

7. heartrending (härt′ ren diŋ)

(*adj.*) causing mental pain or grief

The survivor told a **heartrending** story about the shipwreck and the days she spent alone on the island.

SYNONYMS: moving, sad, heartbreaking, poignant
ANTONYMS: amusing, funny, hilarious

CCSS Vocabulary: 4.c., 4.d. (See pp. T14–15.)

8. leisurely (lē′ zhər lē)

(*adj.*) unhurried, taking plenty of time; (*adv.*) in an easygoing or unhurried way

My parents enjoy taking a ___leisurely___ stroll through the park on a Sunday afternoon.

We ate ___leisurely___ and spent hours talking about old times.

SYNONYMS: (*adj.*) slow, relaxed
ANTONYMS: (*adj.*) hasty, hurried, rushed, hectic

9. lethargic (lə thär′ jik)

(*adj.*) unnaturally sleepy; dull, slow moving; indifferent

The twins often become ___lethargic___ after eating a large meal at their grandmother's house.

SYNONYMS: lazy, sluggish, listless
ANTONYMS: wide-awake, alert, energetic, dynamic

10. malady (mal′ əd ē)

(*n.*) a sickness, illness, disease, disorder

Rheumatic fever, usually a childhood ___malady___, can cause permanent damage to the heart.

SYNONYMS: ailment, affliction
ANTONYMS: health, well-being

11. mellow (mel′ ō)

(*adj.*) ripe, well-matured; soft, sweet, and rich; gentle, pleasant; (*v.*) to become gentle and sweet

Hawaii is known for its ___mellow___ fruit, all of which is ripe and juicy.

Mom continued to hope that her upstart brother would ___mellow___ with age and experience.

SYNONYMS: (*adj.*) dulcet, creamy
ANTONYMS: (*adj.*) unripe, green, harsh, grating, strident

12. nomadic (nō ma′ dik)

(*adj.*) wandering, moving about from place to place

Many groups in the desert live a ___nomadic___ life, traveling from place to place in search of water and grazing land.

SYNONYMS: roaming, vagrant, migratory, itinerant
ANTONYMS: stationary, settled, rooted, fixed

13. piecemeal (pēs′ mēl)

(*adj.*) one piece at a time; (*adv.*) gradually

The committee's ___piecemeal___ approach to the problem was taking more time and money than the school board could afford.

Patchwork quilts are sewn ___piecemeal___.

SYNONYM: (*adv.*) bit by bit
ANTONYM: (*adv.*) all at once

CCSS Vocabulary: 4.c., 4.d. (See pp. T14–15.)

14. quest (kwest)

(*n.*) a search, hunt; (*v.*) to search, seek, ask

In ___quest___ of a safe water route to the Pacific, Lewis and Clark journeyed more than three thousand miles.

Diplomats ___quest___ for peaceful solutions to global problems.

SYNONYMS: (*n.*) pursuit, venture

15. random (ran′ dəm)

(*adj.*) by chance, not planned or prearranged; irregular

According to a ___random___ sampling of voters, Proposition 10 will be approved by a wide margin.

SYNONYMS: haphazard, accidental
ANTONYMS: planned, systematic

16. rant (rant)

(*v.*) to speak wildly and noisily; (*n.*) loud, violent talk

When the speaker began to ___rant___ like a rabble-rouser, the crowd shouted him down.

Listening to the ___rant___ of that radio personality makes me want to give up on talk shows.

SYNONYMS: (*v.*) rave, fume, spout
ANTONYMS: (*v.*) whisper, murmur

17. reinforce (rē in fôrs′)

(*v.*) to make stronger with new materials or support

They used steel beams to ___reinforce___ the structure of the building.

SYNONYMS: strengthen, bolster, prop up
ANTONYMS: weaken, undermine, sap, impair

18. seclusion (si klü′ zhən)

(*n.*) isolation from others, solitude

Some actors choose to live in ___seclusion___, away from the prying eyes of journalists.

SYNONYMS: aloneness, solitariness
ANTONYM: the thick of things

19. status (stā′ təs)

(*n.*) a person's condition or position in the eyes of the law; relative rank or standing, especially in society; prestige

Winning the prestigious book award boosted the young writer's literary ___status___.

SYNONYMS: recognition, standing

20. turmoil (tər′ moil)

(*n.*) a state of great confusion or disorder; mental strain or agitation

For many years after the Civil War, the South remained a society in ___turmoil___.

SYNONYMS: upheaval, tumult; ANTONYMS: peace and quiet, order

CCSS Vocabulary: 4.c., 4.d. (See pp. T14–15.)

Choosing the Right Word

*Select the **boldface** word that better completes each sentence. You might refer to the passage on pages 146–147 to see how most of these words are used in context.*

1. (**Nomadic, Despondent**) groups of horse breeders still wander the plains of Central Asia in search of pasturage for their herds.

The nomadic horse riders of Central Asia move from place to place as seasons change.

2. As soon as I opened the book, I realized that I had stumbled on a rich (**cache, braggart**) of useful information for my report.
3. In the (**heartrending, lethargic**) conclusion of the film, the hero dies in the arms of his beloved friend.
4. Although she appeared calm and composed, her mind was in (**turmoil, status**).
5. As I was in no hurry to get where I was going, I decided to set a rather (**random, leisurely**) pace for myself.
6. The eternal (**quest, seclusion**) for youth and beauty explains the huge sales of cosmetics, to men as well as to women.
7. There is a great difference between being quietly confident of your own ability and being an obnoxious (**nomad, braggart**).
8. Our present policy appears to be so contradictory that I believe some (**clarification, turmoil**) of it is in order.
9. Over the years, I have learned one thing about rumors: Where the facts are few, fictions (**abound, clarify**).
10. My experience on my summer job has (**reinforced, abounded**) many of the lessons I learned in the classroom.
11. Only the fact that they cannot see the seriousness of the emergency can explain their (**lethargic, nomadic**) response to our appeal for help.
12. Why would a world-famous writer choose to live in the (**quest, seclusion**) of a country village far from the "madding crowd"?
13. At the time of our very public argument, I was angry, but over the years my emotions have (**mellowed, reinforced**).
14. I believe that education, understanding, and experience provide the only cure for the (**malady, status**) of prejudice.
15. Many doctors believe that when sick people become (**heartrending, despondent**) over their health, it is more difficult for them to recover.

CCSS Vocabulary: 4.d. (See pp. T14–15.)

16. After receiving his paper marked with a big red *D* in his teacher's handwriting, the student sulked (**despondently, leisurely**) for hours.

17. For weeks, a gang of muggers wandered the streets aimlessly, choosing their victims at (**random, piecemeal**) from those who happened by.

18. The least useful thing you could do at this moment is to deliver a long, loud (**rant, turmoil**) against your opponents.

19. People say that Brianna is a (**mellow, status**) person, but I've seen her lose her temper too often to believe them.

20. Though he (**rants, embezzles**) and raves about the problems of the world, he has little to offer in the way of solutions to them.

21. They drove (**piecemeal, leisurely**) through the countryside, taking time to view hills, woods, and meadows full of blooming wildflowers.

22. The president went on the air to inform the general public of the present (**malady, status**) of the negotiations with the enemy.

23. Instead of such (**mellow, piecemeal**) efforts to prevent air pollution, we need a unified campaign that will be continued for as long as necessary.

24. People who waste the natural resources of this country are in a sense (**embezzling, reinforcing**) the wealth of future generations.

25. We repaired the house (**randomly, piecemeal**), doing one small task after another.

Synonyms

*Choose the word from this Unit that is the same or most nearly the same in meaning as the **boldface** word or expression in the phrase. Write that word on the line. Use a dictionary if necessary.*

1. was among the last **roving** groups in Lapland ____nomadic____
2. achieved a well-regarded **situation** among her peers ____status____
3. a loud **harangue** that persuaded no one ____rant____
4. legal terms that will need **explication** ____clarification____
5. attempted to **make off with** money from the fund ____embezzle____
6. made an **arbitrary** search for the lost keys ____random____
7. was caught up in the **chaos** left by the storm ____turmoil____
8. is just another conceited **showoff** ____braggart____
9. rehearsed the play **little by little** ____piecemeal____
10. suffers from a serious **indisposition** ____malady____

 CCSS Vocabulary: 5. (See pp. T14–15.)

The synonyms and antonyms here do not appear on the Definitions page.

Antonyms

Choose the word from this Unit that is most nearly opposite in meaning to the **boldface** *word or expression in the phrase. Write that word on the line. Use a dictionary if necessary.*

1. **confusion** resulting from my explanation ____clarification____
2. will **safeguard** the company's money ____embezzle____
3. unwisely chose to **mumble** at the crowd ____rant____
4. a **unified** effort to complete the task ____piecemeal____
5. witnessed a **deliberate** act of kindness ____random____

Completing the Sentence

From the words in this Unit, choose the one that best completes each of the following sentences. Write the correct word form in the space provided.

1. Apparently, the man could pay off his staggering gambling debts only by ____embezzling____ funds from the company that employed him.

2. Though Ponce de León's ____quest____ for the Fountain of Youth proved futile, he did explore Florida and claim it as territory for the Spanish.

3. In order to prevent the bridge from collapsing, it has been necessary to ____reinforce____ its girders and foundations.

4. The lake so ____abounds____ with trout and pickerel that even a person with my limited skill in fishing can catch them easily.

5. Most detectives solve crimes in a(n) ____piecemeal____ fashion, as clues come to light, rather than all at once.

6. The ____turmoil____ of the French Revolution and the Napoleonic Era was succeeded by 100 years of relative peace and quiet in Europe.

7. Every once in a while, I like to take time out from my busy schedule to have a ____leisurely____ dinner with old friends.

8. The park is always full of soapbox orators ____ranting____ about the inequality of government or society.

9. Arthritis is a(n) ____malady____ that attacks many millions of people, especially in middle and old age.

10. After putting up all week with the noise and confusion of life in the big city, I enjoy the ____seclusion____ of my mountain retreat on weekends.

CCSS Vocabulary: 4.a., 5. (See pp. T14–15.)

11. Though I am always full of energy in the morning, I start to become a little ___**lethargic**___ as the day wears on.

12. The tenor's voice was rich and ___**mellow**___, but the baritone's sounded somewhat harsh and unpleasant.

13. Instead of trying to decide which applicants were best suited for the job, he selected two at ___**random**___.

14. It's natural for you to feel a little ___**despondent**___ over not getting the job, but don't let that prevent you from applying for other positions.

15. At first, when I couldn't make out what she wanted me to do, I asked her for some ___**clarification**___ of her instructions.

16. Yesterday, I read a truly ___**heartrending**___ account of the plight of millions of people suffering from the effects of a severe famine.

17. When I first entered this country, I was classified as a "resident alien," but my ___**status**___ has changed since then.

18. The two brothers are both fine athletes, but one is quiet and modest, while the other is an awful ___**braggart**___.

19. Many homeless people now lead essentially ___**nomadic**___ existences on the streets of our major cities.

20. During warm months, foxes bury many animals they have killed, with the result that they have ___**caches**___ to tide them over the winter.

Writing: Words in Action

Answers to both prompts will vary.

1. Look back at "Hero From the Wrong Side of the Track Retires" (pages 146–147). Notice how the author describes Seabiscuit over the course of his career in racing. Think of at least three more words or phrases to describe the horse's character and physique, including at least two Unit words. Then write a brief description of Seabiscuit, using the details you think are most essential to convey the horse's notable traits.

2. Many athletes become national heroes and inspire people. Seabiscuit inspired people, but he was an animal. Do you consider a racehorse to be an athlete, like a baseball player or a runner? Write a persuasive essay in which you state why you think Seabiscuit was, or was not, an athlete. Support your opinion with specific examples from your observations, reading (refer to pages 146–147), or personal experience. Use three or more Unit words.

Writing prompt #2 is modeled on that of standardized tests.

CCSS Vocabulary: 6; Writing: 1.c., 2.d., 3.d., 4. (See pp. T14–15.)

Vocabulary in Context: Informational Text for Unit 12 is available online at **vocabularyworkshop.com**.

Vocabulary in Context

Literary Text

The following excerpts are from Victor Hugo's novel Les Misérables. *Some of the words you have studied in this Unit appear in* **boldface** *type. Complete each statement below the excerpt by circling the letter of the correct answer.*

1. An aged and falling apple-tree leans far over to one side, its wound dressed with a bandage of straw and of clayey loam. Nearly all the apple trees are falling with age. . . . The skeletons of dead trees **abound** in this orchard. Crows fly through their branches, and at the end of it is a wood full of violets.

Trees that **abound** are

a. widespread **c.** tall
b. rare **d.** valuable

Hugo's novel tells the story of Inspector Javert's pursuit of the thief Jean Valjean.

2. Once as he sat with his knees pressed together, and his eyes almost closed, in a **despondent** attitude, his daughter ventured to say to him, "Father, are you as angry with him as ever?"

Someone who is **despondent** feels

a. sleepy **c.** humble
b. enthusiastic **d.** hopeless

3. All heads were raised: the sensation was indescribable; there was a momentary hesitation in the audience, the voice had been so **heartrending**; the man who stood there appeared so calm that they did not understand at first. They asked themselves whether he had indeed uttered that cry; they could not believe that that tranquil man had been the one to give that terrible outcry.

A **heartrending** voice is one that

a. frightens others **c.** stirs deep emotions
b. depresses others **d.** makes no impression

4. She did not know what name to give to what she now felt. Is anyone the less ill because one does not know the name of one's **malady**?

Another word for **malady** is

a. feeling **c.** weakness
b. disease **d.** grief

5. A little beyond the barricade, it seemed to him that he could make out something white in front of him. He approached, it took on a form. It was two white horses . . . who had been straying at **random** all day from street to street, and had finally halted there.

An event that happens at **random** is NOT

a. timely **c.** accidental
b. enjoyable **d.** planned

Interactive Quiz

Snap the code, or go to **vocabularyworkshop.com**

CCSS Vocabulary: 4.d.; Reading (Literature): 4. (See pp. T14–15.)

Vocabulary for Comprehension

Read the following passage in which some of the words you have studied in Units 10–12 appear in ***boldface*** *type. Then answer the questions on page 157.*

This passage discusses how, long before the civil rights movement of the 1950s and 1960s, African Americans worked to end racial discrimination and segregation.

(Line)

Have you ever heard the term the *Great Migration*? If so, you may know that between 1870 and 1920, hundreds of thousands of African Americans moved from rural areas in the Southeast to the industrialized urban areas in the Northeast and Midwest. For most, this huge migration meant an escape from poverty and the **malady** of discrimination, of being treated unfairly. To these African Americans, the movement north was a **quest** for a better life, as northern factory jobs were a great improvement over farm work.

As more industrial jobs became available during World War I, about half a million African Americans went north. Although their economic **status** improved during the war years, African Americans in both the North and the South were still denied many basic rights. As a result, some notable African Americans rose to the challenge of righting injustices and achieving equal opportunity.

One African American who fought to end injustice was Booker T. Washington. Born enslaved, Washington taught himself to read. Years later, in 1891, he founded the Tuskegee Institute in Alabama. There, African Americans were taught skills such as bricklaying, printing, and teaching, which would help them improve their lives as they worked peacefully toward equality.

African American women also struggled for justice. Ida B. Wells, for example, strove to end the **notorious** practice of segregation—that is, of separating African Americans from other groups in society—and other forms of racial injustice. For Wells, her pen and her resolve were her only weapons. As editor of the newspaper *Free Speech*, which she founded in Memphis, Tennessee, Wells fought to end **random** acts of violence against African Americans. "Can you remain silent," she wrote ". . . when such things are done in your own community and country?"

As these African American leaders and others lectured across the country, they inspired the growth of the civil rights movement. In fact, even today, their words and deeds still motivate organizations to continue the struggle for justice.

CCSS Vocabulary: 4.a.; Reading (Informational Text): 2, 4, 6. (See pp. T14–15.)

1. The main purpose of the passage is to
   a. inform about African Americans' early struggles to end injustice
   b. describe African American life in the North from 1870 to 1920
   c. entertain the reader with several fictional anecdotes
   d. tell a personal story about the writer's ancestors
   e. persuade the reader to take action

2. The question in lines 1–2 functions as the focus for
   a. paragraph 1
   b. paragraph 2
   c. paragraphs 3 and 4
   d. paragraph 5
   e. the entire passage

3. **Malady** (line 10) most nearly means
   a. humiliation
   b. stigma
   c. sickness
   d. oppression
   e. crime

4. **Quest** (line 13) is best defined as
   a. request
   b. search
   c. victory
   d. competition
   e. hope

5. In lines 12–16, it is clear that the main motivation for African Americans moving to the North from the South was their search for
   a. political representation
   b. sturdy housing
   c. family and friends
   d. a better life
   e. a college education

6. **Status** (line 21) most nearly means
   a. education
   b. condition
   c. skills
   d. opportunities
   e. successes

7. **Notorious** (line 42) is best defined as
   a. haphazard
   b. widespread
   c. official
   d. cruel
   e. disgraceful

8. The meaning of **random** (line 51) is
   a. planned
   b. brutal
   c. arbitrary
   d. shocking
   e. shameful

9. The author's attitude toward Booker T. Washington and Ida B. Wells is best described as one of
   a. disbelief
   b. hostility
   c. indifference
   d. admiration
   e. sympathy

10. From the sentence "For Wells, her pen and her resolve were her only weapons" (lines 46–47), you can infer that Wells
    a. gave in to pressure to stop writing
    b. wrote countless editorials
    c. defended herself against enemies
    d. was weak and easily intimidated
    e. kept her opinions to herself

11. Which of the following states something that both Washington and Wells had in common?
    a. They founded newspapers.
    b. They visited the White House.
    c. They wrote best-selling books.
    d. They lectured all across the country.
    e. They founded schools.

12. Which paragraph tells about the efforts of African American women to fight injustice?
    a. paragraph 1
    b. paragraph 2
    c. paragraph 3
    d. paragraph 4
    e. paragraph 5

CCSS Vocabulary: 4.a.; Reading (Informational Text): 2, 4, 6. (See pp. T14–15.)

Two-Word Completions

Select the pair of words that best completes the meaning of each of the following sentences.

1. A communication between the warring factions' two leaders was the ____________ to a bold new peace ____________ that would end a twenty-year-long conflict.

a. beneficiary . . . veto
b. stalemate . . . status
c. overture . . . pact
d. surplus . . . farce

2. Before we can even think about renovating this ____________ old house, we must remove all the worthless ____________ that is strewn around the rooms and blocking the entrances.

a. gigantic . . . cache
b. dilapidated . . . clutter
c. mellow . . . havoc
d. futile . . . surplus

3. Among law enforcement, his ____________ is that of a ____________ con artist who targets segments of the population that are likely to fall prey to his convincing words.

a. havoc . . . braggart
b. misdemeanor . . . narrative
c. dialogue . . . grueling
d. status . . . notorious

4. "I am still ____________ the matter over in my mind," the president told the press. "When I have reached a decision, I will either sign the bill or ____________ it."

a. mellowing . . . botch
b. narrating . . . dismantle
c. mulling . . . veto
d. clarifying . . . mar

5. As he sat by the fire that glowed in the ____________, the old sailor entertained the children with a(n) ____________ of his adventures on the high seas, beginning when he was a boy of twelve, almost sixty years before.

a. lair . . . farce
b. cache . . . dialogue
c. hearth . . . narrative
d. clutter . . . overture

6. The earliest inhabitants of North America lived ____________ lives. They were constantly moving from place to place in search of the game that made up the greater part of their diet. This endless ____________ for food eventually took them to all parts of the continent.

a. nomadic . . . quest
b. grueling . . . cache
c. pampered . . . malady
d. lethargic . . . status

7. Since the soil is so remarkably rich and fertile, a variety of crops can be grown in ____________. The farmers keep what they need for themselves and sell off the ____________ at a handsome profit.

a. abundance . . . surplus
b. seclusion . . . reinforcements
c. lavishness . . . hospitality
d. leisure . . . adequacy

 CCSS Vocabulary: 4.a. (See pp. T14–15.)

In the passage about Babe Didrikson Zaharias (see pages 136–137), the author notes that the athlete would not be slowed by serious illness because she had "other fish to fry."

"Other fish to fry" is an idiom that means "more important things to do." An **idiom** is an expression that uses figurative language to express an idea. The meaning of an idiom can't be guessed from the literal meaning of its words. An idiom must be learned, as if it were a new word or phrase.

Choosing the Right Idiom

*Read each sentence. Use context clues to figure out the meaning of each idiom in **boldface** print. Then write the letter of the definition for the idiom in the sentence.*

1. You complain so much; must you always have **an ax to grind**? __g__
2. Don't ask me why she did it; **your guess is as good as mine**. __c__
3. Because we can never know **what lies in store**, I think we're better off not worrying about the future. __j__
4. **The ball is in your court** now, so I hope you'll give me an answer soon. __a__
5. Please tell us more about the **wild and woolly** days of the Old West. __b__
6. **Keep an eye on** that snake; don't let it slither away. __h__
7. The sound of those cats wailing in the middle of the night **drives me up the wall**. __d__
8. **Keep your eyes peeled** for Aunt Nina; she should be waiting for us in Terminal B. __f__
9. She really **hit the nail on the head** when she said that some people learn best in groups. __e__
10. **Lend me your ear**, and I'll tell you a tale. __i__

a. It's your turn; it's time for you to make a decision or make a move.

b. untamed, uncivilized

c. I don't know any more about the subject being discussed than you do.

d. makes me feel crazy

e. made the exactly right point

f. watch for

g. a readiness to quarrel or find fault

h. watch carefully

i. Listen to me.

j. what unforeseen events will occur later

CCSS Vocabulary: 5.a. (See pp. T14–15.)

WORD STUDY

Writing with Idioms

Find the meaning of each idiom. (Use a dictionary if necessary.) Then write a sentence for each idiom. **Answers will vary.**

1. a chip on one's shoulder **Sample response: Susan has had a chip on her shoulder ever since she found out she was not picked for the tennis team.**

2. brush up on

3. learn the ropes

4. living on borrowed time

5. keep your chin up

6. run circles around

7. toot your own horn

8. over the top

9. put up a fight

10. smell a rat

11. until the cows come home

12. out of steam

 CCSS Vocabulary: 5. (See pp. T14–15.)

Denotation and Connotation

When you look up a word in the dictionary, you get its **denotation**, or literal meaning. Many words also have **connotations**—implied meanings that we commonly associate with them.

Connotations may be positive, negative, or neutral. A word's synonyms—words that mean nearly the same thing—can have very different connotations, some more positive or more negative than others. Consider these synonyms for the neutral word *avoid*.

sidestep *evade* *shirk* *neglect*

Sidestep and *evade* have neutral to mildly negative connotations, but *shirk* and *neglect* have strongly negative connotations.

Think: To sidestep or evade an issue you don't want to talk about shows avoidance, but to shirk or neglect an important duty shows irresponsibility and a lack of trustworthiness.

Look at these examples of words that are similar in denotation but have different connotations.

NEUTRAL	POSITIVE	NEGATIVE
difficult	**challenging**	**grueling**
slowly	**leisurely**	**slothfully**
soft	**mellow**	**slack**

Whether you are reading a text or writing one, you will do a better job if you understand the connotations of words. As a reader, you will sense the underlying meanings associated with a word. As a writer, you will know which word to choose to accurately express your meaning.

Shades of Meaning

Write a plus sign (+) in the box if the word has a positive connotation. Write a minus sign (–) if the word has a negative connotation. Put a zero (0) if the word is neutral.

1. hospitable +	**2.** clutter –	**3.** quest +	 **4.** abound  +
5. botch  –	**6.** narrative 0	**7.** emblem 0	**8.** lair 0
9. adequate 0	**10.** morbid –	**11.** cache +	**12.** surplus +
13. vindictive –	**14.** status +	**15.** hearth +	**16.** infamous –

CCSS Vocabulary: 5.c. (See pp. T14–15.)

Expressing the Connotation

Read each sentence. Select the word in parentheses that better expresses the connotation (positive, negative, or neutral) given at the beginning of the sentence.

negative **1.** Melinda goes about her chores in a(n) (**lethargic, unhurried**) way.

neutral **2.** As a youth, Mr. Fredericks had pursued a (**vagrant, nomadic**) way of life.

negative **3.** The attack from Planet X-5155 created (**havoc, disorder**) in Earth's cities.

neutral **4.** A mysterious (**illness, malady**) forced me to miss class that day.

positive **5.** The care he received in the hospital after his accident was completely (**satisfactory, adequate**).

positive **6.** She was the (**recipient, beneficiary**) of the valuable knowledge passed down by her mother, a famous scholar.

positive **7.** Even after the "once in a lifetime" sales event, there was a (**surplus, glut**) of merchandise left in the furniture store.

negative **8.** Trying to find a gift he'll like is a(n) (**futile, ineffective**) exercise.

Challenge: Using Connotation

Choose vocabulary words from Units 10–12 to replace the ***boldface*** *words in the sentences below. Then explain how the connotation of the replacement word changes the tone of the sentence.* Answers will vary.

gigantic	**heartrending**	**innumerable**
dismantle	**lax**	**shirk**

1. Looking up at the black sky, we gaped at the **many** innumerable bright, twinkling stars.
Sample response: *Innumerable* is a stronger word with a positive connotation that creates a tone of awe.

2. It's natural to want to **avoid** shirk your chores, but completing them will make you feel good.
Sample response: *Shirk* is a word with a more negative connotation than *avoid*. It casts a worse light on the person who doesn't want to do the work.

3. In the show's final episode, the main character faced a **sad** heartrending outcome to his love story.
Sample response: *Heartrending* is a more emotionally powerful word than *sad*, and makes the episode sound more dramatic.

 CCSS Vocabulary: 5, 5.c. (See pp. T14–15.)

Classical Roots

note, not—to know, recognize, or mark

This Latin root appears in **notorious** (page 130), which means "widely and unfavorably known." Some other words based on the same root are listed below.

connote	**notary**	**noteworthy**	**notion**
denote	**notation**	**notify**	**notoriety**

From the list of words above, choose the one that corresponds to each of the brief definitions below. Write the word in the blank space in the illustrative sentence below the definition. Use a dictionary if necessary.

1. to point out, give notice of, inform
   We will ___notify___ our attorney of your intention to sue us.

2. a public official who certifies statements and signatures
   The ___notary___ public witnessed the signing of Grandfather's will.

3. remarkable, outstanding because of some special excellence (*"worthy of being recognized"*)
   The senator made ___noteworthy___ remarks about the importance of reducing air pollution.

4. a record; a note to assist memory, memorandum; a set of symbols or expressions
   Good students often write ___notations___ in the margins of books.

5. an idea; a foolish idea or opinion; a small useful item
   She has the odd ___notion___ that no one in her class likes her.

6. ill fame; being famous for something bad
   Jesse James achieved ___notoriety___ as an outlaw in the Old West.

7. to suggest or imply in addition to giving an exact meaning
   The name *Angela* means "angel," but it also ___connotes___ goodness.

8. to indicate, be the sign of, mean exactly
   The child's high temperature and chills ___denote___ severe illness.

CCSS Vocabulary: 4.b. (See pp. T14–15.)

UNIT 13

Note that not all of the 20 Unit words are used in this passage. *Grovel*, *handicraft*, *hilarious*, *maternal* and *revere* are not included.

Read the following passage, taking note of the ***boldface*** *words and their contexts. These words are among those you will be studying in Unit 13. As you complete the exercises in this Unit, it may help to refer to the way the words are used below.*

CCSS Vocabulary: 4; Reading (Informational Text): 4, 6. (See pp. T14–15.)

The Last Flight of the *Hindenburg*

<Radio Broadcast Transcript>

In 1936 the biggest airship (also called a dirigible or zeppelin) the world has ever seen took to the skies. The German *Hindenburg* could cross the Atlantic in just two days. It was filled with highly-flammable, lighter-than-air hydrogen gas. The following transcript describes the events of May 6, 1937.

Harold Bickerson for WLEN in Springfield: *Hello everyone. This is Harold Bickerson speaking to you from the naval airbase at Lakehurst, New Jersey, where the giant* Hindenburg *airship is about to land. While that great dirigible circles overhead, I'll recount the* ***chronological*** *sequence of its travels. After departing from Frankfurt, Germany, the airship spent two days speeding over miles of ocean. Though the* Hindenburg *was scheduled to land at dawn, its travel time* ***fluctuates*** *with wind conditions. Favorable conditions reduce the travel time, while unfavorable headwinds* ***diminish*** *its speed and increase travel time considerably. The ship appeared over the New York metropolitan area around noon, but the crew could not* ***countenance*** *a landing at that time. Shifting surface winds and air* ***agitation*** *at the time made landing too dangerous.*

It's just about sunset and raining fairly heavily. I'll say a few words about the preparations that have been made on the ground. The Lakehurst airbase has played a great part in the ***saga*** *of lighter-than-air transportation in this country, and it's well equipped to handle large hydrogen-filled airships of the* Hindenburg*'s* ***magnitude****. The ground crew have been preparing the field. They're a* ***reputable*** *staff, well-known and trained to ease the giant zeppelin onto the ground. When the airship arrives, it will drop heavy ropes to the men below,*

The first *Hindenburg* flight, March 1936

A Ball of Fire: The *Hindenburg* in flames after its disaster, May 6, 1937

and these ropes will be affixed to the **massive** *mooring mast to anchor the 804-foot-long ship.*

Here comes the Hindenburg *now: It's a beautiful sight, enough to* **enchant** *the most sober observer and* **foster** *a feeling of excitement in the most jaded and* **stodgy** *onlooker. The* Hindenburg *is pointed directly at the mooring mast. I can see the passenger quarters and the observation deck, where the passengers must be gazing down at the great mass of humanity below them. The propellers are moving just a little to keep the ship….*

It burst into flames! It burst into flames! The Hindenburg *is burning, and it's falling, it's crashing to the ground! Watch out, watch out, folks! Oh, it's horrible, it's… The* Hindenburg *is crashing into the mooring mast, and all the people on the field are running for their lives and screaming. This is the making of a catastrophe, ladies and gentlemen. There's no chance anyone could survive this… I can't… The flames are swelling perhaps five hundred feet up in the sky and a smoky* **pall** *is spreading over the field, and I'm sorry, ladies and gentlemen, I can hardly breathe or talk because of the smoke. I have to move inside.*

I'm back now. The wreckage is still flaming and crackling out there. We're not sure what **ignited** *the ship, but something may have slipped on the craft and caused a spark, or caused the highly-flammable hydrogen gas to leak. But I have some good news related to something I hurriedly* **blurted** *out earlier. Ambulances have arrived, and I'm told that the ground crew managed to get out of the way unharmed. And of the 97 people on board, at least 25 have been rescued. Evidently many jumped out of the windows as the ship fell to the ground. And now I'll have to pause again, because they're asking for help out there and I must to do my part.*

Of the 97 people on board, 35 died, as did one person on the ground. The era of commercial airships was over.

For iWords and audio passages, snap the code, or go to vocabularyworkshop.com.

Definitions

Note the spelling, pronunciation, part(s) of speech, and definition(s) of each of the following words. Then write the appropriate form of the word in the blank spaces in the illustrative sentence(s) following. Finally, study the lists of synonyms and antonyms.

1. agitation (aj i tā′ shən)

(*n.*) a violent stirring or movement; noisy confusion, excitement; a stirring up of public enthusiasm

The ____agitation____ for campaign finance reform was gaining widespread support in Congress.

SYNONYMS: disquiet, uneasiness, upset
ANTONYMS: peace of mind, composure, calm

2. blurt (blərt)

(*v.*) to say suddenly or without thinking

The detective was fairly certain that, after hours of interrogation, the suspect would ____blurt____ out the truth.

SYNONYMS: blab, let slip

3. chronological (krän əl äj′ i kəl)

(*adj.*) arranged in order of time of occurrence

The importance of a time line is that it arranges historical events in ____chronological____ order.

SYNONYMS: in time sequence, consecutive

4. countenance (kaůn′ tə nəns)

(*n.*) a face, facial expression; (*v.*) to tolerate or approve

The teacher's smiling ____countenance____ reassured us that the rehearsal was going well.

The new boss is strict and does not ____countenance____ lateness or absenteeism.

SYNONYMS: (*v.*) support, condone
ANTONYM: (*v.*) disapprove of

5. diminish (di min′ ish)

(*v.*) to make or become smaller, reduce in size

It takes no time at all for a fad to ____diminish____ in popularity.

SYNONYMS: lessen, decrease, dwindle
ANTONYMS: increase, enlarge, augment

6. enchant (en chant′)

(*v.*) to please greatly; to charm, put under a magic spell

The singer proceeded to ____enchant____ the audience with her beautiful voice and engaging style.

SYNONYMS: delight, thrill, bewitch
ANTONYMS: bore, nauseate, disgust

CCSS Vocabulary: 4.c., 4.d. (See pp. T14–15.)

7. fluctuate (flək′ chü āt)

(*v.*) to change continually; to move up and down

Stock prices ___fluctuate___ daily.

SYNONYMS: waver, seesaw, oscillate
ANTONYMS: stay put, remain unchanged

8. foster (fôs′ tər)

(*v.*) to bring up, give care to; to promote, encourage; (*adj.*) in the same family but not related by birth

The American ambassador worked to ___foster___ positive relations with the newly formed republic.

It is important for ___foster___ children to be placed with loving families.

SYNONYMS: (*v.*) support, nurture, cultivate
ANTONYMS: (*v.*) stifle, smother, quash, discourage

9. grovel (gräv′ əl)

(*v.*) to humble oneself, act in a fearful and servile way; to lie face downward; to indulge in something base or unworthy

Afraid of punishment, the Roman slave began to ___grovel___ at the feet of the emperor.

SYNONYMS: crouch, cringe, wallow

10. handicraft (han′ dē kraft)

(*n.*) work done by hand; a trade requiring hand skill

Making apple-head dolls is a ___handicraft___ still enjoyed in the Arkansas River Valley, among other places.

SYNONYMS: manual art, artisanship

11. hilarious (hi lâr′ ē əs)

(*adj.*) extremely funny, causing loud amusement

The comedian told a ___hilarious___ story that had the audience laughing hysterically.

SYNONYMS: highly amusing, side-splitting
ANTONYMS: boring, dull, heartrending, humorless

12. ignite (ig nīt′)

(*v.*) to set on fire, cause to burn; to heat up, excite

We used lighter fluid to ___ignite___ the charcoal in the outdoor grill.

SYNONYMS: inflame, light, kindle
ANTONYMS: quench, extinguish, douse, put out

13. magnitude (mag′ nə tüd)

(*n.*) the great size or importance of something

At first, the ___magnitude___ of the task seemed to be overwhelming for a group as small as ours.

SYNONYMS: extent, immensity
ANTONYMS: smallness, unimportance, insignificance

CCSS Vocabulary: 4.c., 4.d. (See pp. T14–15.)

14. massive (mas′ iv)

(*adj.*) large and heavy; great in size or scope

A ___massive___ boulder still blocks the entrance to the secret cave.

SYNONYMS: bulky, immense
ANTONYMS: flimsy, frail, thin

15. maternal (mə tər′ nəl)

(*adj.*) of or like a mother

The kittens' mother took her ___maternal___ responsibilities very seriously.

SYNONYMS: protective, sympathetic
ANTONYM: paternal

16. pall (pôl)

(*v.*) to lose in interest, attraction, or effectiveness; to become tiresome; (*n.*) a dark covering, something that conceals

When the excavation yielded only pieces of pottery, the archaeologist's optimism began to ___pall___.

News of the surprise attack on Pearl Harbor cast a ___pall___ over the nation on December 7, 1941.

SYNONYMS: (*v.*) bore, weary; (*n.*) gloom, shadow
ANTONYMS: (*v.*) intrigue, fascinate; (*n.*) light, brightness

17. reputable (rep′ yət ə bəl)

(*adj.*) well thought of, having a good reputation

A list of ___reputable___ lawyers is available through the local bar association.

SYNONYMS: reliable, respectable, trustworthy
ANTONYMS: shady, unsavory, questionable

18. revere (ri vēr′)

(*v.*) to love and respect deeply, honor greatly

The elderly teacher was ___revered___ by a whole generation of students.

SYNONYMS: esteem, cherish
ANTONYMS: scorn, disdain, mock

19. saga (säg′ ə)

(*n.*) a narrative of heroic exploits; a long, detailed account

Although written in Old English, *Beowulf* is very much like a Norse ___saga___ in that it details the colorful deeds of a legendary hero.

SYNONYMS: heroic tale, epic, chronicle

20. stodgy (stäj′ ē)

(*adj.*) dull, boring; old-fashioned, hidebound; lumpy, thick

The ___stodgy___ politician showed little inclination to listen to the speeches of junior senators.

SYNONYMS: stuffy, tiresome, blah
ANTONYMS: forward-looking, avant-garde, progressive

CCSS Vocabulary: 4.c., 4.d. (See pp. T14–15.)

Choosing the Right Word

*Select the **boldface** word that better completes each sentence. You might refer to the passage on pages 164–165 to see how most of these words are used in context.*

1. For more than a hundred years, the delightful *Alice's Adventures in Wonderland* has been (**palling, enchanting**) readers young and old.

2. I have difficulty remembering the correct (**chronology, handicraft**) of the many battles that took place during the Civil War.

3. Some controversial figures are both (**fostered, revered**) as saints and despised as villains.

4. Many older people complain that the warm spirit of neighborliness has greatly (**diminished, ignited**) under the conditions of city living.

5. The speaker warned that our whole system of handling lawbreakers has (**massive, stodgy**) faults that will be difficult to correct.

6. She kept us in stitches with her (**chronological, hilarious**) jokes.

Charles L. Dodgson wrote two Alice books under the name Lewis Carroll.

7. Any editorial about pollution appearing in such a (**maternal, reputable**) newspaper is bound to make a strong impression on many citizens.

8. My love of reading, (**fostered, diminished**) by my parents since early childhood, has continued to grow through the years.

9. Many professionals and executives today have made enjoyable hobbies of such (**handicrafts, sagas**) as carpentry and weaving.

10. The movie was difficult to follow because its many short scenes did not follow a traditional (**chronological, reputable**) order.

11. I'm writing a (**saga, handicraft**) that depicts one courageous soldier's devotion to the cause of freedom during the Civil War.

12. Rather than (**diminish, grovel**) in your self-pity and play the role of the victim, why don't you take a stand and confront your accuser.

13. In my excitement, I accidentally (**blurted, agitated**) out the very thing that I was trying so hard to conceal.

14. (**Fostered, Ignited**) by the civil rights movement, the students organized several sit-ins and challenged the status quo.

15. One of the sure signs of a country that is not free is that the people in power will not (**countenance, blurt**) any criticism of their acts.

CCSS Vocabulary: 4.d. (See pp. T14–15.)

16. As the game proceeded, and the ball continued to change hands, our feelings (**fostered, fluctuated**) from joy to despair and back again.

17. Though there has of late been a good deal of (**countenance, agitation**) for tax reform, nothing much has come of it so far.

18. For a long time my favorite TV entertainment was police and detective programs, but now they are beginning to (**pall, enchant**).

19. Her charming personality and sparkling wit brought a breath of fresh air into the (**stodgy, hilarious**) atmosphere of the stuffy old club.

20. When the Wright brothers made the first successful airplane flight, few people realized the (**pall, magnitude**) of their achievement.

21. If it were not for the strong (**maternal, hilarious**) instinct to protect their young, many species of animals could not survive.

22. The Tea Act of 1773 was one of the sparks that helped (**enchant, ignite**) the American Revolution.

23. Like everyone else, I want to be well liked, but I will not (**grovel, fluctuate**) before public opinion when I am firmly convinced that it is wrong.

24. The cowboy on his trusty quarter horse plays a prominent part in the (**magnitude, saga**) of the Old West.

25. Marta refuses to swim in the ocean as she is fearful of (**stodgy, massive**) sharks.

Choose the word from this Unit that is the same or most nearly the same in meaning as the ***boldface*** *word or expression in the phrase. Write that word on the line. Use a dictionary if necessary.*

1. a **manual trade** like blacksmithing — handicraft
2. launched a **monumental** attack — massive
3. watched an **extremely comical** play — hilarious
4. will **accept** the president's proposal — countenance
5. guided by her **motherly** instinct — maternal
6. to **reveal** the truth — blurt
7. the **enormity** of an earthquake — magnitude
8. a leader who is loved and **admired** — revered
9. temperatures that **vary** wildly — fluctuate
10. will **cower** before the king — grovel

CCSS Vocabulary: 5. (See pp. T14–15.)

Antonyms

Choose the word from this Unit that is most nearly opposite in meaning to the **boldface** *word or expression in the phrase. Write that word on the line. Use a dictionary if necessary.*

1. to **deride** the Romantic poets ______ revere
2. a meeting to address a **serious** matter ______ hilarious
3. **bragging** to the media ______ groveling
4. known for their **machine-made products** ______ handicraft
5. inheriting a **fatherly** trait ______ maternal

Completing the Sentence

From the words in this Unit, choose the one that best completes each of the following sentences. Write the correct word form in the space provided.

1. The waves of laughter from the audience indicated that those around me found the clown's antics as ______ hilarious ______ as I did.
2. His attitudes are so incredibly ______ stodgy ______ and hidebound that they would have been considered old-fashioned 100 years ago!
3. Even though I need a job badly, I still have my self-respect, and I am not going to ______ grovel ______ just to get work.
4. How can you ______ countenance ______ such rude behavior in a young child!
5. All of a sudden, from out of the fog loomed a(n) ______ massive ______ ocean liner bearing down on our small boat.
6. The two little girls playing house fussed over their dolls with all the ______ maternal ______ attention that their own mothers bestowed on them.
7. In the ______ Saga ______ *of Eric the Red*, there is a very interesting account of the Norse discovery of North America in A.D. 1000.
8. The number and the ______ magnitude ______ of the problems faced by the President of the United States are almost beyond our imagination.
9. The pilot light of the stove will automatically ______ ignite ______ the burner when the handle is turned to the "on" position.
10. With no money coming in and my daily expenses continuing to mount, my savings have ______ diminished ______ at an alarming rate.

CCSS Vocabulary: 4.a., 5. (See pp. T14–15.)

11. Can you imagine my ______agitation______ when I was told I would have to take over the lead role in the play immediately, with no rehearsals!

12. Our study of American history has taught us to ______revere______ the great men and women who founded this nation.

13. Instead of moving steadily upwards or steadily downwards, the price of oil has been ______fluctuating______ all year.

14. We will donate the proceeds of the cake sale to any ______reputable______ charity you may select.

15. "When I was living in the Australian outback, I learned many curious skills and ______handicrafts______ from the local people," the explorer said.

16. We had hoped to have a wonderful time at the party, but the sad news of the principal's accident cast a(n) ______pall______ over the gathering.

17. She was very fortunate to have had talented and sympathetic teachers who ______fostered______ her career.

18. The audience was ______enchanted______ not only by the lovely voice of the soprano but also by her youthful good looks.

19. Statements ______blurted______ out in anger may often be regretted for a long time afterward.

20. Educators report that there is often a vast difference between a child's mental age and his or her ______chronological______ age.

Writing: Words in Action

Answers to both prompts will vary.

1. Look back at "The Last Flight of the *Hindenburg*" (pages 164–165). Think about how air travel has changed since the flight of the *Hindenburg*. Do you think air travel is safer today than it was in 1936? Write a persuasive essay in which you state and support your opinion, using at least two details from the passage and three Unit words.

2. People often face both man-made and natural disasters. What should people do to prepare for disasters? How can people help others after a disaster? Write a brief essay about disaster preparedness and assistance. Support your ideas with specific examples, observations, your studies, the reading (refer to pages 164–165), or personal experience. Write at least three paragraphs, and use three or more words from this Unit.

Writing prompt #2 is modeled on that of standardized tests.

 CCSS Vocabulary: 6; Writing: 1.c., 2.d., 3.d., 4. (See pp. T14–15.)

Vocabulary in Context: Informational Text for Unit 13 is available online at **vocabularyworkshop.com**.

Vocabulary in Context

Literary Text

The following excerpts are from Around the World in 80 Days *by Jules Verne. Some of the words you have studied in this Unit appear in* ***boldface*** *type. Complete each statement below the excerpt by circling the letter of the correct answer.*

1. His **countenance** possessed in the highest degree what physiognomists call "repose in action," a quality of those who act rather than talk. Calm and phlegmatic, with a clear eye, Mr. Fogg seemed a perfect type.

A **countenance** is a(n)

a. expression **c.** advantage
b. behavior **d.** reputation

2. The crowd swayed back . . . . The undulations of the human surge reached the steps, while all the heads floundered on the surface like a sea agitated by a squall. Many of the black hats disappeared, and the greater part of the crowd seemed to have **diminished** in height.

When something is **diminished**, it

a. strengthens **c.** shrinks
b. expands **d.** prospers

David Niven played the role of Phileas Fogg, who traveled around the world in eighty days.

3. Aouda, leaning upon Mr. Fogg's arm, observed the tumultuous scene with surprise, while Fix asked a man near him what the cause of it all was. Before the man could reply, a fresh **agitation** arose; hurrahs and excited shouts were heard.

An **agitation** is a(n)

a. ceremony **c.** understanding
b. commotion **d.** mystery

4. Passepartout was delighted. His master's last exploit, the consequences of which he ignored, **enchanted** him. Never had the crew seen so jolly and dexterous a fellow.

If a person is **enchanted**, he or she is

a. saddened **c.** mocked
b. valued **d.** captivated

5. The **massive** walking-beam rose and fell above the deck; at one end a piston-rod worked up and down; and at the other was a connecting-rod.

Something that is **massive** is NOT

a. small **c.** nearby
b. substantial **d.** noticeable

Snap the code, or go to **vocabularyworkshop.com**

CCSS Vocabulary: 4.d.; Reading (Literature): 4. (See pp. T14–15.)

UNIT 14

Note that not all of the 20 Unit words are used in this passage. *Akin*, *gaudy*, *impostor*, and *nutritious* are not included.

Read the following passage, taking note of the ***boldface*** *words and their contexts. These words are among those you will be studying in Unit 14. As you complete the exercises in this Unit, it may help to refer to the way the words are used below.*

CCSS Vocabulary: 4; Reading (Informational Text): 4, 6. (See pp. T14–15.)

Celebrating the Death of a Killer

<Online Article>

by Aisha B. Boulos

GENEVA, SWITZERLAND The year 2012 marks the thirty-fifth anniversary of the last naturally occurring case of the highly contagious smallpox virus on the planet. The victim of the disfiguring and sometimes deadly **affliction** was a young man in the East African country of Somalia. Fortunately, after prompt treatment, the patient survived this deadly disease that has plagued humanity for centuries.

Two and a half years later, at a **gala** celebration at its headquarters in Geneva, Switzerland, the World Health Organization (WHO) officially declared that the disease had finally been eradicated. The history of smallpox stretches back over 3,500 years. The peoples of the world owe a debt of **gratitude** to WHO.

How did a single agency of the United Nations, with very little money and only a limited, **meager** staff, **vanquish** this killer disease in only a decade (1967–1977)? The story of the eradication of smallpox might seem like a **hoax**, if it were not for the fact that it is entirely true. It is a tale of persistence, determination, and the imaginative handling of stiff challenges.

In 1959, smallpox was present in 59 countries, all of them located in Latin America, Asia, and Africa. Experts have estimated that there were about 10 million new cases annually. Approximately one third were fatal. In the previous century, the smallpox virus had caused the deaths of at least half a billion people. This staggering total may be compared with the roughly 150 million deaths caused by warfare during the same period. For many of those **meditating** a global attack on smallpox, their intentions and hopes must have seemed **wan** and weak indeed. No other disease had ever been eradicated worldwide before. Even the director-general of WHO suggested that such an **inflated** goal might lie beyond the pale.

Nevertheless, the WHO team, refusing to **heed** conventional wisdom, sallied forth in January 1967. It was led by the American epidemiologist D.A. Henderson. His study of smallpox and its characteristics convinced Henderson that the team could meet the challenge. First, the virus infected only humans, so there was no reservoir in nature. Each infected person exhibited a telltale rash. If victims were isolated immediately, they could be prevented from **transmitting** the virus to others. Perhaps most critical of all, experts had developed a stable, inexpensive, freeze-dried vaccine against smallpox. A single vaccination provided immunity for at least ten years.

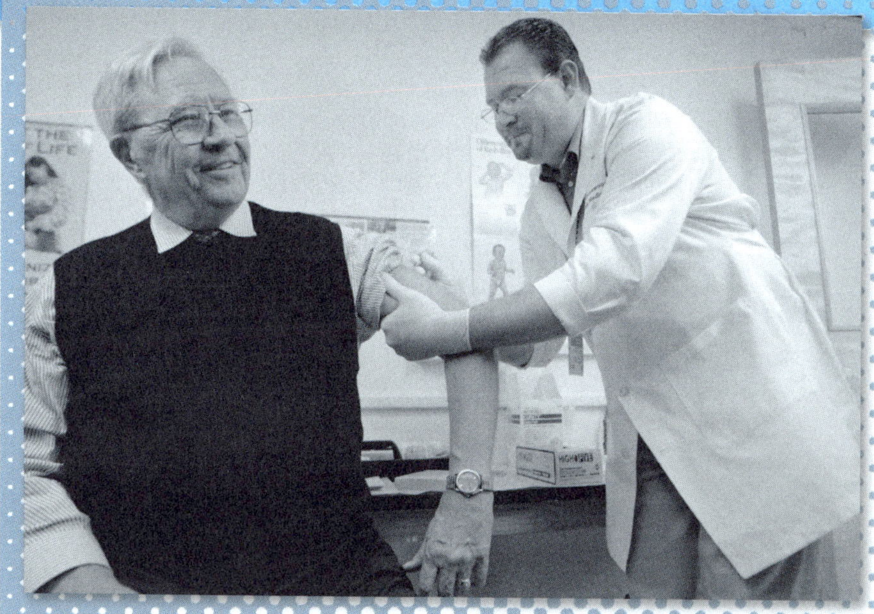

Dr. Henderson, leader of the WHO team against smallpox, receives his smallpox vaccine.

Despite these advantages, however, the WHO team had to confront formidable obstacles. Besides the skepticism of senior officials, the WHO staff members had to deal with roads in terrible disrepair, broken-down vehicles, war zones, and cultural opposition to vaccination. There were also geographical barriers. Large mountainous areas of Ethiopia, for instance, were inaccessible except for **pedestrians** or for travelers on mule-back. Communications were an ongoing problem. Drought, famine, and tides of refugees **oppressed** the team's efforts in some areas.

Yet somehow the team got it done. By 1980, a **cosmopolitan** and **impartial** killer with billions of victims around the world, including emperors and monarchs, was gone. Ramses V of Egypt, Joseph I of Austria, Louis XV of France: All their wealth and power did little to **elongate** their lives once they contracted smallpox. A small but intrepid team from WHO turned out to be the disease's most potent adversary.

This article appeared in section B, page B5 of the January 4, 2012, print edition of the Times.

WHO kept meticulous track of which areas were still being infected by smallpox.

Audio

For iWords and audio passages, snap the code, or go to vocabularyworkshop.com.

Definitions

Note the spelling, pronunciation, part(s) of speech, and definition(s) of each of the following words. Then write the appropriate form of the word in the blank spaces in the illustrative sentence(s) following. Finally, study the lists of synonyms and antonyms.

1. affliction (ə flik′ shən)
(*n.*) a physical ailment; a cause of pain or trouble, misfortune

Lupus is a dreadful **affliction** that kills nearly 5,000 people, mostly women, each year.

SYNONYMS: illness, woe, torment, anguish
ANTONYMS: blessing, boon, joy

2. akin (ə kin′)
(*adj.*) related by blood; having similar qualities or character

Our neighbors seem to have ideas **akin** to ours about landscaping.

SYNONYMS: kindred, like
ANTONYMS: unrelated, different

3. cosmopolitan (käz mə päl′ ə tən)
(*adj.*) found in most parts of the world; having many fields of interest; of worldwide scope; sophisticated

It does not surprise us that our cousin, a big-city dweller, has a **cosmopolitan** outlook.

SYNONYMS: global, international, polished
ANTONYMS: narrow, unsophisticated, provincial

4. elongate (i lôŋ′ gāt)
(*v.*) to grow in length, become longer; to extend the length of

The artist sought to **elongate** the trunk of the elephant in her caricature in order to amuse the children.

SYNONYMS: lengthen, stretch, protract
ANTONYMS: shorten, abbreviate, contract, curtail

5. gala (gā′ lə)
(*n.*) a public entertainment marking a special event, a festive occasion; (*adj.*) festive, showy

The inexperienced reporter had never seen such finery as was worn at the **gala**.

The President and the First Lady attended a **gala** performance at the Kennedy Center in Washington, D.C.

SYNONYMS: (*n.*) extravaganza, fête; (*adj.*) spectacular, grand

6. gaudy (gô′ dē)
(*adj.*) flashy, showy; not in good taste

The singer's **gaudy** outfit was totally inappropriate for a command performance before the queen.

SYNONYMS: loud, vulgar
ANTONYMS: restrained, quiet, sober, sedate

CCSS Vocabulary: 4.c., 4.d. (See pp. T14–15.)

7. gratitude
(grat′ ə tüd)

(*n.*) appreciation, thankfulness

Be sure to express your **gratitude** to your teacher for having written you a letter of recommendation.

SYNONYMS: thanks, gratefulness

8. heed
(hēd)

(*v.*) to pay careful attention to, notice; to be guided by; (*n.*) close attention or consideration

My parents are always telling me to **heed** their advice.

Pay no **heed** to old superstitions.

SYNONYMS: (*v.*) listen to, attend
ANTONYMS: (*v.*) ignore, disregard

9. hoax
(hōks)

(*n.*) an act intended to trick or deceive, a fraud; (*v.*) to trick, deceive

Their plan was to **hoax** people into believing that they had found a masterpiece.

SYNONYMS: (*n.*) deception, ruse, fake; (*v.*) dupe

10. impartial
(im pär′ shəl)

(*adj.*) just, unbiased, fair, not taking sides

The defense attorney knew it would be difficult to find **impartial** jurors to serve on such a celebrated case.

SYNONYMS: disinterested, neutral, objective
ANTONYMS: one-sided, prejudiced, biased, partial

11. impostor
(im päs′ tər)

(*n.*) a swindler, deceiver; one who uses a false name or character in order to cheat

After having posed as a doctor for five years, the man was finally exposed as an **impostor**.

SYNONYMS: cheat, trickster

12. inflate
(in flāt′)

(*v.*) to fill with air or gas; to swell or puff out; to make something appear larger than it is

On the evening before the big parade, we watched the workers **inflate** the huge balloons.

SYNONYMS: blow up, pump up, enlarge
ANTONYMS: deflate, flatten, diminish

13. meager
(mē′ gər)

(*adj.*) poor, scant, unsatisfactory; thin, slight

My brother, a high school student, is always complaining that he cannot live on the **meager** allowance our parents give him.

SYNONYMS: scanty, skimpy, sparse
ANTONYMS: ample, plentiful, abundant

CCSS Vocabulary: 4.c., 4.d. (See pp. T14–15.)

14. meditate (med′ ə tāt)

(*v.*) to think about deeply and quietly, reflect upon; to plan, intend

Many ancient philosophers would seek peaceful surroundings in which to ___meditate___ on the meaning of life.

SYNONYMS: ponder, contemplate, ruminate

15. nutritious (nü trish′ əs)

(*adj.*) nourishing, valuable and satisfying as food

My mother cooks ___nutritious___ meals to ensure that we have a balanced diet.

SYNONYMS: wholesome, healthful

16. oppress (ə pres′)

(*v.*) to govern or rule cruelly or unjustly; to weigh heavily upon

Too many dictators have used their absolute power to ___oppress___ the people they govern.

SYNONYMS: mistreat, persecute, grind underfoot
ANTONYMS: pamper, coddle, free, liberate

17. pedestrian (pə des′ trē ən)

(*n.*) one who goes on foot; (*adj.*) relating to walking; on foot; ordinary, unimaginative

The driver slammed on the brakes and swerved so as not to hit the ___pedestrian___.

Critics denounced his ___pedestrian___ literary style, but his book sales were high.

SYNONYMS: (*adj.*) commonplace, prosaic
ANTONYMS: (*n.*) driver, rider; (*adj.*) original, novel

18. transmit (tranz mit′)

(*v.*) to send on, pass along, send out

In the Old West, local sheriffs would ___transmit___ messages by telegraph to the marshal of the territory.

SYNONYMS: pass on, convey, relay, deliver

19. vanquish (vaŋ′ kwish)

(*v.*) to defeat in a battle or contest, overthrow; to overcome a feeling or condition

The general's goal was to ___vanquish___ his country's enemies.

SYNONYMS: beat, conquer; ANTONYMS: succumb to, yield to

20. wan (wän)

(*adj.*) unnaturally pale or sickly looking; lacking vitality; dim, faint; weak, ineffectual

The patient was so weak that all she could give the nurse was a ___wan___ smile.

SYNONYMS: ashen, pasty, bloodless, gaunt
ANTONYMS: rosy, ruddy, blooming, radiant

CCSS Vocabulary: 4.c., 4.d. (See pp. T14–15.)

Choosing the Right Word

*Select the **boldface** word that better completes each sentence. You might refer to the passage on pages 174–175 to see how most of these words are used in context.*

A sideshow barker in the 1930s tries to persuade an audience to see the exhibits.

1. Try as he might, the sideshow barker couldn't convince me that the "real live mermaid" inside the tent wasn't just a clever (**hoax, gala**).

2. After a lifetime of travel in dozens of countries all over the world, she is highly (**cosmopolitan, akin**) in her tastes and ideas.

3. Mere words cannot express our (**affliction, gratitude**) for your splendid services to our school.

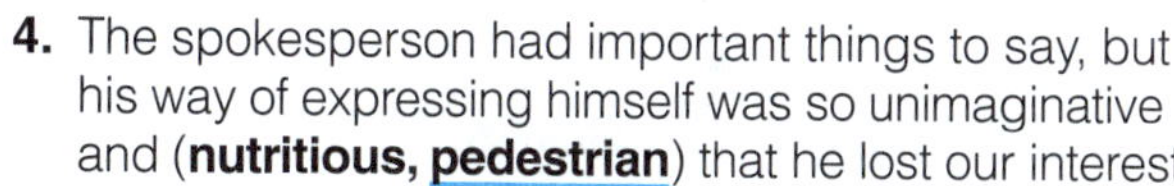

4. The spokesperson had important things to say, but his way of expressing himself was so unimaginative and (**nutritious, pedestrian**) that he lost our interest.

5. The speaker was greeted by a (**meager, gaudy**) round of applause, but before she left the stage, she had the audience cheering.

6. My mind and body were so (**oppressed, heeded**) by the stifling heat that afternoon that I couldn't do anything at all.

7. Such extravaganzas as the "Night of 100 Stars" are usually designed to be (**wan, gala**) charity benefits for worthy causes.

8. Each scholarship candidate was identified by a number so that the people doing the grading would be absolutely (**impartial, pedestrian**).

9. Is it necessary for you to go into the woods to (**inflate, meditate**) every time you have to make a routine decision?

10. By continuing to praise his extremely modest accomplishments, you are helping to (**inflate, transmit**) his already oversized ego.

11. He claimed to be a famous multimillionaire, but when he tried to borrow bus fare, we realized he was a(n) (**pedestrian, impostor**).

12. Education and compassion are the only weapons by which we will (**heed, vanquish**) prejudice and superstition once and for all.

13. The glowing review of my performance must be accurate, as critics do their best to be (**impartial, oppressive**) in their reviews.

14. The man's pathetically (**wan, elongated**) personality is matched only by the hopelessly bland and lifeless statements that issue from his mouth.

15. I'd describe nostalgia as a feeling more (**meager, akin**) to yearning than to grief.

CCSS Vocabulary: 4.d. (See pp. T14–15.)

16. Regardless of whether the light is green, (**cosmopolitans, pedestrians**) always have the right of way, according to the law.

17. We won the game because we kept our heads and paid no (**gratitude, heed**) to the insulting remarks made by our opponents.

18. (**Transmitting, Meditating**) every day not only lowers stress, but it also reduces the risk of a heart attack.

19. Is there any country in the world in which the terrible (**affliction, impostor**) of poverty has been entirely overcome?

20. In order to express my (**affliction, gratitude**) for all the help Mrs. Schroeder had given me, I made a donation to her favorite charity.

21. Have you ever noticed that as the sun sinks lower in the sky, shadows become (**elongated, cosmopolitan**)?

22. Shakespeare's advice about dressing—"rich, not (**gaudy, akin**)"—still holds true in today's sophisticated world.

23. We are so accustomed to television that we tend to forget what a marvel it is to (**oppress, transmit**) colored images from one place to another.

24. A viewing diet made up entirely of game shows may be entertaining, but it is not particularly (**meager, nutritious**), mentally speaking.

25. Had you (**heeded, vanquished**) my advice, you would be finished by now.

Synonyms

*Choose the word from this Unit that is the same or most nearly the same in meaning as the **boldface** word or expression in the phrase. Write that word on the line. Use a dictionary if necessary.*

1. would never wear such **garish** shoes — gaudy
2. had an **exaggerated** sense of her importance — inflated
3. attended a **dull** series of lectures — pedestrian
4. will **subdue** all foes of the realm — vanquish
5. ate a **healthy** meal before the game — nutritious
6. sharing **comparable** traits — akin
7. had light hair and a **pallid** complexion — wan
8. must **obey** the captain's command — heed
9. would **muse** on the meaning of the universe — meditate
10. was taken in by the **pretender** — impostor

CCSS Vocabulary: 5. (See pp. T14–15.)

Antonyms

*Choose the word from this Unit that is most nearly opposite in meaning to the **boldface** word or expression in the phrase. Write that word on the line. Use a dictionary if necessary.*

1. was **dissimilar to** the views she held ____akin (to)____
2. refuses to eat **toxic** foods ____nutritious____
3. was surprised by the **tasteful** furnishings in his home ____gaudy____
4. cooked with a **lavish** amount of spices ____meager____
5. a treat to meet an **honest person** ____impostor____

Completing the Sentence

From the words in this Unit, choose the one that best completes each of the following sentences. Write the correct word form in the space provided.

1. Modern medical science can do wonders for people suffering from various physical or emotional ____afflictions____.
2. "Although these two words are not related etymologically," the professor observed, "they are ____akin____ to each other in meaning."
3. The distraught mother's ____wan____ expression reflected her sense of anxiety over her lost child.
4. With a population made up of people from many different lands, New York City is one of the most ____cosmopolitan____ places in the world.
5. Most cities have now passed laws to discourage ____pedestrians____ from crossing against the light or jaywalking.
6. The big clown's ____gaudy____ costume was in sharp contrast to the simple white outfits worn by the trapeze artists.
7. Though the newspapers hailed the find as the "discovery of the century," it turned out to be nothing but an outrageous ____hoax____.
8. Unfortunately, the region cannot support a very large population because its natural resources are so ____meager____.
9. Junk food may look attractive and taste great, but it is by no means as ____nutritious____ as much plainer fare.
10. If you had only ____heeded____ my warnings, all this trouble could easily have been avoided.

11. An earthworm moves by first ___elongating___ and then contracting its wonderfully elastic body.

12. Modern technology has provided us with the computer, a device for collecting, sorting, and ___transmitting___ information quickly.

13. I don't expect you to throw yourself on your knees, but I wish you'd show a little ___gratitude___ for the things I've done for you.

14. Refusing to be ___oppressed___ by unjust laws, the American colonists rose in revolt against the British government.

15. Superstars and other celebrities are usually very much in evidence at ___gala___ events, such as opening night of a new Broadway show.

16. Because I am a very close friend of his, you cannot expect me to be totally ___impartial___ in judging your criticisms of him.

17. Have you ever tried to ___inflate___ a bicycle tire with one of those old-fashioned hand pumps?

18. Most of us are so busy with everyday concerns that we can find little or no time to ___meditate___ on the larger issues of life.

19. After beating off the enemy's initial assault, our brave troops delivered a series of crippling counterattacks that ___vanquished___ the foe.

20. The family lawyer proved that the young man claiming to be the missing heir was no more than a(n) ___impostor___.

Writing: Words in Action

Answers to both prompts will vary.

1. Look back at "Celebrating the Death of a Killer" (pages 174–175). Suppose that you were working for Dr. Henderson. You want to persuade others to join the World Health Organization team, travel to different countries, and assist with vaccinations. Write a persuasive editorial stating why this venture is a worthy cause. Use at least two details from the passage and three Unit words.

2. Vaccinations have virtually wiped out certain diseases, yet they have become a source of controversy in recent years. Some people believe that vaccinations can lead to harmful side effects. As a result, some parents are so concerned that they refuse to allow their children to receive required vaccinations. In a brief essay, argue in favor of requiring vaccinations or of exercising the right to refuse them. Consider what might be some of the consequences of not vaccinating children. Support your opinion with specific examples, observations, and the reading (refer to pages 174–175). Write at least three paragraphs, and use three or more words from this Unit.

Writing prompt #2 is modeled on that of standardized tests.

 CCSS Vocabulary: 6; Writing: 1.c., 2.d., 3.d., 4. (See pp. T14–15.)

Vocabulary in Context: Informational Text for Unit 14 is available online at **vocabularyworkshop.com**.

Vocabulary in Context

Literary Text

The following excerpts are from Andersen's Fairy Tales *by Hans Christian Andersen. Some of the words you have studied in this Unit appear in* **boldface** *type. Complete each statement below the excerpt by circling the letter of the correct answer.*

1. The learned man from the cold lands . . . sat in a glowing oven; it took effect on him, he became quite **meager**—even his shadow shrunk in, for the sun had also an effect on it. ("The Shadow")

Someone who becomes **meager** is

a. ancient **c.** wealthy
b. feeble **d.** robust

2. "You are so clever," said the Reindeer. . . . "Will you give the little maiden a potion, that she may possess the strength of twelve men, and **vanquish** the Snow Queen?" ("The Snow Queen")

To **vanquish** is to

a. weaken **c.** torment
b. support **d.** conquer

"The Snow Queen" is one of Hans Christian Andersen's longest fairy tales.

3. "How naughty a boy Cupid is! I will tell all children about him, that they may take care and not play with him."

And all good children to whom he related this story, took great **heed** of this naughty Cupid. ("The Naughty Boy")

Whenever people take **heed** of a story, they

a. ignore it **c.** memorize it
b. listen to it **d.** recite it

4. One of the travelers kept watch while the others slept. . . . How close it was in the chamber! The heat **oppressive** to suffocation. ("The Best That the Galoshes Gave")

Something that is **oppressive** is NOT

a. angry **c.** unfair
b. hot **d.** mild

5. [H]e went to the crafty **impostors**, who, as soon as they were aware of the Emperor's approach, went on working more diligently than ever; although they still did not pass a single thread through the looms. ("The Emperor's New Clothes")

Impostors are people who are

a. devious **c.** honest
b. modest **d.** attentive

Snap the code, or go to **vocabularyworkshop.com**

CCSS Vocabulary: 4.d.; Reading (Literature): 4. (See pp. T14–15.)

UNIT 15

Note that not all of the 20 Unit words are used in this passage. *Mirth*, *officiate*, *partial*, *patronize*, and *sagacious* are not included.

*Read the following passage, taking note of the **boldface** words and their contexts. These words are among those you will be studying in Unit 15. As you complete the exercises in this Unit, it may help to refer to the way the words are used below.*

CCSS Vocabulary: 4; Reading (Informational Text): 4, 6. (See pp. T14–15.)

A Brief History of Gold

<Informational Essay>

Has there ever been a more precious commodity than gold? One of the rarest metals in the world, gold has been treasured, **hoarded**, sought after, and **feuded** over. It was highly prized long before the concept of exchanging money began. A ruler's wealth and power **coincided** with how much gold he had: More gold equaled more power. Even now, some view owning gold as the ultimate in financial security.

Recent scientific research suggests that gold and other metals were transported to the earth's surface by meteors billions of years ago (though there is not yet **authoritative** evidence to confirm this theory). Gold is found in the form of dust, grains, flakes, or nuggets. Surprisingly, gold is also found in seawater. Extracting it from water is expensive. Entrepreneurs attempting to recover gold from the sea would likely go **bankrupt**.

The mining of gold began many thousands of years ago. Some of the oldest gold artifacts have been unearthed in the Varna Necropolis. This ancient burial site is near Varna, Bulgaria. It contained an astounding cache of treasures. Skilled goldsmiths of that era hammered gold into exquisite pieces, including solid-gold masks, goblets, and jewelry.

Prospectors rest by a sluice box in California during the gold rush.

Solid gold Thracian king's mask from the 5th century BCE

The world's oldest-known geological map, the Turin papyrus map (created circa 1150 BCE or Before the Common Era), indicates where the early Egyptians excavated their gold mines. Egyptians were so enamored of gold that they believed it to be a physical manifestation of the sun and the "flesh of the gods." Their pharaohs' coffins were made out of solid gold. Because of its beauty and indestructible nature, it was valued by numerous other early civilizations, from the ancient Mediterranean civilizations of the Minoans and Etruscans to the ancient American Aztecs and Incas. Gold was also used in religious **rites**. The **legacy** of age-old folk and fairy tales from around the world is full of wishes and dreams for gold.

But how did gold change from an object of beauty and worship to a **legitimate**, official form of currency? Early on, people used the barter system to get most goods and services they needed. When **haggling** proved less than **harmonious**, people moved on to primitive forms of payment such as shells, stones, beads, and fur. This system evolved over time, and many societies switched to using pieces of gold. The pieces were marked with weight and then turned into coins. The first gold coins were minted around 640 BCE in the ancient Roman province of Lydia. The Greeks also used gold coins. Goldsmith Ephraim Brasher created the first United States gold coin in 1784.

Man's greed for gold inspired European explorations and violent conquests in Central and South America. **Despots** and tyrants on all sides had "gold fever," **clamoring** loudly for more and more riches. Fortunes were quickly made, and even more quickly lost.

The discovery of gold around the world led to gold rushes, including the famous California gold rush of the 1840s. The wild outpost of Sutter's Mill attracted more than 40,000 **hardy** prospectors. Few found the mother lode. Those who did were **indisposed** to share it. Many failed prospectors returned home **cynical**, sadder, and wiser, no doubt appreciating the saying, "Better an ounce of happiness than a pound of gold."

Audio

For iWords and audio passages, snap the code, or go to vocabularyworkshop.com.

Definitions

Note the spelling, pronunciation, part(s) of speech, and definition(s) of each of the following words. Then write the appropriate form of the word in the blank spaces in the illustrative sentence(s) following. Finally, study the lists of synonyms and antonyms.

1. authoritative
(ə thär′ ə tā tiv)

(*adj.*) official, coming from a source that calls for obedience or belief; dictatorial

A dictionary is an __authoritative__ source for the spelling, pronunciation, and definition of words in a language.

SYNONYMS: reliable, authoritarian; ANTONYMS: unofficial, unreliable

2. bankrupt
(baŋk′ rəpt)

(*adj.*) in a state of financial ruin; (*v.*) to ruin financially; (*n.*) one who has been ruined financially

The __bankrupt__ company was closing its doors for the last time.

Another bad sales year will __bankrupt__ the failing firm.

A __bankrupt__ will have trouble getting credit.

SYNONYMS: (*adj.*) flat broke, insolvent
ANTONYMS: (*adj.*) financially sound, solvent

3. clamor
(klam′ ər)

(*n.*) a public outcry; any loud and continued noise; (*v.*) to call for by loud, continued outcries

The coal miners began to __clamor__ for better working conditions in the mine.

The __clamor__ of the trumpets was piercing.

SYNONYMS: (*n.*) uproar, din, racket; (*v.*) cry out for

4. coincide
(kō in sīd′)

(*v.*) to be in full agreement; to be the same in nature, character, or function; to happen at the same time

Our political beliefs would __coincide__ with theirs on the issues of term limits and tax reform.

SYNONYMS: concur, match

5. cynical
(sin′ ə kəl)

(*adj.*) inclined to believe the worst of people; bitterly mocking or sneering

The radio personality's __cynical__ attitude made it difficult for the station manager to find advertisers.

SYNONYMS: skeptical, sarcastic, contemptuous
ANTONYMS: hopeful, optimistic

6. despot
(des′ pət)

(*n.*) a ruler who oppresses his or her subjects, a tyrant

That film director is known for acting like a __despot__ on the movie set.

SYNONYMS: dictator, autocrat, strongman

CCSS Vocabulary: 4.c., 4.d. (See pp. T14–15.)

7. feud
(fyüd)

(*n.*) a bitter, long-term quarrel; (*v.*) to fight or quarrel with

A senseless ___feud___ caused the division between the two clans.

What originally caused the clans to ___feud___ has long been forgotten.

SYNONYMS: (*n.*) grudge, vendetta
ANTONYMS: (*n.*) pact, agreement, harmony, concord

8. haggle
(hag′ əl)

(*v.*) to argue in a petty way, especially about a price

Let's not ___haggle___ over the price of admission until we finish writing the play!

SYNONYMS: bargain with, wrangle

9. hardy
(här′ dē)

(*adj.*) able to bear up under difficult conditions or harsh treatment; brave and tough

The saguaro is a ___hardy___ variety of the cactus family.

SYNONYMS: rugged, sturdy, resolute, stalwart
ANTONYMS: feeble, weak

10. harmonious
(här mō′ nē əs)

(*adj.*) able to get along together well; combining different elements that blend pleasingly; melodious

The two companies' negotiations were ___harmonious___ and resulted in a merger.

SYNONYMS: agreeable, compatible, tuneful
ANTONYMS: harsh, grating, discordant

11. hoard
(hôrd)

(*v.*) to store up, save; (*n.*) a hidden store or supply

Where did the miser keep his ___hoard___ of money?

SYNONYMS: (*v.*) amass, reserve, cache
ANTONYMS: (*v.*) waste, throw away, squander

12. indisposed
(in dis pōzd′)

(*adj., part.*) slightly ill; disinclined to do something

My sister was ___indisposed___ with a bad head cold.

SYNONYMS: (*adj.*) unwell, reluctant
ANTONYMS: (*adj.*) healthy, willing, eager

13. legacy
(leg′ ə sē)

(*n.*) an inheritance; something handed down from an ancestor or from the past

The ___legacy___ from her grandmother made her a wealthy woman.

SYNONYMS: bequest, heritage

CCSS Vocabulary: 4.c., 4.d. (See pp. T14–15.)

14. legitimate (lə jit′ ə mət)

(*adj.*) lawful, rightful; reasonable, justifiable

There is a new committee that rules on whether complaints are **legitimate**.

SYNONYMS: legal, right, proper, genuine
ANTONYMS: unlawful, illegal, improper, unauthorized

15. mirth (mərth)

(*n.*) merry fun, gaiety; laughter

The children were filled with **mirth** as they exited the Fun House.

SYNONYMS: merriment, glee
ANTONYMS: gloom, sorrow

16. officiate (ə fish′ ē āt)

(*v.*) to perform the duties of an office; to conduct a religious ceremony; to referee

Will a judge **officiate** at the ceremony?

SYNONYMS: chair, emcee, moderate

17. partial (pär′ shəl)

(*adj.*) not complete; favoring one side over another; showing a strong liking for someone or something

To say that she is **partial** to sweets would be an understatement.

SYNONYMS: biased, prejudiced, fond of
ANTONYMS: complete, fair, just, unbiased

18. patronize (pa′ trə nīz)

(*v.*) to give one's business to regularly as a customer; to support, provide financial help; to treat someone as an inferior while making a show of being kind or gracious

We like to **patronize** the family-owned stores in the neighborhood.

SYNONYMS: do business with, deal with, trade with
ANTONYMS: boycott, refuse to deal with

19. rite (rīt)

(*n.*) a ceremony; the customary form of a ceremony; any formal custom or practice

A minister will perform the marriage **rites**.

SYNONYMS: observance, liturgy

20. sagacious (sə gā′ shəs)

(*adj.*) shrewd; wise in a keen, practical way

History has shown that **sagacious** leaders exercise tolerance and fairness, along with good judgment.

SYNONYMS: smart, astute
ANTONYMS: silly, ill-advised, dopey

CCSS Vocabulary: 4.c., 4.d. (See pp. T14–15.)

Choosing the Right Word

*Select the **boldface** word that better completes each sentence. You might refer to the passage on pages 184–185 to see how most of these words are used in context.*

1. The city is hosting a conference to celebrate Mark Twain's (**legacy, feud**) and discuss his landmark novels and witty essays.
2. In the period ahead, there may be shortages of some foodstuffs, but we will only make things worse if we resort to (**patronizing, hoarding**).
3. Life cannot be all happiness; we must expect tears as well as (**legacies, mirth**).
4. The (**clamor, feud**) that the two sides of the family have been waging for years is about whether chili should be made with beans.
5. Learning to drive, graduating from high school, and entering college or the job market are all part of a teenager's (**rites, hoards**) of passage.

Mark Twain's most famous creations are the characters Tom Sawyer and Huck Finn.

6. We cannot accept the idea that capital and labor must constantly (**feud, coincide**) with each other.
7. One reason the coach is so popular is that he is firm and even tough with his players but never acts like a (**bankrupt, despot**).
8. I was (**hardy, indisposed**) to accept the halfhearted invitation that reached me only a day before the party.
9. During the winter, there are always a few (**hardy, partial**) souls who take a dip in the icy waters off Atlantic Beach.
10. No matter how efficient the new chairperson may be, the meeting will not proceed (**authoritatively, harmoniously**) unless the members cooperate.
11. The jury was impressed by the fact that the testimony of two witnesses who were complete strangers (**coincided, clamored**) in every detail.
12. Although Aunt Helen serves delicious pumpkin pie on Thanksgiving, I must say that I am (**partial, harmonious**) to apple pie.
13. A party that cannot offer new ideas to deal with the pressing problems of the day must be considered politically (**legitimate, bankrupt**).
14. Why (**haggle, officiate**) over minor details when we are in agreement overall?
15. If you're looking for a witty, charming personality to (**officiate, coincide**) at the awards dinner, need I say that I'm available?

CCSS Vocabulary: 4.d. (See pp. T14–15.)

16. Your healthy body is a (**legacy, rite**) you have received from your parents, and you should strive to protect it from harmful influences.

17. Did you know that our play-off game (**officiates, coincides**) with spring break, and the players on the roster can't be changed?

18. We will give careful attention to (**cynical, legitimate**) complaints, but we will not be influenced by silly faultfinding.

19. The (**harmonious, authoritative**) tone in which she gave the order left no doubt in anyone's mind that she expected full obedience.

20. Isn't it (**cynical, feuding**) of you to ask other people to support a candidate in whom you yourself have no confidence?

21. A good sports official pays no attention to the (**clamor, mirth**) of the crowd when a decision goes against the home team.

22. Each answer will be considered either right or wrong; no (**sagacious, partial**) credit will be given.

23. I am annoyed by the (**haggling, patronizing**) way in which they keep reminding me "how a well-bred person behaves."

24. She may give the impression of being simple and uncomplicated, but we have found her to be unusually (**sagacious, indisposed**) in judging people.

25. In the winter, Alice grows kale, as it is such a (**hardy, sagacious**) vegetable.

Synonyms

*Choose the word from this Unit that is the same or most nearly the same in meaning as the **boldface** word or expression in the phrase. Write that word on the line. Use a dictionary if necessary.*

1. broadcast **incomplete** details of the tragedy — partial
2. will undergo a **ritual** of initiation — rite
3. was behaving in a highly **bossy** manner — authoritative
4. would **quibble** over a penny — haggle
5. asked a substitute to **preside** — officiate
6. was **ailing** with a headache — indisposed
7. proved to be a **clever** ruler — sagacious
8. was filled with joy and **cheerfulness** — mirth
9. would **shop at** the local businesses — patronize
10. had taken sides in the bitter **dispute** — feud

CCSS Vocabulary: 5. (See pp. T14–15.)

The synonyms and antonyms here do not appear on the Definitions page.

Antonyms

*Choose the word from this Unit that is most nearly opposite in meaning to the **boldface** word or expression in the phrase. Write that word on the line. Use a dictionary if necessary.*

1. someone who is **respectful** — patronizing
2. would **follow along** during the religious services — officiate
3. was **foolish** in the choices she made — sagacious
4. a situation that is one of **sadness** — mirth
5. submitted the **entire** report — partial

Completing the Sentence

From the words in this Unit, choose the one that best completes each of the following sentences. Write the correct word form in the space provided.

1. When you say that "everyone is out to take advantage of everyone else," I think you're being much too __cynical__.

2. The students were urged to __patronize__ the local merchants who advertised in the school paper.

3. About five minutes before feeding time, all the babies in the nursery start to __clamor__ for their bottles.

4. The referee who __officiates__ at a hockey game needs the stamina to keep up with the players and the patience to put up with them.

5. I think your price for the tennis racket is too high, but as I'm in no mood to __haggle__ with you, I'll take it.

6. Where can I get a(n) __authoritative__ estimate of how the population of the United States is likely to change in the years ahead?

7. We must be prepared to defend the __legacy__ of freedom that we have inherited from earlier generations of Americans.

8. My aunt called to say that she would not be able to visit us today because she was __indisposed__ with an asthma attack.

9. Historians are still examining the deadly __feud__ that arose between the Hatfield and McCoy families more than 100 years ago.

10. Nothing will be accomplished unless the members of the committee work together in a(n) __harmonious__ fashion.

CCSS Vocabulary: 4.a., 5. (See pp. T14–15.)

11. Is it true that squirrels ___hoard___ nuts and other foods that they can use during the winter?

12. Although she had no previous experience as a treasurer, she showed herself to be highly ___sagacious___ in the way she handled money.

13. The pioneers who settled the West were ___hardy___ people who could cope with difficulties and dangers of all kinds.

14. Our supervisor became extremely unpopular with us because he acted like a(n) ___despot___ toward everyone in the department.

15. True, business has been poor, but we are covering our expenses and can assure you that there's no danger of our going ___bankrupt___.

16. Your program for cleaning up the neighborhood ___coincides___ with ours, so why don't we work together?

17. The fact that the baseball season is opening today is certainly not a(n) ___legitimate___ excuse for being absent from school.

18. I am making only a(n) ___partial___ payment at the present time and will pay off the balance in installments.

19. I like a good laugh as much as anyone, but I realized that such a solemn ceremony was not the time for ___mirth___.

20. The pagan religions of ancient times revolved around the performance of various ___rites___ designed to ensure the fertility of the land.

Writing: Words in Action

Answers to both prompts will vary.

1. Look back at "A Brief History of Gold" (pages 184–185). Suppose that people used gold instead of paper money as currency today. People's wealth would actually be measured by their "weight in gold." Do you think people would be more conscientious about spending and saving if this were the case? Write a persuasive essay in which you support your opinion, using at least two details from the passage and three Unit words.

2. *"All that glitters is not gold."—William Shakespeare*

   Shakespeare's famous quotation from *The Merchant of Venice* suggests that some things we desire may not actually be valuable. In a brief essay, state whether you agree with Shakespeare on this point. Support your ideas with specific examples, observations, your studies, personal experiences, or the reading (refer to pages 184–185). Write at least three paragraphs, and use three or more words from this Unit.

Writing prompt #2 is modeled on that of standardized tests.

CCSS Vocabulary: 6; Writing: 1.c., 2.d., 3.d., 4. (See pp. T14–15.)

Vocabulary in Context: Informational Text for Unit 15 is available online at **vocabularyworkshop.com**.

Vocabulary in Context

Literary Text

The following excerpts are from The Hound of the Baskervilles *and* The Adventures of Sherlock Holmes *by Sir Arthur Conan Doyle. Some of the words you have studied in this Unit appear in* **boldface** *type. Complete each statement below the excerpt by circling the letter of the correct answer.*

1. Some, too, have baffled his analytical skill, and would be, as narratives, beginnings without an ending, while others have been but **partially** cleared up, and have their explanations founded rather upon conjecture and surmise than on that absolute logical proof which was so dear to him. ("The Five Orange Pips")

If something is **partially** resolved, it is done

a. openly **c.** rationally
b. incompletely **d.** cautiously

2. He rushes to some secret **hoard**, where he has accumulated the fruits of his beggary, and he stuffs all the coins upon which he can lay his hands into the pockets to make sure of the coat's sinking. ("The Man with the Twisted Lip")

A **hoard** is a

a. friend **c.** stockpile
b. cellar **d.** dwelling

3. His plans were suddenly brought to a head by his knowledge that Sir Charles was about to leave the Hall on the advice of Dr. Mortimer, with whose opinion he himself pretended to **coincide**. (*The Hound of the Baskervilles*)

To **coincide** with others is to

a. challenge them **c.** be fond of them
b. avoid them **d.** agree with them

In the 1959 film adaptation of *The Hound of the Baskervilles*, Peter Cushing plays Sherlock Holmes.

4. "I hope," said Dr. Mortimer, "that you do not look with suspicious eyes upon everyone who received a **legacy** from Sir Charles, for I also had a thousand pounds left to me." (*The Hound of the Baskervilles*)

A **legacy** is a(n)

a. misgiving **c.** invitation
b. inheritance **d.** souvenir

5. "I have cross-examined these men . . . who all tell the same story of this dreadful apparition . . . I assure you that there is a reign of terror in the district, and that it is a **hardy** man who will cross the moor at night." (*The Hound of the Baskervilles*)

Someone who is **hardy** is definitely NOT

a. frail **c.** courageous
b. pleasant **d.** stubborn

Snap the code, or go to **vocabularyworkshop.com**

Vocabulary for Comprehension

*Read the following passage in which some of the words you have studied in Units 13–15 appear in **boldface** type. Then answer the questions on page 195.*

This passage discusses Jim Thorpe (1888–1953), one of America's greatest and most versatile athletes.

(Line)

Voted the greatest male athlete of the first half of the twentieth century by the Associated Press in 1950, Jim Thorpe received **massive** praise and criticism in his lifetime. Thorpe was born in Indian Territory (now Oklahoma) in 1888. In 1904, Thorpe was sent to the Carlisle Indian School in Pennsylvania, where his astounding athletic ability was first discovered by Glenn S. "Pop" Warner, the legendary coach of the school. When the coach spotted Thorpe high-jumping six feet, he offered him a place on the track team, where he instantly became a star. He also became a football hero. In fact, in one of his best games, he helped the Carlisle football team **vanquish** its rival Harvard by booting four field goals. For his efforts on the football field, he was named to the All-American team.

Jim Thorpe left Carlisle in 1909 to play baseball for two seasons in the East Carolina minor league, a decision that would affect his whole life. His greatest achievement would come, however, in the 1912 Olympic Games in Stockholm, Sweden. There, he would win two gold medals—in the pentathlon and the decathlon. "Sir, you are the greatest athlete in the world," said King Gustav V of Sweden, who was **officiating** at the games. Yet as events would show, Thorpe's triumph would be only a **partial** victory.

Shortly after the Olympic games were held, a sportswriter who had seen Thorpe play baseball in the minor leagues exposed him as a professional athlete, making him ineligible for Olympic competition. The Amateur Athletic Union stripped Thorpe of his Olympic records and medals in 1913, casting a **pall** over his achievements.

Thorpe joined the baseball New York Giants in that same year. The versatile Thorpe played professionally in both baseball and football. He was named the first commissioner of the new National Football League in 1920.

For his achievements in football, he was inducted into the College and Pro Football Halls of Fame. In 1982, nearly 30 years after his death, the International Olympic Committee restored Thorpe's medals, thereby preserving his status as one of the world's greatest athletes.

CCSS Vocabulary: 4.a.; Reading (Informational Text): 2, 4, 6. (See pp. T14–15.)

1. Which of the following would make the best title for this passage?
   a. "Famous Native Americans"
   b. "Pop Warner and Jim Thorpe"
   c. "The Olympic Games of 1912"
   (d.) "The Athletic Career of Jim Thorpe"
   e. "Great Male Athletes of the Twentieth Century"

2. The meaning of **massive** (line 4) is
   (a.) great
   b. reliable
   c. enthusiastic
   d. widespread
   e. unjustified

3. **Vanquish** (line 20) most nearly means
   a. challenge
   (b.) conquer
   c. welcome
   d. persecute
   e. succumb to

4. The criticism of Thorpe mentioned in line 5 had to do with
   a. his personal life
   b. his conduct as a football commissioner
   c. his professional behavior as a baseball player
   d. his professional behavior as a football player
   (e.) his professional career before the 1912 Olympic Games

5. **Officiating** (line 36) is best defined as
   a. observing
   b. competing
   c. announcing
   (d.) presiding
   e. voting

6. **Partial** (line 38) most nearly means
   a. small
   b. instant
   c. elusive
   d. fond of
   (e.) incomplete

7. Thorpe's athletic ability was first recognized when he was
   a. a professional football player
   b. a minor league baseball player
   (c.) a child at the Carlisle Indian School
   d. a player for the New York Giants
   e. a gold medal winner

8. From lines 39–48, you can infer that
   (a.) Olympic competitors had to be amateur athletes
   b. Olympic competitors had to be professional athletes
   c. Thorpe had a spectacular career in the minor leagues
   d. Thorpe did not know about the Olympic committee's rules
   e. sportswriters were biased against Thorpe

9. **Pall** (line 47) is best defined as
   a. bore
   b. light
   (c.) shadow
   d. scandal
   e. fascination

10. Thorpe was all of these EXCEPT
    a. a member of the Football Hall of Fame
    (b.) the most valuable player in the 1912 World Series
    c. the winner of the decathlon in the 1912 Olympics
    d. the winner of the pentathlon in the 1912 Olympics
    e. a commissioner of the National Football League

11. The author organized the information
    (a.) in chronological order
    b. in spatial order
    c. using cause-effect
    d. in order of importance
    e. using comparison-contrast

12. The author's tone is best described as
    a. critical
    (b.) respectful
    c. indifferent
    d. skeptical
    e. enthusiastic

C CCSS Vocabulary: 4.a.; Reading (Informational Text): 2, 4, 6. (See pp. T14–15.)

Two-Word Completions

Select the pair of words that best completes the meaning of each of the following sentences.

1. "I hate to ______________ over minor details," the fussy little prince remarked to the court magician. "But I'm hungry, and bouquets of fake flowers aren't particularly ______________. Do you have any carrot sticks?"
   a. haggle . . . nutritious
   b. meditate . . . massive
   c. grovel . . . pedestrian
   d. clamor . . . gaudy

2. "If we are to win this important election," the senator said, "we must put aside our private ______________ and present a united front. Those who ______________ this advice will be helping our cause."
   a. afflictions . . . diminish
   b. legacies . . . revere
   c. handicrafts . . . countenance
   d. feuds . . . heed

3. Betty's grandfather was a ______________ young man who traveled alone on a ship from Ireland to the United States. Although he worked years for ______________ wages, he eventually saved up enough money to buy a farm and start a family.
   a. cynical . . . stodgy
   b. hilarious . . . bankrupt
   c. hardy . . . meager
   d. wan . . . inflated

4. The tragic news of our friend's death in an automobile accident cast a(n) ______________ of gloom over our little gathering that evening and turned our ______________ to tears.
   a. affliction . . . rite
   b. clamor . . . agitation
   c. saga . . . countenance
   d. pall . . . mirth

5. "I'm happy to shop at any establishment that is owned by a ______________ businessperson," Mom declared. "But I absolutely refuse to ______________ a store that is run by people who are out to cheat me."
   a. despotic . . . bankrupt
   b. reputable . . . patronize
   c. cosmopolitan . . . foster
   d. legitimate . . . transmit

6. The referees who ______________ at hockey games are like judges presiding over trials. For that reason, they and their assistants must be as ______________ as possible. If they show any favoritism in their calls, they'll hear about it from the fans.
   a. officiate . . . impartial
   b. agitate . . . authoritative
   c. clamor . . . cosmopolitan
   d. haggle . . . partial

7. "You certainly don't have to ______________ your money the way a miser would," I observed, "but if you continue to throw it around quite so freely, you'll soon be ______________."
   a. transmit . . . stodgy
   b. hoard . . . bankrupt
   c. revere . . . pedestrian
   d. foster . . . indisposed

 CCSS Vocabulary: 4.a. (See pp. T14–15.)

In the passage "Celebrating the Death of a Killer" (see pages 174–175), the writer states that the World Health Organization's goal to eradicate smallpox was considered by many to be "beyond the pale."

"Beyond the pale" is an idiom that means the idea was so extreme, it was unacceptable to many people. An **idiom** is an expression that does not make sense if you define it literally. Idioms work their way into our daily language. The best way to learn idioms is to understand the context in which they are used.

Choosing the Right Idiom

*Read each sentence. Use context clues to figure out the meaning of each idiom in **boldface** print. Then write the letter of the definition for the idiom in the sentence.*

1. If Mark thinks I will lend him money, he's **barking up the wrong tree**. ___h___
2. John will do anything for Brenda **at the drop of a hat**. ___a___
3. With the flu going around, students at our school are **dropping like flies**. ___j___
4. With increased gas and food prices, we must **tighten our belts** around here. ___c___
5. "Quit **horsing around** before you knock over the display!" Maya said. ___d___
6. When Dana takes over Jessica's job, she will have some pretty **big shoes to fill**. ___f___
7. Your stationary bike is a **white elephant** that sits in the garage collecting dust. ___b___
8. I'm not sure why Steve called this meeting, but I think he has **something up his sleeve**. ___e___
9. Whenever Carlos is out of town, Sheila acts as if she is **top dog**. ___i___
10. Did you hear that Jack **threw his hat into the ring** and decided to run for class president? ___g___

a. promptly or immediately

b. possession that cost too much but has little value

c. spend less money than usual

d. playing rowdily or acting silly

e. a secret plan or scheme

f. huge expectations in taking the place of another

g. announced a run for office

h. looking for something in the wrong place

i. the person who is in charge

j. becoming ill or dying in large numbers

CCSS Vocabulary: 5.a. (See pp. T14–15.)

Writing with Idioms

Find the meaning of each idiom. (Use a dictionary if necessary.) Then write a sentence for each idiom. **Answers will vary.**

1. take a catnap **Sample answer: I feel so sleepy after lunch that I wish I could just take a catnap at my desk.**

2. lose one's shirt

3. wag the dog

4. buckle down

5. roll up your sleeves

6. the lion's share

7. a night owl

8. on a shoestring

9. the shoe's on the other foot

10. a fat cat

11. ride on someone's coattails

12. bright-eyed and bushy-tailed

 CCSS Vocabulary: 5. (See pp. T14–15.)

Denotation and Connotation

The dictionary meaning of a word is its **denotation**. This meaning is literal and has a neutral tone.

Words also have emotional associations, or **connotations**. These associations can be positive or negative.

Consider these synonyms for the neutral word *worldly*.

urbane *cosmopolitan* *cultured* *slick*

Urbane, cosmopolitan, and *cultured* are words with a positive connotation, but *slick* has a negative connotation.

> **Think:** It is a compliment to be considered urbane, cosmopolitan, or cultured because those words imply maturity and sophistication. It is an insult to be considered slick, as that word suggests a surface glossiness and superficiality.

Look at these examples of words that are similar in denotation but have different connotations.

NEUTRAL	POSITIVE	NEGATIVE
store	**save**	**hoard**
noise	**excitement**	**clamor**
maternal	**caring**	**overprotective**

It is important for readers and writers to know the connotations of words, since a single word can alter the emotional tone of a sentence. For example, if a character in a story *closes* a door, the action seems neutral, and there is no reason to question the character's motivations. But if a character *secures* a door, readers might infer that the character is frightened, and they might wonder what danger is looming.

Shades of Meaning

Write a plus sign (+) in the box if the word has a positive connotation. Write a minus sign (–) if the word has a negative connotation. Put a zero (0) if the word is neutral.

1. chronological [0]	**2.** hilarious [+]	**3.** wan [–]	**4.** coincide [0]
5. grovel [–]	**6.** pedestrian [0]	**7.** handicraft [0]	**8.** hoax [–]
9. gratitude [+]	**10.** stodgy [–]	**11.** ignite [–]	**12.** gala [+]
13. despot [–]	**14.** rite [0]	**15.** nutritious [+]	**16.** feud [–]

CCSS Vocabulary: 5.c. (See pp. T14–15.)

Expressing the Connotation

Read each sentence. Select the word in parentheses that better expresses the connotation (positive, negative, or neutral) given at the beginning of the sentence.

negative 1. A (**strong, massive**) snowstorm caused hundreds of airline delays.

neutral 2. Rather than get married by a city official, some people go to Las Vegas and have an Elvis impersonator (**officiate, perform**) the ceremony.

positive 3. In some markets, customers are encouraged to (**negotiate, haggle**) for the best price.

negative 4. You know things must be bad when Joyce, the optimist, views the news in a (**cynical, doubtful**) light.

neutral 5. Lou's interest in the new girl began to (**lessen, pall**) when he realized she was a snob.

negative 6. "We will (**vanquish, tame**) this corrupt regime!" the protestors cried from the tower.

positive 7. I love to watch the awards shows on television and see the (**gaudy, colorful**) outfits the actors wear.

positive 8. The announcement that the school was in lock-down caused (**concern, agitation**) among the students.

Challenge: Using Connotation

Choose vocabulary words from Units 13–15 to replace the highlighted words in the sentences below. Then explain how the connotation of the replacement word changes the tone of the sentence. Answers will vary.

impostor	**oppressed**	**blurted**
cosmopolitan	**despot**	**indisposed**

1. The announcement read: "Madame Laurent sends her regrets. She will not be able to attend this evening's gala, as she is presently **nauseated** indisposed."
Sample response: *Indisposed* makes the tone of the sentence more formal, less explicit, and more appropriate to the context of the announcement.

2. Everyone at dinner was stunned when my sister **said** blurted that she was quitting her job to join a rock band.
Sample response: *Blurted* makes the action sound more forceful, suggesting that the sister's news was abrupt and even shocking to the listeners.

3. I'm reading a novel about a medieval **monarch** despot who forcibly gained control of the throne and imprisoned those who did not accept his rule.
Sample response: *Despot* creates a more negative tone, suggesting that the ruler was cruel and oppressive.

 CCSS Vocabulary: 5, 5.c. (See pp. T14–15.)

Classical Roots

rupt—to break

This Latin root appears in **bankrupt** (page 186). Literally, the word means "bank broken"—that is, "unable to pay one's debts." It also means "one who is unable to pay his or her debts" or "to ruin financially and thus make unable to pay debts." Some other words based on the same root are listed below.

abrupt	**disruptive**	**incorruptible**	**irruption**
corrupt	**erupt**	**interrupt**	**rupture**

From the list of words above, choose the one that corresponds to each of the brief definitions below. Write the word in the blank space in the illustrative sentence below the definition. Use a dictionary if necessary.

1. not open to immoral behavior, honest; unbribable

He remained a(n) ____incorruptible____ public official despite the many attempts of the crime boss to bribe him.

2. a breaking or bursting in; a violent invasion

The ____irruption____ of the Goths into Roman territory led to the collapse of the Roman Empire.

3. sudden, short, blunt; very steep

The car made a(n) ____abrupt____ stop at the crosswalk to avoid hitting the pedestrian.

4. causing disorder or turmoil (*"to break apart"*)

His late arrival had a(n) ____disruptive____ influence on the meeting.

5. to break in upon; to stop, halt

All day long she has to ____interrupt____ her work in order to answer telephone calls from clients.

6. rotten, wicked, dishonest; to make evil; to bribe

The ____corrupt____ dictatorship was replaced by a democratic republic.

7. to burst forth (*"to break out"*)

Boiling streams of lava ____erupted____ from the exploding volcano, causing the population to flee.

8. a breaking; to break

The engineers worked frantically to repair the ____rupture____ in the wall of the dam.

CCSS Vocabulary: 4.b. (See pp. T14–15.)

FINAL MASTERY TEST

Synonyms

Select the two words or expressions that are most nearly the same in meaning.

1.	a. erode	b. renovate	c. indulge	d. pamper
2.	a. nurture	b. disrupt	c. foster	d. haggle
3.	a. pact	b. alliance	c. wrath	d. potential
4.	a. turmoil	b. dynasty	c. regime	d. despot
5.	a. spirited	b. available	c. animated	d. reputable
6.	a. remnant	b. cache	c. void	d. hoard
7.	a. docile	b. fickle	c. vital	d. indispensable
8.	a. decrease	b. diminish	c. capsize	d. lubricate
9.	a. fruitless	b. harmonious	c. mellow	d. futile
10.	a. verify	b. implore	c. entreat	d. goad
11.	a. preview	b. overture	c. foretaste	d. magnitude
12.	a. seethe	b. quench	c. bewilder	d. stifle
13.	a. ultimate	b. cynical	c. inimitable	d. unique
14.	a. brood	b. meditate	c. hinder	d. mortify
15.	a. orthodox	b. quaint	c. customary	d. notorious

Antonyms

Select the two words that are most nearly opposite in meaning.

16.	a. swerve	b. veto	c. maul	d. ratify
17.	a. entice	b. accelerate	c. dissuade	d. insinuate
18.	a. peevish	b. puny	c. disputatious	d. gigantic
19.	a. hostile	b. hardy	c. hilarious	d. heartrending
20.	a. humdrum	b. leisurely	c. grueling	d. miscellaneous
21.	a. hanker	b. grovel	c. hurtle	d. patronize
22.	a. graphic	b. random	c. chronological	d. pending
23.	a. inflammable	b. meager	c. nutritious	d. lavish
24.	a. flourish	b. flounder	c. singe	d. wilt
25.	a. enchant	b. presume	c. trickle	d. pall

Analogies

Select the item that best completes the comparison.

26. **barren** is to **produce** as
    a. inhumane is to abuse
    b. timid is to fear
    c. poised is to enjoy
    (d.) ignorant is to know

27. **résumé** is to **career** as
    a. truce is to war
    b. speaker is to oration
    (c.) synopsis is to plot
    d. paragraph is to sentence

28. **scurry** is to **walk** as
    a. dive is to swim
    (b.) chatter is to talk
    c. listen is to hear
    d. demonstrate is to show

29. **simultaneous** is to **time** as
    a. regal is to power
    (b.) contemporary is to period
    c. coincidental is to luck
    d. abnormal is to health

30. **hearth** is to **heat** as
    (a.) lamp is to light
    b. sink is to kitchen
    c. door is to lock
    d. bed is to blanket

31. **basket weaving** is to **handicraft** as
    a. profession is to medicine
    (b.) carpentry is to trade
    c. skill is to talent
    d. hobby is to stamp collecting

32. **laugh** is to **mirth** as
    (a.) yawn is to boredom
    b. frown is to delight
    c. tear is to suspense
    d. gasp is to disappointment

33. **caterer** is to **refreshments** as
    a. chef is to restaurant
    b. seamstress is to needle
    c. baker is to oven
    (d.) tailor is to clothing

Two-Word Completions

To complete the sentences, select the best word pair from among the choices given.

34. The man was sure the watch was a valuable collectible, and was shocked to find out that he had been ________________ as it was nothing but a ________________.
    a. flustered … farce
    (b.) duped … counterfeit
    c. evicted … firebrand
    d. heeded … drone

35. Although the experienced ________________ had a highly marketable idea, he ________________ in the recession.
    (a.) entrepreneur … went bankrupt
    b. bystander … was sullen
    c. fugitive … was vigilant
    d. beneficiary … was controversial

36. The editor's comment about the novel's "________________" narrative ________________ the writer.
    a. gruesome … marred
    b. notable … frustrated
    c. unscathed … inflated
    (d.) stodgy … disheartened

37. With her ________________ complexion and ________________ dress, the actress resembled the ghost of a vaudevillian entertainer.
    a. wayward … trivial
    b. dynamic … maternal
    c. lethargic … grimy
    (d.) wan … gaudy

FINAL MASTERY TEST

Supplying Words in Context

To complete each sentence, select the best word from among the choices given. Not all words in the word bank will be used. You may modify the word form as necessary.

indignant	**botch**	**blurt**	**nub**
dominate	**adjacent**	**fledgling**	**impostor**
nomadic	**mull**	**malignant**	**flagrant**
uncertainty	**pervade**	**inflict**	**interrogate**

38. When I was just a(n) ___fledgling___ in my very first pro season, one of the veteran players took me under his wing.

39. Although I realize you have many interesting stories to tell, I do wish you wouldn't always ___dominate___ the conversation.

40. Even though he lives in a house ___adjacent___ to the school, he is often late for his first class.

41. Inexperienced as we were, we knew we would ___botch___ the preparation of the meal, so we decided to go out to eat.

42. Instead of giving me all those unimportant details, let's get right to the ___nub___ of the matter.

43. I know I would have to ___mull___ over the events of the evening before I could determine if I had acted inappropriately.

downright	**interminable**	**recompense**	**affliction**
insubordinate	**dilapidated**	**malady**	**elongate**
transmit	**iota**	**morbid**	**incentive**
utmost	**snare**	**alight**	**casual**

44. Luckily, the communications officer was able to ___transmit___ an SOS signal just before the ship's radio stopped working.

45. The smile of joy she gave me when she received the award was ample ___recompense___ for all the time and effort I had spent in helping her.

46. It was ___downright___ rude of her to ignore my kind offer of help.

47. If you had a(n) ___iota___ of consideration for us, you would turn down the volume on the television set.

48. The trick was to ___snare___ him in his own web of lies and deceit.

49. The deserted cabin was so ___dilapidated___ that it looked as though any strong breeze would cause it to collapse.

Word Associations

*Select the word or expression that best completes the meaning of the sentence or answers the question, with particular reference to the meaning of the word in **boldface** type.*

50. Which of the following would be most likely to create **havoc**?
a. a summer breeze
b. a game of volleyball
c. a school assembly
d. a tornado

51. An example of a **grim** event is a
a. graduation
b. fatal accident
c. family reunion
d. holiday

52. If there is **mutual** admiration between two people,
a. the admiration is not genuine
b. they admire each other
c. the admiration is one-sided
d. the admiration will not last

53. Which of the following is likely to be **sodden**?
a. a desert
b. a high school musical
c. a rain-soaked field
d. a driver's test

54. A **stalemate** lacks
a. a solution
b. a sense of humor
c. freshness
d. opponents

55. Which of the following would *not* be likely to **canvass** an area?
a. an interviewer
b. a homebody
c. a pollster
d. a door-to-door salesperson

56. A **braggart** would be most likely to
a. grin and bear it
b. stick to his or her guns
c. fly off the handle
d. toot his or her own horn

57. Which of the following would *not* be found in **rural** areas?
a. skyscrapers
b. water
c. cows
d. people

58. You would be most likely to **browse**
a. in a library
b. on the tennis court
c. when you are asleep
d. during a test

59. A person facing the **hazards** of life is
a. making money
b. tackling perils
c. winning victories
d. playing golf

60. Which of the following is *not* **transparent**?
a. a pane of glass
b. a feeble excuse
c. air
d. a wooden door

61. A person who receives a **legacy** has gained something as a result of
a. inheriting it
b. hard work
c. dishonesty
d. gambling

Choosing the Right Meaning

Read each sentence carefully. Then select the item that best completes the statement below the sentence.

62. The dogs scattered out of the house once they saw that the door had been left **ajar**.

In line 1 the word **ajar** most nearly means

a. alone **b.** partly open **c.** untouched **d.** sealed

63. The guidance counselor assured the student that she would develop a more **cosmopolitan** point of view by travelling abroad.

In line 2 the word **cosmopolitan** most nearly means

a. mechanical **b.** sophisticated **c.** false **d.** oppressed

64. In looking for work, the fisherman decided to move to a port town that was rumored to **abound** with fish.

In line 2 **abound** most nearly means

a. leap **b.** produce young **c.** are protected **d.** are plentiful

65. Realizing her brother was the defendant, she knew she would not be able to provide an **impartial** decision, and asked to be removed from the case.

In line 2 **impartial** most nearly means

a. unbiased **b.** incomplete **c.** unhurried **d.** effective

66. The longer two people carry on a **feud**, the harder it becomes for them to reconcile with one another.

In line 1 **feud** most nearly means

a. machine **b.** quarrel **c.** movement **d.** constituent

67. Thousands of **downtrodden** workers met in the square to talk about the possibility of creating a union.

In line 1 **downtrodden** most nearly means

a. well-paid **b.** happy **c.** skillful **d.** oppressed

68. Because the pledge had been left by an **anonymous** donor, the organization could not send out a letter of thanks.

In line 1 **anonymous** most nearly means

a. innocent **b.** eager **c.** unnamed **d.** angry

69. Because both children loved broccoli, their mother did not expect them to **detest** cauliflower.

In line 1 **detest** most nearly means

a. know **b.** hate **c.** welcome **d.** understand

70. As he had been found guilty of **perjury** in the past, his testimony could not be considered reliable, and he was dismissed from the case.

In line 1 **perjury** most nearly means

a. kidnapping **b.** stealing **c.** killing **d.** lying

WORD LIST

The following is a list of all the words taught in the Units of this book. The number after each entry indicates the page on which the word is defined.

INDEX